Invisible on the Web

INVISIBLE ON THE WEB

A Guide to Online Privacy and Security

Andrea Ciarrocchi

MERCURY LEARNING AND INFORMATION
Boston, Massachusetts

MERCURY LEARNING AND INFORMATION
121 High Street, 3rd Floor
Boston, MA 02110
info@merclearning.com

A. Ciarrocchi. *Invisible on the Web: A Guide to Online Privacy and Security*
ISBN: 978-1-5015-2588-9

Library of Congress Control Number: 2026941396

242526321 This book is printed on acid-free paper in the United States of America.

To my family

CONTENTS

Preface

We live in an age in which being connected has become synonymous with being alive. Our work, relationships, entertainment, health, and even our identities are increasingly mediated by digital systems that promise convenience, efficiency, and speed. Yet this same digital environment quietly records, analyzes, and stores traces of our behavior with a persistence and scale unprecedented in human history. Privacy, once protected by physical distance, walls, and social conventions, has become fragile, negotiable, and often invisible.

This book was born from a simple but urgent observation: most people care deeply about privacy, yet few truly understand how it is compromised, how it can be defended, or what trade-offs are involved in protecting it. Online privacy is often discussed in extremes, either as something already lost beyond recovery or as a purely technical problem solvable by a single tool or setting. Reality is more complex. Privacy is neither dead nor guaranteed; it is a dynamic condition shaped by technology, law, economics, and individual choices.

The aim of this book is not to instill fear, nor to promote digital withdrawal, but to provide clarity. Understanding privacy requires crossing disciplinary boundaries: history explains how the concept evolved; law defines its protections and limits; technology reveals how data is collected and exploited; cybersecurity shows how that data can be stolen or abused; and ethics frames why privacy matters beyond compliance and convenience. Only by connecting these perspectives can we move from abstract concern to informed action.

Throughout these chapters, privacy is treated not as an absolute state of secrecy but as a form of control: control over personal information, over one's digital footprint, and over how identity is shaped and interpreted by machines and institutions. This includes understanding everyday technologies (cookies, browsers, encryption, and cloud services) as well as the less visible infrastructures that enable surveillance, profiling, and large-scale data aggregation. Defensive tools and secure practices are presented not as guarantees but as risk-reduction strategies that empower users without creating false expectations of invulnerability.

A central theme of this book is responsibility—not only the responsibility of governments and corporations to respect rights and protect data but also the responsibility of individuals to understand the systems they use daily. Digital literacy has become a prerequisite for personal autonomy. Choosing a browser, a password manager, or a messaging app is no longer a neutral decision; it is a statement about trust, transparency, and control.

This book is intended for readers who want to go beyond headlines and slogans. No advanced technical background is required, but curiosity and critical thinking are essential. Whether you are a student, a professional, a developer, or simply a conscious user of digital tools, the goal is to help you see the Internet not as a black box but as an environment whose risks and possibilities can be understood and navigated.

Privacy has always adapted to social change. The challenge of our time is ensuring that it adapts without disappearing. This book is a contribution to that effort: a guide, a reference, and an invitation to remain visible by choice, not by default.

CHAPTER 1

The History and Evolution of Privacy and Data Protection

Privacy is a multifaceted and diverse concept. It represents the right to safeguard the most personal aspects of one's life from unauthorized interference by governments, corporations, or individuals. Over time, the understanding and significance of privacy have shifted dramatically, influenced by societal changes and advancements in technology. The idea of privacy often stems from the distinction between "private" and "public," reflecting an individual's natural tendency to establish boundaries between themselves and the external world. In principle, numerous countries have enacted laws designed to uphold and protect citizens' privacy rights.

The distinction between private and public has always been influenced by the cultural and historical context, leading to continuous shifts in what people perceive as private. Even Aristotle, in his work *Politics*, differentiated between the public sphere and the private sphere associated with domestic life. Legally, the concept of privacy dates back to ancient times, with the Code of Hammurabi prohibiting unauthorized entry into a person's home, and Roman law also addressing similar issues. For the ancient Greeks, active participation in public life was highly valued, yet they still acknowledged the individual's right to manage personal matters. The modern understanding of privacy began to emerge after the decline of feudalism. The Roman philosopher Marcus Tullius Cicero emphasized the value of personal independence, championing an individual's right to live free from external interference. In the Middle Ages, Islamic scholars expanded on the notion of privacy by codifying laws concerning contracts, property ownership, and personal relationships. By the nineteenth century, urbanization had brought on rapid population growth in cities, leading to more crowded living conditions. Yet, this shift also granted individuals a novel sense of privacy, as they escaped the relentless moral scrutiny and surveillance of small village communities. The rise of tabloid newspapers, which thrived on gossip and photography, marked another pivotal change in the concept of privacy. In 1890, American jurists Louis Brandeis and Samuel Warren authored the essay *The Right of Privacy*, articulating the right to "be let alone" and introducing the idea of inviolable personal intimacy. This essay quickly became a landmark work, celebrated by legal historians as one of the most influential and enduring law review articles in history. The researchers concluded that for the law to adequately address societal needs and fully protect individuals and their property, it must evolve alongside political, social, and economic changes. They identified two major threats to privacy: technological advancements, such as instant photography, and the commercialization of gossip in newspapers. Warren and Brandeis viewed an existing common law right as a foundation for the right to be left alone, as it allowed individuals to decide how much of their thoughts, emotions, and experiences to share with others. The right to privacy offered protection against the unauthorized disclosure of personal information, including private facts, feelings, and ideas. Since then, this right has gained universal recognition, developed further, and become a fundamental human right in many Western nations.

The universal recognition of privacy as a fundamental right was solidified in 1948 with the adoption of Article 12 of the Universal Declaration of Human Rights. It declares that no one shall face arbitrary interference with their privacy, family, home, or correspondence, nor suffer attacks on their honor or reputation. Historically, privacy was primarily focused on protecting physical spaces, such as homes and possessions. Advancements in technology and easier access to information have, however, broadened privacy concerns to include the collection, storage, and use of personal data. Privacy remains closely linked to human dignity, personal freedom, and individual autonomy. The term now also encompasses the right to data secrecy, reflecting its close connection to privacy. In recent decades, the concept has significantly evolved to emphasize individuals' control over their personal data. The protection of personal data seeks to prevent individuals from being subjected to constant surveillance aimed at predicting behavior and creating detailed profiles. While monitoring has always existed as a socially recognized phenomenon, it was particularly evident in small communities where neighbors closely observed one another, applying moral pressure to maintain communal values.

Modern monitoring differs fundamentally from traditional observation, as it not only involves being watched but also includes the collection, storage, and documentation of various aspects of our lives (e.g., through security cameras, credit card transactions, and airline bookings). The proliferation of new technologies in the twenty-first century has significantly eroded the barriers to privacy, enabling easy access to vast amounts of personal information, much of which may be sensitive. Collected data can be quickly transferred, systematically organized, and stored in massive databases, facilitating unprecedented levels of surveillance and data analysis. With the advent of modern communication technologies and the ease of information sharing and replication, it has become evident that protecting the right to privacy requires more than shielding individuals from unwanted intrusions. It is equally essential to prevent the misuse of personal information, particularly when it is collected without consent and used for purposes not explicitly authorized by the individual. Beyond choosing what data to share, users must have the ability to control its usage and analysis, fostering an understanding of both its benefits and potential risks. This is especially relevant in the context of the data we share on social media, our purchasing habits, the movies we watch, the ads we engage with, and the Web sites we visit. This vast amount of shared data creates a detailed profile of an individual, revealing aspects such as political and spiritual beliefs, interests, hobbies, and health conditions.

Posting an image or video online often leads to a loss of control over that content, which can have severe consequences for the mental well-being of those involved. Recent cases highlight the spread of intimate videos online without consent, where the material circulates uncontrollably, becoming public. The sheer volume of information flowing through the Internet daily and the absence of a central authority or specific target to address make it nearly impossible to halt the dissemination of such content. Data-sharing systems are frequently decentralized, exemplified by peer-to-peer (P2P) sharing methods. Given the Internet's architecture and the wide range of data dissemination options, no regulation or preventive measure can be entirely foolproof. Nonetheless, numerous nations are now enacting laws that broaden the definition of private information to include biometric data, which relies on distinctive physical characteristics for identification. These regulations also address the use of surveillance tools such as drones and facial recognition technology, aiming to safeguard anonymity despite the rapid evolution of emerging technologies and future advancements.

Both public and private databases increasingly gather vast amounts of personal information, making privacy more fragile and exposing individuals to cybercrime risks. This growing vulnerability highlights the need to redefine the right to privacy, extending it beyond matters of personal intimacy. It must now encompass Internet activity, mobile devices, social media, drones, biometric identification, and the Internet of Things (IoT). Today, it is nearly impossible to exist without leaving a digital trace. Sensitive data, such as information on racial or ethnic background, religious or philosophical beliefs, political affiliations, or membership in organizations, is protected because it can be exploited to discriminate or control individuals through actions such as wrongful termination, employment rejection, or denial of services such as insurance. Despite privacy laws, debates persist about what aspects of privacy require protection and how to define privacy itself. Professor Alan Westin, for instance, highlights that privacy involves a choice between openness and various degrees of social withdrawal and personal concealment, while scholars such as Solove acknowledge privacy as a complex, elusive concept. Westin identifies three factors (political, socio-cultural, and personal) that shape privacy norms, emphasizing the individual's role in maintaining a figurative *aura* that separates them from the external world. This boundary is fluid, varying across contexts and individuals, which necessitates creating an average standard to be legally protected. The standards shift, however, for public figures, such as politicians, actors, or athletes, whose privacy rights often clash with the public's right to information and the formation of socially significant opinions. Generally, the right to report takes precedence if the information is truthful, relevant, and presented appropriately. Conversely, stricter safeguards apply to certain groups, such as minors or individuals with mental illnesses, and to specific sensitive details, including health and sexual life.

People disclose personal information for various reasons, despite surveys consistently showing that privacy is highly valued. Many individuals routinely share sensitive details about their lives online or provide personal information in everyday situations. For example, applying for loans, mortgages, or credit cards often requires revealing identity details, addresses, Social Security numbers, job histories, and financial information. Other instances include sharing information during confessions, medical consultations, or legal discussions. Interestingly, there is often a disconnect between people's stated privacy concerns and their actual behaviors. Practically speaking, individuals may choose or feel compelled to exchange personal data for specific benefits, such as completing an online purchase. Similarly, people accept or permit surveillance in the interest of maintaining social order. For example, it is widely regarded as normal for cameras to monitor public spaces such as government buildings, airports, and banks to deter criminal activity. Furthermore, societies may decide through laws and regulations to curtail certain privacy rights in specific contexts, such as during criminal investigations or intelligence operations, to protect public safety and prevent potential threats. Our concern for privacy often relates to our desire to control our accessibility to others: how much others know about us, their physical access to us, and the degree of attention we receive. In today's digital age, however, it has become nearly impossible to exist without leaving some form of personal record behind.

Expanding privacy to include the protection of sensitive data brings two major challenges. First, it is crucial to prevent companies from profiling users in ways that could lead to discrimination. Second, there is the persistent risk of sensitive information being stolen, such as login credentials or, even more critically, financial data. While online security is inherently complex, understanding and using tools that promote safe practices is essential to reducing vulnerability to attacks. No one, however, is entirely immune to the risk of malicious targeting. Data breaches frequently occur at the server level of the services individuals rely on, rather than on personal devices. This means that, in many cases, users are neither responsible for nor capable of preventing such breaches, leaving them both blameless and powerless against these threats.

When taken out of context, seemingly harmless personal information can become damaging when combined with other personal or non-personal data. Uncertainty about the likelihood of data misuse or security breaches may make individuals less cautious in managing their personal information. The information society we inhabit profoundly shapes our lives, with significant implications for privacy. On one hand, technological advancements increasingly encroach on private spheres, making personal life more transparent and accessible. On the other, as more aspects of life shift online, individuals may withdraw from in-person interactions, leading to less intimate relationships and greater privacy in the offline world. Technological progress has made it possible to live nearly entirely online: working, socializing, shopping, and more. This shift redefines individuals, who are no longer seen solely as themselves but as the data collected about them. Online interactions often lack a full understanding of someone's physical form, rendering the person virtual and recognized primarily as a collection of data. Despite this virtualization, the individual remains a real human being, though their online presence creates a perception that this digital version mirrors their offline identity.

Inadequate privacy protections can lead to various harms. One classification, proposed by Hoven, highlights information inequality, where individuals face price discrimination without their knowledge or ability to influence it.

This occurs when data about purchases and preferences is used for marketing, enabling businesses to offer the same products or services at different prices based on behavioral monitoring and analysis. For instance, past purchase history or habits may determine the cost presented to a specific consumer. Discrimination is another potential consequence, where individuals or social groups face unfavorable treatment based on false or misleading assumptions.

Additionally, the restriction of moral autonomy arises when people's ability to define themselves is constrained by the pervasive availability of personal information. This limitation infringes on freedoms protected by the right to privacy. For example, behavioral profiling and targeted advertising can result in persistent profiles spanning multiple domains, or individuals may feel compelled to create distinct online personas tailored to specific contexts, such as social networking, professional use, or creative expression. Information damage refers to harm that becomes possible only after the collection of personal data, with identity theft being a prominent example in the digital age. Such harm can be direct or indirect, potentially damaging relationships, intensifying conflicts, or causing individuals to fear misuse of their personal information in situations such as stalking or personal surveillance. Immediate consequences may also include credit card theft, physical harm, or property loss.

When privacy protections are compromised, it becomes challenging to quantify the extent of potential harm. Damage can manifest in financial, social, emotional, or physical ways, often in unpredictable forms. Beyond personal impacts, the erosion of trust in entities handling personal data can have broader societal repercussions, undermining confidence in systems that rely on responsible data usage.

Various socioeconomic forces shape the societal demand for privacy and the pursuit of a balance between privacy and security. Governments increasingly use personal data to provide societal goods, often deemed acceptable intrusions into privacy by either authorities or society at large.

Social attitudes toward privacy are also shifting, with individuals becoming more willing to share personal information for modest benefits, such as joining communities of like-minded people or using accessible platforms to share content more freely. When managed appropriately, personal data processing can benefit society as a whole. For instance, the public sector increasingly relies on personal data to enhance services such as social security and tax administration. Integrating government services through centralized systems, such as one-stop shops that consolidate data from multiple sources, simplifies citizen access and improves service efficiency. The growing application of data in fields such as healthcare, sociology, and economics, however, highlights the need for stronger data protection frameworks.

The tension between privacy and security is a key topic in policy discussions, but these often overlook human rights considerations. In democratic societies, privacy intrusions are justified only when necessary. Tools such as data sharing and biometrics are increasingly utilized to combat serious crime and terrorism, demonstrating their value in identifying threats. It is, however, crucial to recognize that protecting personal data has inherent societal value. Privacy enables individuals to freely express themselves, associate with others, and practice their beliefs without fear of undue intrusion, serving as a foundation for exercising other freedoms. Not only is privacy protection essential for individual well-being, but it also fosters freedom and creativity that benefit society as a whole. Importantly, data protection and privacy are not a zero-sum game; enhancing one does not necessarily diminish the other. Instead, they work together to create a society where personal freedoms are respected and societal progress is achieved.

While concerns around privacy have deep historical roots, it remains a pressing issue today. Definitions of privacy and the right to privacy initially captured the attention of legal scholars and were later addressed through regional and international human rights agreements. Yet, significant challenges persist in protecting privacy. Media discussions suggest that privacy invasions are evolving, from clear and overt violations to subtle, persistent, and often unnoticed intrusions. The once-clear boundaries of privacy, previously defined by physical barriers such as property lines, walls, or the human body, are now increasingly shaped by an individual's information, ideas, and movements. These more abstract aspects of privacy are being encroached upon by powerful social forces that individuals have little ability to influence or control. As technology advances, participation in modern society increasingly requires sharing personal data. This evolution brings new categories and types of personal information, alongside an exponential increase in the volume of data processed online.

Rapid technological developments present significant challenges for data protection authorities, who must craft adaptable laws capable of addressing these emerging realities. Consequently, privacy policies remain a contentious area of debate, as society grapples with balancing privacy, data protection, and other objectives. Discussions often focus on the interplay between privacy, data protection, and security. Public opinion, as reflected in surveys, reveals diverse and complex perspectives, often highlighting trust or mistrust in authorities and a nuanced, context-dependent view of security measures. This variability underscores the ongoing tension between individual privacy rights and societal goals in an era of rapid technological change.

DATA PROTECTION AND CYBERSECURITY

Cybersecurity, also referred to as computer security, encompasses tools, technologies, and practices designed to safeguard computer systems by ensuring the availability, confidentiality, and integrity of information assets. To achieve this, a system must exhibit resilience, robustness, and responsiveness, critical traits for withstanding attacks that threaten its functionality and performance. Cybersecurity has become increasingly important in the economic and information technology (IT) sectors, driven by the rapid digitalization of public and private services, the proliferation of devices and systems, and the growing sophistication of cyberattackers. This heightened reliance on technology has amplified concerns about securing computer systems, reflecting their vital role in modern society. It is essential to distinguish cybersecurity from information security. Cybersecurity focuses on protecting IT assets such as infrastructure, networks, devices, systems, applications, and services. In contrast, information security aims to safeguard the information itself across organizational, physical, environmental, and logical dimensions, including IT and telecommunications technologies. Cybersecurity functions as a component of information security, serving as a means to achieve its broader goals, though not the ultimate purpose. Furthermore, individuals with access to sensitive data must uphold privacy, ensuring its use complies with legal requirements and aligns with the purposes explicitly authorized by the data owner. Cyberattacks are a daily occurrence, targeting sensitive and valuable information from companies, institutions, and government organizations. Evaluating security requires identifying the threats, vulnerabilities, and risks tied to information assets to protect them from potential attacks (both internal and external) that could cause significant harm, whether economic, socio-political, or reputational, beyond acceptable limits. Beyond the foundational principles of availability, confidentiality, and integrity, additional factors such as authenticity, non-repudiation, accountability, and reliability are often considered. The increasing sophistication of cyber threats has underscored the critical role of data protection in preventing costly breaches. Data protection is now a central focus of cybersecurity, intertwining with compliance and privacy efforts. Data protection goes beyond technologies designed to secure sensitive information, however. While traditional cybersecurity approaches primarily safeguarded localized data, modern enterprise strategies also address the flow of data across wireless devices and cloud servers, reflecting the evolving nature of digital threats and the interconnected nature of today's information systems. Cybersecurity encompasses legal, human, technical, and organizational dimensions, all aimed at identifying system vulnerabilities, associated threats, and potential risks. It involves practices and processes designed to promptly detect attacks and implement recovery measures. By employing effective systems and strategies, both organizations and individuals can mitigate the risk of data theft, safeguarding against data loss and operational disruptions. Data breaches and corruption cost companies billions annually, with a single cybersecurity incident potentially incurring significant financial losses. Expenses often include litigation, compliance penalties, and investment in upgraded cybersecurity measures, making preventive controls a sound investment.

Private citizens are not immune to such attacks, with personal devices often targeted. Many data breaches stem from inadequate password protection and poorly encrypted database credentials. Viruses and malware are particularly dangerous when targeting devices used for banking or storing sensitive information, such as login credentials. Malware, encompassing worms, ransomware, spyware, and viruses, is designed to harm systems by modifying or deleting files, extracting sensitive data, or facilitating malicious activities such as spam emails or traffic generation. Malware can infiltrate systems through malicious actors or be inadvertently spread by users clicking on harmful links or downloading infected files. Ransomware encrypts files, rendering them inaccessible until a ransom is paid, while social engineering attacks exploit trust to manipulate individuals into sharing sensitive data or installing malware. For instance, attackers may impersonate trusted entities, such as brands, colleagues, or friends, using tactics such as urgency to coerce victims. Phishing, a common form of social engineering, employs emails, SMS, or voice messages to trick users into revealing information or clicking on malicious links. These campaigns range from mass phishing attempts to targeted spear phishing, where attackers focus on specific individuals, such as posing as job seekers to send infected résumés. Advanced persistent threats (APTs) represent another sophisticated attack method. In these, malicious actors gain prolonged access to systems, conducting reconnaissance and stealing data while remaining undetected. These stealthy operations allow attackers to extract valuable information without triggering defense mechanisms, highlighting the need for robust cybersecurity measures. Malicious actors frequently exfiltrate data during ransomware attacks, leveraging the threat of public disclosure to extort payment, often in cryptocurrency, in exchange for a decryption key. Paying the ransom does not guarantee successful data recovery, however, as decryption keys may fail.

Data protection aims to prevent theft before organizations or individuals face the high costs of a successful breach. It also safeguards customers from data loss, identity theft, and fraud. Achieving comprehensive data protection is an ongoing process involving multiple strategies and tools. Key elements of data protection include storage, which involves archiving outdated data separately to free space while retaining it for future needs, such as investigations; backups, which involves creating copies of data for recovery in case of loss or corruption; and snapshots, which include system configurations for restoring functionality.

Data duplication across environments ensures redundancy, and production data must remain accessible for daily operations. A disaster recovery plan is essential to address data loss and restore normalcy swiftly, minimizing downtime and maintaining productivity. Modern systems span multiple operating systems and platforms, including cloud environments. While data portability ensures continuity across these platforms, it also increases the risk of interception, theft, and corruption. Cloud integration is especially crucial, as many organizations now use the cloud for backups and archives. Note, however, that restoring data from the cloud during a disaster requires careful planning, including secure configurations and robust access controls to prevent unauthorized access.

The growing number of network-connected devices has expanded the attack surface, complicating the creation of effective data protection plans. A solid plan must address potential issues, such as data corruption. Backups must be verified to ensure they are uncompromised and reliable. Backup locations must also be accessible to facilitate quick recovery. Since ransomware often targets backups, securing these files and locations is critical. Redundancy is a key principle of data protection, but poor backup management, such as overwriting active backups, can lead to significant data loss.

Data encryption is a foundational defense against attackers. Encryption should protect data at rest (e.g., stored on devices) and in transit (e.g., during Internet transfers). Encrypted data remains unreadable even if intercepted or stolen. Mobile devices with encrypted storage protect sensitive information in the event of physical theft. As technology evolves, data protection strategies must keep pace with emerging threats. Organizations increasingly turn to the cloud for backup and storage, recognizing its efficiency and scalability. Ensuring proper integration, security, and access control in cloud environments is, however, vital to maintain data availability and protection. Effective data protection requires a balance of redundancy, secure encryption, and adaptable solutions to combat ever-changing cybersecurity threats.

As cyber threats become more sophisticated, it is crucial for users to adopt advanced tools and strategies for data protection and information security. Backup and recovery systems automate the process of securing critical data and enable swift restoration in the event of a breach or disaster. Encryption protects sensitive information by converting it into a format that only authorized individuals can access. Data discovery and classification tools help organizations identify and organize sensitive information, making it easier to protect effectively. Endpoint security systems safeguard individual devices, such as laptops, desktops, and mobile phones, against various threats. Data loss prevention protocols focus on monitoring and managing data access and usage to prevent theft or compromise. Firewalls act as protective barriers, filtering network traffic to block unauthorized access. Additionally, antivirus, anti-malware, and anti-ransomware software detect and neutralize malicious programs that pose risks of data breaches or leaks.

The rising use of computing tools and the Internet has intensified attention on software security from developers. Secure software is designed to minimize vulnerabilities that could lead to severe or irreparable damage to a system. In the process of software design, achieving a balance between ease of use and resistance to external threats and critical errors is vital. This balance ensures programs are both functional and resilient against potential attacks.

The security of application programs fundamentally relies on the robustness of the operating system. Two key aspects define software security: *safety*, which focuses on eliminating risks of irreversible harm to the system, and *reliability*, which aims to mitigate events that could cause any level of damage. A program is considered more secure when the probability of failure is low and the impact of any potential failure is minimal. Ensuring this involves verifying program specifications, identifying and resolving code defects, and thoroughly analyzing system functions for vulnerabilities.

Basic measures to enhance security include regularly updating operating systems with security patches and installing reliable antivirus software. Effective antivirus programs should offer real-time scanning and frequent updates. Users are advised to perform routine scans of devices, including hard drives and removable media, to detect and eliminate threats such as viruses and worms. Scanning email attachments for malware before opening or sending files is another critical practice, ensuring the antivirus is appropriately configured for these tasks.

Risk analysis forms the foundation of a sound cybersecurity strategy. It begins by identifying valuable assets, assessing potential threats based on their likelihood and severity, and then devising a risk management plan. This plan dictates the necessary countermeasures to protect against identified risks. Conducting risk assessments is especially important during the early stages of deploying IT systems.

Cybersecurity efforts focus on safeguarding data from unauthorized access, not only by external attackers but also by users with limited permissions. These measures aim to prevent unauthorized copying, modification, or deletion of data. Security violations can include attempts to access restricted areas, identity theft, unauthorized use of resources, and other breaches.

Additionally, cybersecurity seeks to avert denial-of-service (DoS) attacks, where malicious actors disrupt system resources to render them inaccessible to users. Such attacks can significantly impact system functionality and user operations, highlighting the importance of robust preventive measures.

In addition to risk analysis, penetration testing, commonly referred to as pentesting or ethical hacking, plays a crucial role in evaluating the security of computer systems. Unlike a basic vulnerability assessment, which focuses on identifying weaknesses, penetration testing actively exploits these vulnerabilities to assess the effectiveness of the system's defenses. This method provides a more comprehensive evaluation of risks but requires careful planning as part of an established security strategy.

Computer systems face a variety of threats that exploit vulnerabilities, leading to unauthorized access, data breaches, or disruptions in functionality. Threats and vulnerabilities, though closely related, are distinct concepts. Threats represent potential dangers, while vulnerabilities are weaknesses within the system that threats can exploit. Most protective measures aim to address vulnerabilities, as threats themselves are often beyond direct control.

The causes of system unavailability or compromise can generally be divided into two main categories: accidental events and adverse events. Accidental events are non-malicious incidents, such as user errors, hardware malfunctions, software glitches, or accidental deletions. These events primarily affect the availability of systems and can be mitigated by regular backups and disaster recovery procedures. While they cannot always be prevented, proactive measures such as system monitoring and user training can reduce their likelihood. Adverse events, on the other hand, involve intentional actions, such as malicious attacks or unauthorized use of access privileges. These include activities such as exploiting vulnerabilities to infiltrate systems, escalating privileges to gain control over restricted areas, and causing data loss or theft. Malicious attacks are often carried out remotely using specialized software designed to bypass protections and compromise systems. Examples of adverse events include malware infections, theft of devices containing sensitive information, unintentional disclosure of data, and payment card fraud. To address adverse events, organizations need to implement a range of strategies, such as improving access controls to prevent unauthorized actions, regularly updating software to address vulnerabilities, and restricting access permissions to minimize potential misuse.

Monitoring systems for unusual activity can also help detect and respond to threats in real time, further reducing risks. Backups are a vital component of safeguarding systems against both accidental and adverse events. They enable data recovery and continuity in the event of system failure or data corruption. Disaster recovery plans should include frequent backups to maintain current data, secure storage to prevent unauthorized access, and regular testing to ensure backups remain viable for restoration when needed. These measures enhance resilience against threats, ensuring that organizations and individuals can quickly recover from incidents while minimizing damage and downtime.

There is a wide range of tactics used during cyberattacks that can compromise systems and data. Buffer overflow occurs when a program writes more data to a memory buffer than it can hold, potentially allowing an attacker to execute arbitrary code. DoS attacks aim to overwhelm a system, rendering it unavailable. Social engineering manipulates individuals into divulging confidential information, often leveraging trust or creating a sense of urgency. Keylogging captures keystrokes to gather sensitive data such as passwords. Backdoors provide attackers with unauthorized access to systems or networks, bypassing standard security measures. Spoofing involves impersonating a trusted source to deceive users, while social network poisoning introduces malicious links or misinformation into social platforms. Spyware monitors user activity to collect sensitive data without their knowledge.

A related but distinct issue is unauthorized access to systems, where users gain entry to resources without permission. Unlike attacks over a network, this involves direct physical access to the system, often exploiting vulnerabilities or using shellcode to manipulate the system. These types of breaches can lead to significant consequences, including the disruption of critical infrastructure such as hospitals, underscoring the potential societal impact of these threats.

Cybersecurity measures operate on several levels. Physical security focuses on safeguarding the tangible infrastructure, including servers and facilities, by using controlled access points, surveillance, and protection against environmental hazards such as fire or water damage. This level also includes environmental security measures applied to buildings and technological systems, such as barriers, electronic access keys, and fire sensors in data centers.

Logical security pertains to protecting digital resources through techniques such as authentication and authorization. These ensure that only verified users or services can access, modify, or utilize data and applications. Activities during the authentication process are logged, creating an accountability trail that can be reviewed during audits. These audits evaluate compliance with security policies and help identify potential vulnerabilities.

Passive security encompasses preventative measures to deny unauthorized access to systems and data. For example, reinforced doors with personal identification systems fall under passive security, as do tamper-proof cable ducts and climate control systems for server rooms. While passive security focuses on preventing incidents, it is critical not to over-rely on these measures, as they can create a false sense of safety and lead to the neglect of active defenses.

Active security, by contrast, involves dynamic measures to ensure the confidentiality, integrity, and availability of information. This includes tools such as firewalls, intrusion detection systems (IDSs), and real-time monitoring solutions. Active security measures adapt to emerging threats and play a crucial role in maintaining system resilience.

The human factor also plays a significant role in cybersecurity. Many attacks exploit human error or lack of awareness, making education and training essential components of a robust security strategy. By combining physical, logical, and human-centric measures, organizations can create a comprehensive approach to defending against cyber threats while fostering trust in the systems upon which modern life relies. Active and passive security work in tandem to establish a robust security framework, each addressing different facets of system protection.

Complementing these measures is the IT security audit, which straddles the line between logical and organizational security. IT security audits utilize built-in tools within operating systems or specialized software to evaluate the security posture of devices, services, and terminals. By analyzing logs and comparing them against predefined rules, audits can assess compliance with internal policies, regulatory standards, and best practices.

Automated auditing systems, often integrated into IT environments, monitor logs and events, comparing results to benchmarks set by industry guidelines, vendor advisories, and security organizations. These systems differ from manual audits, which involve human inspectors evaluating management processes and systems. Both approaches play a crucial role in identifying vulnerabilities, ensuring compliance, and maintaining overall system security.

A significant aspect of modern cybersecurity is addressing the human factor, which has been identified as a critical vulnerability. Studies suggest that over 90% of security incidents originate from human error, including poor password management, failure to recognize phishing attempts, and falling prey to deceptive URLs. These behaviors highlight the importance of cybersecurity awareness training. Such training helps users identify potential threats, mitigates risks, and aligns with global security guidelines advocating for a security-conscious culture within organizations. This cultural shift emphasizes the role of informed end-users as a vital line of defense against cyber threats. Cybersecurity risk analysis must consider not only technical vulnerabilities but also potential errors and non-compliance by privileged roles, such as system administrators or developers. These roles, if mismanaged, can introduce significant threats.

Moreover, factors such as geographic location, socioeconomic conditions, and technological adoption levels also influence cybersecurity risks. A study conducted by NordVPN and Statista ranks countries based on these variables, revealing that highly developed and digitally advanced nations face a greater risk of cyberattacks. For example, Iceland, with its high income and technological infrastructure, ranks as the most vulnerable, while Italy occupies a mid-level position in the global ranking.

The foundation of cybersecurity lies in safeguarding the CIA triad: confidentiality, integrity, and availability. Confidentiality ensures that sensitive information is accessible only to authorized individuals. Integrity guarantees the accuracy and completeness of data, while availability ensures timely access to data as needed. These principles are complemented by non-repudiation, which ensures the ability to attribute actions or data to a specific individual or entity, and immutability, which prevents unauthorized alteration of critical information such as administrator logs. The CIA triad, along with supporting principles such as non-repudiation and immutability, forms the core of security assessments and measures. By combining technical safeguards, organizational policies, and user awareness, organizations can establish a comprehensive cybersecurity strategy to address evolving threats while maintaining trust in their digital systems.

Achieving availability in an IT system involves a combination of technical, organizational, and environmental factors. The robustness of software, the reliability of hardware, and secure environments where systems operate all contribute to maintaining availability. A well-functioning system ensures that data integrity and confidentiality are preserved alongside uninterrupted access. Since data security often hinges on the system's operational state, measures that enhance system reliability, such as redundancy and disaster recovery plans, play a vital role. Multiple defensive strategies are essential to guard against the variety of attack techniques that could threaten an IT system. Implementing layers of protection creates barriers between potential attackers and their targets. These layers must safeguard against both intentional and accidental threats, including unauthorized access and accidental alteration of information.

Relying solely on implemented countermeasures, however, can lead to complacency. Instead, robust systems are designed with the assumption that vulnerabilities may still exist, necessitating continuous monitoring and adaptation. To mitigate the risk of system failures or physical damage, redundancy is frequently employed. This could involve server clusters or distributed systems to provide fault tolerance, ensuring that business operations and information systems continue uninterrupted. Preventive strategies, such as disaster recovery and prevention plans, address potential disruptions, enhancing both reliability and availability. Logical countermeasures are a crucial component of a comprehensive security framework.

Authentication systems form the first line of defense, with secure software and advanced methods such as multi-factor authentication (MFA) ensuring that only authorized users access the system. Grid-based password systems, fingerprint recognition, and biometric authentication enhance security by providing additional verification layers. User management and access controls further refine system security. Mandatory access control (MAC) systems restrict access based on predefined rules, ensuring that users interact only with data and resources for which they are authorized. Firewalls, when correctly configured, provide an essential network security function by monitoring and regulating incoming and outgoing traffic, shielding systems from external threats and unauthorized communications.

IDSs play a vital role in identifying and responding to unauthorized access attempts. These systems typically consist of sensors that gather network or system data, a console for monitoring, an analysis engine to detect potential breaches, and a database of rules to evaluate threats. IDSs are versatile tools capable of recognizing diverse attack methods, from sophisticated hacker exploits to automated and semi-automated intrusion attempts.

Honeypots offer an innovative way to detect and analyze cyber threats. Acting as decoys, these systems mimic valuable network assets while being intentionally isolated and devoid of sensitive data. Honeypots attract attackers, providing valuable insights into their methods and intentions while diverting them away from critical systems. By combining these strategies, organizations can achieve a balance of availability, security, and reliability, ensuring that systems remain operational and protected against a wide range of threats.

Anti-spyware tools are another essential countermeasure. These software applications identify and remove spyware, malicious programs designed to monitor and transmit user activities for exploitative purposes. By eliminating these threats, anti-spyware tools protect user privacy and prevent unauthorized data harvesting.

Steganography and cryptography offer sophisticated methods for securing information. Steganography conceals the existence of information, making it invisible to unauthorized users, while cryptography ensures that data is incomprehensible without the correct decryption key. Both techniques enhance data confidentiality, though they serve distinct purposes in information security.

Network intrusion detection systems (NIDSs) analyze traffic within network segments to identify anomalies or potential threats. A NIDS typically operates with probes strategically placed across the network, relaying data to a centralized server and database for analysis. These systems detect activities such as unauthorized access, malware proliferation, privilege escalation, traffic interception, and DoS attacks. By monitoring network traffic, NIDS provide a proactive layer of defense against cyber threats.

To safeguard sensitive documents and data, encryption technologies, digital signatures, and cryptographic certificates are used. Encryption prevents unauthorized access by transforming data into unreadable formats for anyone without the decryption key. Digital signatures verify the authenticity and integrity of documents, while certificates authenticate entities such as Web sites, individuals, and software systems. These tools ensure secure data transmission and protect against tampering or forgery.

In the domain of secure communication, data-in-transit protection ensures that confidential information remains secure during transmission over networks or telecommunications systems. This includes employing secure communication protocols, such as Transport Layer Security (TLS), to prevent interception and unauthorized access.

Product and system certifications further reinforce cybersecurity measures. Certifications serve as a quality assurance mechanism, demonstrating that a product or system meets defined security standards. The certification process involves a thorough evaluation of the object of evaluation (OoE), as specified by the client or developer in a security target (ST). This document outlines the security requirements and assurance levels expected of the product. Accredited laboratories conduct evaluations to verify compliance, culminating in a final report and certificate. These certifications not only attest to the security capabilities of a product but also enhance its credibility in the market, reassuring users of its reliability.

By integrating these additional countermeasures, organizations can strengthen their overall security posture, addressing vulnerabilities and ensuring the resilience of their systems and data.

REFERENCES

1. Bratman B. Brandeis and Warren's The Right to Privacy and the Birth of the Right to Privacy. Tenn L Rev. 2001;69:623.
2. Van Den Hoven J. Information Technology, Privacy, and the Protection of Personal Data [Internet]. na; 2008 [cited 2024 Dec 14]. Available from: *https://www.cambridge.org/core/services/aop-cambridge-core/content/view/17E12096D1BA1F8E376703AFE18784FF*

3. Solove DJ. Nothing to Hide: The False Tradeoff between Privacy and Security [Internet]. 2012 [cited 2024 Dec 14]. Available from: *https://scholarlypublishingcollective.org/information-policy/article-pdf/doi/10.5325/jinfopoli.2.2012.0103/1610491/jinfopoli_2_2012_103.pdf*

4. Privacy. In: Wikipedia [Internet]. 2024 [cited 2024 Dec 14]. Available from: *https://it.wikipedia.org/w/index.php?title=Privacy&oldid=142485293*

5. Gavison R. Privacy and the Limits of Law. The Yale Law Journal. 1980;89(3):421–71.

6. Bloustein EJ. Privacy as an aspect of human dignity: An answer to Dean Prosser. NYUL rev. 1964;39:962.

7. Fogarty EA. Protectors of privacy: Regulating personal data in the global economy. The Review of Policy Research. 2009;26(6):886–9.

8. Gerety T. Redefining privacy. Harv CR-CLL Rev. 1977;12:233.

9. Computer security. In: Wikipedia [Internet]. 2024 [cited 2024 Dec 14]. Available from: *https://en.wikipedia.org/wiki/Computer_security*

10. Westin AF. Social and Political Dimensions of Privacy. Journal of Social Issues. 2003 Jul;59(2):431–53.

11. Bennett CJ, Raab CD. The Governance of Privacy: Policy Instruments in Global Perspective [Internet]. Routledge; 2017 [cited 2024 Dec 14]. Available from: *https://www.taylorfrancis.com/books/mono/10.4324/9781315199269/governance-privacy-colin-bennett-charles-raab*

12. West R. The psychology of security. Commun ACM. 2008 Apr;51(4):34–40.

13. Warren S, Brandeis L. The Right to Privacy. In: Goldstein T, editor. Killing the Messenger [Internet]. Columbia University Press; 1989 [cited 2024 Dec 14]. p. 1–21. Available from: *https://www.degruyter.com/document/doi/10.7312/gold91730-002/html*

14. Whitman JQ. The two western cultures of privacy: Dignity versus liberty. Yale LJ. 2003;113:1151.

15. Post RC. Three concepts of privacy. Geo LJ. 2000;89:2087.

CHAPTER 2

PRIVACY ON THE WEB

In today's interconnected world, where almost every aspect of our daily lives involves the Internet, online privacy has become a cornerstone of personal security and freedom. Whether shopping online, engaging on social media, streaming videos, or simply browsing for information, our digital footprint grows with every click, keystroke, and tap. Yet, as our dependence on the Web expands, so too do the risks to our privacy. For the individual user, understanding and safeguarding online privacy is no longer optional—it is essential.

For individual users, the Internet offers immense convenience and opportunities, but it also comes with challenges. Web sites track user behavior to tailor content and advertisements, often storing vast amounts of data. Cybercriminals target vulnerable users to steal sensitive information. Even seemingly benign activities, such as joining an online forum or posting on social media, can reveal details about your identity, preferences, or location. Web sites and advertisers use cookies, Web beacons, and tracking pixels to monitor your online activities. This data is often compiled into detailed profiles, which can be used for targeted advertising or even sold to third parties without your explicit consent. Behavioral tracking can feel invasive, as it follows you across platforms and Web sites, often without your awareness. Understanding how your information is collected and used is the first step toward protecting your privacy. Familiarize yourself with the privacy policies of Web sites you use and pay attention to consent prompts for data collection. Only provide the information necessary to access a service. Avoid oversharing on social media and think critically before posting personal details online.

COOKIES

HTTP cookies, more often referred to as Web cookies or simply cookies, are a specific type of magic cookie (a sort of identification token) used by server-side Web applications to store and retrieve long-term information on the client side. The concept of a "cookie" in the context of the Web originates from the magic cookie, a technique used in Unix environments as early as the 1980s. It was typically employed to implement mechanisms for client identification by a server, such as authentication for the X Window System server. The first use of cookies in HTTP dates back to 1994, when they were used to check whether visitors to Netscape's Web site had previously accessed it. In 1995, cookie management was integrated into Internet Explorer 2. Initially, the introduction of cookies was not widely known to the public, but it began to gain attention after an article was published in the *Financial Times* on February 12, 1996. The ensuing debate focused on the implications of cookies for privacy. Cookies became the subject of two hearings by the U.S. Federal Trade Commission in 1996 and 1997, after which their use started being regulated.

Today, the most common applications of cookies involve storing information about users' habits on the Web sites they visit. These applications have often raised concerns among privacy advocates, as cookies can either assist users in navigation or track their behavior. In the latter case, many advertising networks (which sell ads to multiple Web sites) use cookies attached to ad images to correlate visits to different Web sites by the same user, thereby building a profile of their preferred sites. Other uses of cookies are considered beneficial, however, as they provide services to the user, such as saving session data to avoid reauthentication on a subsequent visit or maintaining the contents of a "shopping cart" on e-commerce Web sites.

Servers send cookies to the client as part of the HTTP response, and Web browsers are expected to save and resend these cookies to the server whenever additional requests are made. This recognition mechanism enables functionalities such as authentication (e.g., for login processes), storing session data such as graphical or language preferences for the site, tracking user navigation for statistical or advertising purposes, and associating server-stored data such as the contents of an e-commerce shopping cart.

Due to the privacy implications for Web users, the use of cookies is categorized and regulated in the legal systems of many countries. The security of an authentication cookie typically depends on the security of the issuing site, the user's Web browser, and whether or not the cookie is encrypted. Security vulnerabilities may allow hackers to read cookie data, which could be used to access user data or impersonate the user on the Web site to which the cookie belongs (cross-site scripting (XSS) and cross-site request forgery (CSRF) are examples). Cookies, especially third-party cookies, are commonly used to store users' browsing activity. This sensitive data poses potential privacy risks, prompting European and U.S. authorities to regulate its usage. In 2011, legislation was introduced requiring Web sites to inform users about their use of specific types of cookies. European law mandates that all Web sites in member states notify users when certain cookies are used.

Practically speaking, a cookie is like a small file stored on a user's computer by Web sites during navigation. It saves preferences and enhances site performance, optimizing the user's browsing experience. In detail, a cookie is a small text string sent by a Web server to a Web client (usually a browser) and then sent back to the server (unaltered) every time the client accesses the same part of the same Web domain. Cookies were initially introduced to enable users to store items they wanted to purchase while browsing an e-commerce site (the so-called "shopping cart"). Today, however, shopping cart contents are typically stored in a server-side database rather than in a client-side cookie. To associate a shopping cart with a user, the Web server sends a cookie to the client containing a unique session identifier (usually a long string of letters and numbers). Since cookies are sent to the server with every client request, the session identifier is transmitted whenever the user visits a page on the site, allowing the server to determine which shopping cart belongs to the user.

Because session cookies contain only a unique session identifier, the amount of personal information a Web site can store is virtually unlimited. The site is not restricted by the text length of the cookie itself. Session cookies can also help improve page-loading times, as they require little bandwidth due to their small size. The main cookie used to store preferences for other cookies is called a technical (or consent) cookie, which governs the transmission and receipt of information packets (markers). Every domain or subdomain visited through a browser can set cookies. Since a typical Web page, such as an online news site, contains objects from multiple domains—each of which can set cookies—it's common to have hundreds of cookies stored in a browser.

Cookies are often mistakenly considered programs, leading to misconceptions. In reality, they are simple data blocks incapable of performing any action on their own. Specifically, they cannot act as spyware or viruses. Nonetheless, cookies from certain sites are classified as spyware by many anti-spyware programs because they enable user tracking. Modern browsers allow users to decide whether to accept cookies, though refusal can render some Web site features unusable. For instance, shopping carts that rely on cookies cannot function if cookies are rejected. Cookies are not limited to PCs or similar devices—they are also used on smartphones, tablets, and smart TVs.

A cookie is an additional header present in an HTTP request (`Cookie:`) or response (`Set-Cookie:`). If the server wants to assign a cookie to the user, it will include it in the response headers. The client must detect the presence of the cookie and store it in a dedicated area (usually, a directory where each cookie is saved in a separate file). A cookie consists of an arbitrary text string, an expiration date (beyond which it should no longer be considered valid), and a pattern to identify the domains to which it should be sent back. It is possible to set multiple cookies in a single HTTP response. The Web browser client will resend the cookie, without any modifications, attaching it to all HTTP requests that match the pattern, as long as the expiration date has not passed. The server can then choose to assign the cookie again, overwriting the old one. The pattern-based resend mechanism allows all subdomains of a given domain to receive the cookie, if desired.

Cookies are used to add state to a stateless protocol. Without cookies, there would be no difference between a page loaded before logging in and the same page loaded afterward. Since cookies remain in the system for long periods, Web sites can assign an identifier to the user and track their navigation within the site, usually for statistical purposes. They can also be used to track browsing on third-party sites if those sites use content from the site that set the cookie. Typically, advertisements on Web sites are managed by companies that have ads on multiple Web sites. The advertisement content itself is loaded directly from their server (via an HTTP request) and displayed seamlessly within the Web site the user is visiting. In this way, the advertising company's server will receive the address of the page being viewed from the user's browser and may send a cookie to the client. Through this mechanism, advertising companies can aggregate information about users, build profiles, and show them targeted advertisements.

Since they can be used to monitor online browsing, cookies are often at the center of discussions regarding the right to privacy. Many countries and organizations, including the U.S. and the European Union, have passed legislation on this topic. Cookies have also been criticized for not always accurately identifying users and for being potentially vulnerable to cyberattacks. There are some alternatives to cookies, but all of them come with certain drawbacks in addition to their advantages.

In their cookie policy, Web site administrators must specify in detail the rules governing the use of their own cookies or those of third parties. Cookies are used for various activities, such as authentication, session tracking, and storing specific information about users who access the server, such as favorite Web sites or, in the case of online shopping, the contents of their shopping carts. The search engine Google, for instance, also sends a cookie that stores data about searches, keywords used, and user habits.

Many modern browsers allow users to decide when to accept cookies, though rejecting certain cookies may prevent access to specific functions on a Web site (e.g., registering on a site). Browser settings can often be customized to enable or block cookies permanently, define their lifespan, whitelist or blacklist specific Web sites, or filter cookies based on their origin (same server or linked content such as advertisements from other servers).

It is worth noting that the functionality of cookies depends entirely on the Web browser used by the user. In theory, a browser can give the user complete control over cookies, allowing them to permit or block their creation and use. Other programs, such as those used as proxies, also allow for greater control over what happens with cookies. Using tools such as Tor (which stands for The Onion Router) or a proxy server has the effect of not erasing the user's IP address but rather making a different one appear in its place. This approach ensures that no restrictions are encountered on the number of Web sites browsable while masking the actual IP address.

A cookie can be stored as a text file and typically includes four main attributes. The first is the name/value pair, which is a variable and is a mandatory component. Another attribute is the expiration date, which is optional and determines when the cookie will expire. This can be expressed as a specific date, a maximum number of days, or with special settings such as "Now," which causes the cookie to expire immediately after being created, or "Never," indicating that the cookie will not expire and is therefore considered persistent. The access mode, known as HttpOnly, makes the cookie inaccessible to JavaScript and other client-side scripts, enhancing its security. The secure attribute determines whether the cookie should only be transmitted over an encrypted connection via HTTPS.

Cookies also include information about the domain and path, which define their scope of visibility. These parameters instruct the browser to send the cookie to the server only when the specified domain and path match. If these attributes are not explicitly defined, they default to the domain and path that initially requested the cookie. For example, a cookie created after a user logs in might be set with specific parameters, such as the domain `docs.foo.com` and the path `/accounts`, meaning the cookie will only be used when the browser accesses pages under that specific domain and path. On the other hand, cookies with broader domain definitions, such as `.foo.com`, can be used across all subdomains and paths of that domain. Cookies can, however, only be set by their respective primary domains and subdomains.

The diversity of cookies makes their classification challenging, but they can generally be categorized based on their lifecycle. Session cookies are temporary and are deleted once the browser is closed. These cookies do not have an expiration date, allowing browsers to identify them as session-specific. Persistent cookies, in contrast, remain on the user's device even after the browser is closed and expire on a specified date or after a set duration. Cookies can also be classified based on their origin. First-party cookies are created by the domain displayed in the browser's address bar and are typically used for essential Web site functions, such as remembering user preferences or facilitating navigation. Third-party cookies, however, originate from domains other than the one being visited. These cookies are often used by advertisers to track users across multiple Web sites, enabling targeted advertising by building a profile of their browsing history.

The purpose of cookies also plays a role in their classification. Technical cookies are essential for the proper functioning of a Web site, such as enabling secure transactions or logging in to accounts without repeated credential entries. Statistical cookies help optimize Web sites by collecting aggregated, anonymous data on user behavior. Preference cookies, sometimes called functional cookies, enhance the user experience by storing preferences such as language settings. There are additional types of cookies designed to address specific needs or security concerns. Secure cookies are transmitted only over encrypted HTTPS connections to reduce the risk of interception. HttpOnly cookies are inaccessible to scripts running in the browser, providing protection against attacks such as XSS. SameSite cookies restrict their transmission to requests originating from the same domain, mitigating threats such as CSRF.

Other types of cookies include supercookies and zombie cookies. Supercookies originate from top-level domains, such as `.com` or `.co.uk`, and can interfere with legitimate requests made to these domains, posing significant security risks. Zombie cookies are particularly problematic because they are recreated after being deleted by leveraging stored data in multiple locations, such as browser storage or server-side mechanisms. These cookies can persist even when users attempt to remove them, making them a concern for privacy and security.

A manipulation technique involving cookies is known as cookie poisoning. This method entails altering the contents of a cookie, such as personal information stored on the user's computer, to bypass security mechanisms. Through this technique, an attacker can gain unauthorized access to private information, as well as steal a user's digital identity. Cookies stored on a user's computer contain information that allows applications to authenticate user IDs, monitor user behavior, and personalize Web site content. While this data is often encrypted, the algorithms used are not always secure. As a result, malicious actors can potentially intercept and exploit or modify this information. According to the Open Web Application Security Project (OWASP), cookie manipulation ranks among the twenty most common attacks used by hackers, especially in e-commerce systems, where it is used to identify users.

Most Web sites rely on cookies as the sole identifiers for user sessions, as alternative identification methods come with limitations and vulnerabilities. This practice carries inherent risks, however, as it could enable attackers to steal and impersonate user requests. From the perspective of a Web server, a request made by a malicious user—someone who has stolen another user's cookies—appears indistinguishable from a legitimate request made by the victim.

There are several techniques for stealing cookies, which exploit Web sites that rely on HTTP cookies for user authentication. One method involves network interception. A cookie can be stolen from another computer by intercepting it over the network. Network traffic can be captured and read by a device connected to a network other than that of the sender and receiver, particularly when connected to an unencrypted Wi-Fi network. This traffic may include cookies transmitted over unencrypted HTTP sessions, allowing attackers to read the communications of other users on the network. These intercepted communications include HTTP cookies and the full content of conversations, enabling man-in-the-middle (MITM) attacks. A malicious user can exploit intercepted cookies to impersonate the legitimate owner, carrying out harmful actions. This vulnerability can be mitigated through encrypted communication between the user's device and the Web server using TLS, commonly known as HTTPS. The server can also specify the Secure flag during cookie setup, ensuring that the browser transmits the cookies only over encrypted channels such as Secure Sockets Layer (SSL) connections.

Another method is through fake subdomains and DNS cache poisoning. If a malicious actor can manipulate a DNS server or trick the user into using a fake DNS server, they could gain access to the user's cookies. For instance, an attacker might use DNS cache poisoning to create a fake DNS entry for a subdomain that actually points to the attacker's server. By embedding a URL to their server in content, such as an image URL, the attacker can trick victims into sending all cookies associated with the domain to the attacker's server. This type of attack often occurs due to insufficient security measures by Internet service providers (ISPs) for DNS servers. The severity of such attacks can, however, be reduced if the target site uses secure cookies. In this case, the attacker faces the additional challenge of obtaining the destination site's SSL certificate from a certification authority, as secure cookies can only be transmitted over encrypted connections. Without a valid SSL certificate, the attacker's Web site would trigger browser warnings, potentially alerting users and preventing them from sending cookies to an insecure site.

Cookies can also be stolen through XSS, a technique that exploits Web sites allowing users to submit unfiltered HTML and JavaScript content. By injecting malicious HTML or JavaScript, an attacker can use the victim's browser to capture their cookies. For example, a malicious actor might post a link on a forum that includes JavaScript code to retrieve the victim's cookies and send them to the attacker's server. To mitigate such attacks, developers should filter and sanitize user-generated content. Additionally, HttpOnly cookies can be used to prevent client-side scripts, such as JavaScript, from accessing cookies, making them immune to theft through XSS attacks.

Another exploit involves proxy requests through XSS. In older browser versions, security vulnerabilities allowed attackers to manipulate scripts that generated proxy requests via the XML HttpRequest API. For example, if an attacker's script were executed in the victim's browser, it could create a request to the victim's site while routing the traffic through the attacker's server as a proxy. This would expose the victim's cookies to the attacker. This attack would fail with secure cookies, however, as these can only be transmitted over HTTPS connections, which use end-to-end encryption (E2EE).

CSRF is another way that cookies can be exploited. For instance, if Bob is browsing a forum where Mallory has posted a message containing an HTML image tag linked to a malicious operation on Bob's banking Web site, Bob's browser may unwittingly execute the action. If Bob's authentication is stored in a cookie and the cookie is still valid, the request would be authorized without Bob's explicit consent.

Finally, users can manage or delete cookies through their browser settings, where they can clear browsing history, cache, login data, and form information. Third-party tools such as CCleaner and Spybot – Search & Destroy can also help remove cookies. Once cookies are deleted, however, Web sites may prompt users to reset preferences or re-accept cookies, and browsing may initially feel slower due to the absence of cached data.

PIXEL TRACKERS

A pixel tracker, often referred to as a tracking pixel, is a small, invisible image or code snippet embedded within digital content, such as emails, Web sites, or online advertisements, designed to monitor user behavior and collect data about interactions. At its core, it is a single-pixel transparent image, typically a 1x1 pixel GIF or PNG file, that can be imperceptibly placed within the content. When the content containing the pixel tracker is accessed by a user, the tracker communicates with the server where the image is hosted, sending information about the user's interaction. This process triggers an HTTP request, which carries along data such as the user's IP address, browser type, operating system, screen resolution, and even the timestamp of the interaction.

For instance, in email marketing, pixel trackers are widely employed to confirm when an email is opened and sometimes to track subsequent actions, such as clicks on embedded links. The mechanics of pixel trackers make them a powerful tool for analytics and personalization. On Web sites, they can monitor user journeys—identifying which pages were visited, how long the user stayed, and what actions they took. In advertising, they help measure the effectiveness of campaigns by tracking conversions and user engagement, enabling marketers to refine their strategies for better outcomes.

Pixel trackers have, however, also sparked significant privacy concerns. They often operate discreetly, without explicit user consent or awareness, gathering data that could potentially identify individuals or track their activities across platforms. This has led to debates about ethical usage and the introduction of stricter regulations that mandate transparency and user consent for data collection. Despite their controversial nature, pixel trackers are not inherently malicious. Their effectiveness depends on how they are implemented and the transparency of their usage. Responsible use involves informing users about tracking mechanisms and allowing them to opt out or control their data privacy settings.

Advances in technology, such as browser features that block third-party trackers, and growing awareness among users are also reshaping the landscape of pixel tracking. In essence, while pixel trackers play a critical role in modern digital analytics and marketing, they exist at the intersection of utility and privacy. Their future hinges on striking a balance between leveraging their capabilities for innovation and respecting user rights and preferences.

WEB BEACONS

A Web beacon is a small, often invisible mechanism embedded in digital content that enables the tracking and monitoring of user behavior. While similar to pixel trackers, Web beacons encompass a broader range of tracking methods beyond a single-pixel image, including embedded scripts or HTML elements designed to transmit information about user interactions. They are frequently used in conjunction with cookies to enhance data collection capabilities.

The fundamental operation of a Web beacon involves embedding a tiny, transparent image or code snippet within a Web page, email, or online advertisement. When the content is accessed by a user, the beacon communicates with the server that hosts it, transmitting details such as the user's IP address, browser type, operating system, and the time of the interaction. Additionally, it can reveal whether specific content was viewed or interacted with, making it a powerful tool for analytics and user engagement tracking.

In email marketing, Web beacons are commonly used to determine whether an email has been opened and to track subsequent actions, such as clicking on links or downloading attachments. On Web sites, they provide insights into user behavior by tracking page views, time spent on a site, and navigation patterns. This information is invaluable for improving user experience, tailoring content, and measuring the effectiveness of marketing campaigns.

Web beacons also play a pivotal role in online advertising. They enable advertisers to track conversions, retarget users with personalized ads, and evaluate the performance of ad campaigns. By integrating with cookies, they can follow users across multiple sessions and platforms, building detailed profiles that inform targeted advertising strategies.

Despite their utility, Web beacons have faced criticism due to privacy concerns. Since they often operate covertly, users may be unaware that their activities are being monitored. This has led to debates about the ethical implications of their use and increased scrutiny under privacy regulations. Web beacons themselves are not inherently harmful or invasive. They are tools, and their impact depends on how they are deployed. Responsible use involves maintaining transparency, securing user consent, and adhering to privacy standards. Furthermore, technological advancements, such as browser-based tracking prevention and privacy-focused browsing tools, have given users greater control over their online data.

In summary, Web beacons are essential for understanding and improving user engagement in the digital ecosystem, but their role in data collection demands a careful balance between utility and respect for privacy. As the digital landscape evolves, the conversation around their use will continue to shape the ways organizations interact with and respect their audiences.

PRIVACY-ORIENTED BROWSERS

Privacy-oriented browsers represent a crucial evolution in the way we access the Internet, designed with a fundamental commitment to safeguarding user data, enhancing security, and promoting digital autonomy. These browsers have emerged as a response to growing concerns about the pervasive tracking and surveillance embedded in the modern Web ecosystem, where personal data is routinely harvested, analyzed, and monetized by corporations and governments.

At the heart of privacy-oriented browsers lies the principle of minimizing user exposure to tracking technologies. In the standard browsing experience, Web sites often employ trackers, cookies, and other techniques to collect information about users' behaviors, preferences, and even their physical locations. Privacy browsers, by contrast, actively block these mechanisms. By intercepting third-party trackers and preventing the execution of invasive scripts, these browsers allow users to navigate the Web without leaving behind a detailed digital footprint. This feature alone has made them indispensable to individuals who value their privacy.

Security is another cornerstone of privacy-oriented browsers. In an era where cyber threats are becoming increasingly sophisticated, these browsers integrate cutting-edge technologies to shield users from malicious actors. For instance, many privacy-focused browsers enforce strict encryption protocols such as HTTPS, ensuring that the data exchanged between a user and a Web site remains private and secure from eavesdroppers. Additionally, they often include protections against phishing attempts, malware, and other online threats, creating a safer environment for users to interact with digital content.

One of the defining features of these browsers is their commitment to eliminating intrusive advertising. Online advertisements, while a legitimate source of revenue for many businesses, are often embedded with trackers that harvest user data. Privacy browsers counter this by blocking ads by default, thereby not only protecting user privacy but also enhancing the browsing experience by reducing clutter and improving page load speeds. In cases where advertisements are displayed, they are often curated to respect user privacy, as seen in browsers such as Brave, which reward users for viewing non-invasive ads.

Moreover, privacy-oriented browsers frequently offer private browsing modes that go beyond the superficial protections of standard "Incognito" or "Private" modes. While traditional private browsing merely avoids saving history or cookies locally, many privacy browsers ensure that no trace of the session persists anywhere, either locally or on external servers. This level of privacy is especially valuable for individuals who need to protect sensitive information or who are accessing the Internet from shared devices.

Another remarkable aspect of privacy-oriented browsers is their resistance to browser fingerprinting. Browser fingerprinting is a technique used by Web sites to identify users based on subtle details about their devices and configurations, such as screen resolution, operating system, installed fonts, and extensions. Privacy browsers combat this by standardizing or obscuring these details, making it difficult for Web sites to create a unique identifier for each user. This helps prevent cross-site tracking and ensures a more anonymous browsing experience.

Open-source development is a hallmark of many privacy-oriented browsers, reflecting their ethos of transparency and user empowerment. By allowing anyone to inspect their source code, these browsers invite scrutiny and validation of their privacy claims. This openness fosters trust within the community and ensures that potential vulnerabilities can be identified and addressed promptly. The integration of additional privacy tools, such as virtual private networks (VPNs) and proxies, further distinguishes privacy-oriented browsers from their mainstream counterparts. These tools anonymize a user's IP address, preventing Web sites and services from pinpointing their geographical location. Browsers such as Tor go even further by routing traffic through a network of volunteer-operated servers, obscuring the origin of the connection and providing near-complete anonymity. While this level of protection may slow down browsing speeds, it is indispensable for individuals operating in high-risk environments, such as activists, journalists, or whistleblowers.

Despite their many advantages, privacy-oriented browsers are not without their challenges. For instance, some Web sites may not function correctly when privacy protections block essential scripts or elements. Additionally, the broader adoption of these browsers can be hindered by a lack of awareness or misconceptions about their utility. Mainstream users may perceive them as overly technical or unnecessary, particularly if they are not aware of the extent to which their data is collected in traditional browsing environments. Nonetheless, the importance of privacy-oriented browsers cannot be overstated in today's digital age. They empower users to reclaim control over their online presence, resist the commodification of personal data, and navigate the Web with confidence and autonomy. By prioritizing privacy, these browsers challenge the status quo of data-driven monetization and remind us of the fundamental right to online freedom. As awareness grows and technology evolves, privacy-oriented browsers will undoubtedly play an increasingly pivotal role in shaping the future of the Internet.

The following subsections outline some example privacy-oriented browsers.

Brave

The Brave browser stands out as a groundbreaking tool in the modern Internet landscape, championing privacy, speed, and innovation in a way that few browsers have dared to attempt. At its core, Brave is designed to liberate users from the pervasive surveillance culture of the Web, where data harvesting has become a default practice. By blocking third-party trackers and intrusive advertisements by default, Brave ensures that users can navigate the Internet without the constant background noise of data collection and profiling. This not only preserves privacy but also creates a sense of digital freedom rarely experienced in mainstream browsing.

Brave's commitment to user empowerment extends beyond mere tracker blocking. Its Shields feature gives granular control over site-specific settings, allowing users to decide how much privacy to prioritize without compromising functionality. This adaptability makes Brave suitable for a wide range of users, from casual browsers to those with heightened security needs. Its integration with the Tor network further solidifies its appeal to privacy advocates, providing an additional layer of anonymity that's particularly valuable in restrictive or monitored environments.

Brave's approach to digital advertising marks a revolutionary departure from traditional models. Instead of subjecting users to data-harvesting ads, Brave introduces privacy-respecting advertisements that users can opt into. By participating in the Brave Rewards system, users earn Basic Attention Tokens (BAT), a cryptocurrency that rewards their attention while respecting their privacy. This creates a unique dynamic where users, not corporations, gain value from their online activities. Furthermore, this system offers a direct means of supporting content creators, bypassing the invasive advertising ecosystems that dominate the Web today.

Brave's vision for a fairer Internet is evident in its emphasis on decentralization, as demonstrated by its support for the InterPlanetary File System (IPFS) and its integration of a crypto wallet for managing digital currencies. Performance is another area where Brave excels. By blocking ads and trackers, the browser eliminates many of the elements that slow down Web pages, resulting in significantly faster loading times and a smoother user experience.

Its lightweight design and efficient use of system resources ensure that it performs well on a wide range of devices, making it an excellent choice for users who value speed as much as privacy. Its Chromium-based architecture allows for compatibility with the vast library of Chrome extensions, making it easy for users to transition from other browsers without sacrificing functionality. This reliance on Chromium is not without its drawbacks, however, as it raises questions about Brave's independence from Google's underlying framework.

Brave's user interface is both intuitive and visually appealing, with a clean design that emphasizes ease of use. The homepage dashboard is particularly noteworthy, displaying statistics such as the number of ads blocked and trackers prevented, reinforcing the browser's transparency and effectiveness.

Despite its many strengths, Brave is not immune to criticism. Its focus on cryptocurrency, while innovative, may alienate users who are less familiar with or interested in digital currencies. Some also find its occasional notifications for Brave-sponsored ads, though privacy-respecting, somewhat contradictory to its mission of reducing intrusiveness.

Nonetheless, Brave represents a bold and refreshing alternative to conventional browsers, redefining what it means to browse the Internet responsibly and ethically. Its vision of a private, equitable, and efficient Web positions it as more than just a browser—it's a movement toward reclaiming control in an increasingly commercialized digital world.

DuckDuckGo

DuckDuckGo has emerged as a cornerstone of privacy-first Internet tools, offering users a search engine and browser that reject the pervasive surveillance and data monetization practices that dominate the digital landscape. With its foundational promise of never tracking users, DuckDuckGo sets itself apart as a sanctuary for those seeking anonymity and security in their online interactions. The browser's minimalist design belies the sophisticated protections operating beneath the surface, shielding users from trackers, fingerprinting attempts, and intrusive advertisements without requiring extensive configuration. It provides an accessible gateway to privacy for users at all levels of technical expertise, delivering its features in a manner that feels intuitive and seamless.

Central to DuckDuckGo's appeal is its refusal to store or share user data. Unlike conventional search engines that build detailed profiles to serve targeted ads, DuckDuckGo ensures that each search query is treated as an isolated event. This approach prevents any long-term record of user behavior and nullifies the possibility of profiling. Integrated tracker blocking extends this philosophy, stopping third-party scripts and cookies from monitoring activity across Web sites. This prevents entities from building cross-site user profiles, a common practice in modern digital advertising.

DuckDuckGo's relentless focus on privacy is reinforced by its encrypted search results, ensuring that users' queries are not only untracked but also secure from potential interception. The DuckDuckGo browser takes these principles a step further, embedding its search engine into a browsing experience optimized for privacy. Every session benefits from features such as the automatic enforcement of HTTPS connections, which protects data from being transmitted over insecure channels. The browser's Fire Button allows users to clear all browsing data instantly, offering a straightforward way to ensure no traces of a session remain on the device. This feature is particularly appealing to those who share devices or desire convenience without compromising their security. DuckDuckGo's integration of a privacy grade for Web sites educates users by revealing how well each site protects their data and how its trackers are handled.

DuckDuckGo's simplicity is its strength. Unlike some privacy tools that demand a trade-off in usability or performance, DuckDuckGo is designed to work out of the box without complex setups or extensive user intervention. The browser's straightforward interface emphasizes functionality, ensuring that its privacy features do not overwhelm the core browsing experience. The inclusion of familiar tools such as tabs, bookmarks, and a streamlined settings menu allows users to navigate the Web without sacrificing convenience or ease of use.

Its minimalistic approach has, however, also been met with some criticism. Power users accustomed to more advanced customization options or integrated tools may find DuckDuckGo's feature set somewhat limited. Additionally, its focus on privacy does not always align with compatibility; some Web sites may encounter functionality issues due to the browser's aggressive blocking of trackers and scripts. Nonetheless, these trade-offs are often seen as minor by those who value the robust privacy protections that DuckDuckGo provides.

DuckDuckGo's ethos is not confined to its search engine and browser. It represents a broader commitment to challenging the status quo of data exploitation in the digital age. Its success in carving out a niche in an ecosystem dominated by data-hungry corporations underscores a growing demand for tools that prioritize user autonomy. By making privacy accessible and straightforward, DuckDuckGo has positioned itself not just as a product but as a movement for reclaiming control over personal information. Its steady growth and widespread adoption signal a paradigm shift in how individuals view their online presence, proving that privacy-focused technology can be both practical and impactful.

Firefox

Firefox stands as a symbol of openness and user empowerment in the modern Web, championing privacy, transparency, and adaptability in an era dominated by corporate-controlled browsers. Developed by Mozilla, a nonprofit organization dedicated to maintaining an open Internet, Firefox rejects the pervasive monetization of user data and instead prioritizes control and customization for its users. Its commitment to transparency is exemplified by its open-source nature, allowing anyone to examine its code and verify its privacy claims. This ethos of openness ensures that Firefox remains accountable and aligned with its mission to protect the rights of users in a digital world increasingly shaped by surveillance.

Central to Firefox's appeal is its robust suite of privacy features, which are designed to shield users from the myriad tracking technologies embedded across the Web. Enhanced Tracking Protection is one of its hallmark tools, blocking third-party cookies, social media trackers, cryptominers, and fingerprinters by default. This comprehensive defense ensures that users can browse without the constant specter of data collection looming over their activities. Firefox takes these protections a step further with its Total Cookie Protection feature, which isolates cookies to the sites where they are created, preventing cross-site tracking and limiting the reach of advertising networks. These measures reflect Firefox's unwavering focus on giving users control over their digital identities.

Performance and compatibility are also areas where Firefox excels. Unlike many privacy-focused browsers that sacrifice speed or usability in the pursuit of security, Firefox strikes a balance by delivering fast page loads and smooth performance without compromising its protective measures. Its lightweight design and resource efficiency make it a versatile choice for a wide range of devices, from powerful desktops to low-powered laptops. Firefox's strong adherence to Web standards ensures that users rarely encounter compatibility issues, making it a practical alternative to more ubiquitous browsers such as Chrome.

Customization is another pillar of Firefox's appeal. Its extensive library of add-ons and extensions allows users to tailor their browsing experience to their specific needs. Whether enhancing privacy, boosting productivity, or simply personalizing the interface, Firefox empowers users to create a browser that reflects their unique preferences.

Features such as the Multi-Account Containers extension further enhance functionality by allowing users to separate their online identities, keeping work, personal, and shopping activities isolated from one another. This level of customization, combined with the browser's clean and intuitive interface, ensures that Firefox remains a user-friendly option for individuals across all levels of technical expertise.

In addition to its core functionality, Firefox distinguishes itself through its commitment to innovation and inclusivity. Features such as Pocket, which allows users to save articles for later reading, and its integration of Reader

Mode, which simplifies Web pages for distraction-free consumption, demonstrate Mozilla's dedication to enhancing the overall browsing experience.

Firefox's support for advanced security measures, such as DNS over HTTPS and its partnership with Cloudflare to offer encrypted DNS services, further solidifies its reputation as a browser that prioritizes user safety at every turn.

While Firefox has many strengths, it is not immune to challenges. One of its most persistent struggles is competing in a market dominated by Chromium-based browsers, which have become the standard for Web developers. As a result, Firefox occasionally faces issues with certain Web sites or services optimized solely for Chromium frameworks. Additionally, its market share has declined in recent years, leading to concerns about its long-term sustainability and ability to maintain influence in shaping the Web's future. Mozilla's non-profit status and mission-driven approach, however, provide reassurance that Firefox's goals are rooted in principles rather than profits.

Ultimately, Firefox is more than just a browser; it is a declaration of resistance against the erosion of online privacy and a testament to the importance of an open, user-focused Internet. Its balance of privacy, performance, and customization ensures that it remains a relevant and powerful tool in the hands of those who value their digital freedom. In an age where user data is increasingly commodified, Firefox offers a refreshing alternative, standing as a beacon of trust and transparency in the complex and often opaque world of Web browsing.

LibreWolf

LibreWolf represents the pinnacle of privacy-focused Web browsing, offering users a fortified version of Firefox designed specifically to eliminate any compromises on security, privacy, and freedom. Built as an independent fork of Mozilla Firefox, LibreWolf takes the foundation of one of the most trusted browsers in the world and enhances it by removing telemetry, hardening privacy features, and stripping out corporate-influenced components. It exists as a browser for purists, those who demand uncompromising protection from the invasive practices that have become standard across the Internet.

LibreWolf's modifications begin with the complete removal of Firefox telemetry, ensuring that no data about the user's browsing behavior, system, or interactions is collected or sent back to Mozilla or any other entity. This foundational change establishes a baseline of trust, allowing users to browse with the assurance that their activities remain entirely private.

LibreWolf's dedication to privacy extends to its rigorous blocking of trackers, third-party cookies, and invasive scripts, achieved through built-in configurations and the default integration of privacy-enhancing extensions such as uBlock Origin. These defenses are not optional or watered down; they are the core of the browser's design, ensuring maximum privacy from the moment it is launched.

LibreWolf also addresses vulnerabilities and loopholes that might allow user identification or tracking. Enhanced security settings, such as hardened fingerprinting resistance and stricter cookie isolation, go beyond standard protections, making it exceedingly difficult for Web sites to piece together identifiable information about the user.

LibreWolf's commitment to transparency is evident in its open-source nature, inviting the community to scrutinize and contribute to its development. This open collaboration ensures that the browser remains aligned with its mission to provide a truly private and independent browsing experience.

Performance-wise, LibreWolf maintains the efficiency of Firefox while optimizing it for privacy enthusiasts. It balances resource usage and speed, ensuring that the additional layers of security do not result in noticeable slowdowns. Users benefit from the same fast, standards-compliant browsing experience for which Firefox is known, with the added peace of mind that their data is not being shared or compromised. LibreWolf retains compatibility with Firefox extensions, granting users access to a vast library of tools to further enhance their browsing experience. Its stripped-down design, free from corporate influence, however, makes it leaner and more focused, appealing to those who seek minimalism without sacrificing functionality.

Customization is a key strength of LibreWolf. While it is preconfigured for maximum privacy, advanced users can further tailor the browser to meet their specific needs. The absence of automatic updates—handled manually by the user or through package managers—places full control in the hands of the individual, aligning with the browser's ethos of user autonomy. This manual update system, while a potential hurdle for less tech-savvy users, ensures that updates are transparent and free from unexpected changes.

Despite its many advantages, LibreWolf is not without its challenges. Its focus on privacy and independence from mainstream frameworks means it lacks certain conveniences found in more widely used browsers. Some users may find the lack of synchronization features, such as cloud-based bookmarks or history syncing, to be a drawback, particularly if they are transitioning from services such as Google Chrome. Furthermore, the manual update process can be intimidating for those accustomed to automated updates. Compatibility issues may occasionally arise with Web sites optimized solely for Chromium-based browsers, though these instances are rare given LibreWolf's adherence to Web standards.

LibreWolf is not just a browser; it is a statement of resistance against the normalization of surveillance and data exploitation in the digital age. It provides a robust alternative for individuals who value their privacy above all else and are willing to make minor trade-offs for unparalleled protection. By building on Firefox's legacy and enhancing it with strict privacy measures, LibreWolf offers a browsing experience that is as uncompromising as it is reliable. It stands as a tool for those who refuse to settle for anything less than complete control over their digital presence, embodying the principles of freedom, security, and transparency in every line of its code.

Mullvad

Mullvad Browser stands as a unique and powerful tool in the realm of privacy-focused Web browsing, created through a collaboration between the renowned Mullvad VPN team and the Tor Project. This browser is not just an alternative to mainstream options but a deliberate and highly refined approach to online anonymity, built specifically to counter the pervasive surveillance and data exploitation that define much of the modern Internet. Mullvad Browser's defining characteristic is its alignment with Mullvad's broader ethos: absolute user privacy without unnecessary frills, tracking, or commercial motives.

At its core, Mullvad Browser shares much of its DNA with Tor Browser, offering many of the same robust privacy features while omitting Tor's onion routing network. Instead, it is optimized for use with VPNs, particularly Mullvad's own service. By combining the strong protections of Tor's fingerprinting-resistant browser design with VPN-level encryption and location masking, Mullvad Browser creates an ideal solution for those seeking anonymity without engaging with the complexities of the Tor network. The focus is clear and uncompromising: ensure that users can browse without leaving a trail or being uniquely identifiable.

The fingerprinting resistance in Mullvad Browser is one of its most significant features. By ensuring that all users appear nearly identical to Web sites, it drastically reduces the ability of trackers to build profiles based on unique browser and system configurations. This anonymity by uniformity approach, inherited from the Tor Project, ensures that even advanced tracking techniques struggle to differentiate one user from another.

Mullvad Browser also blocks third-party cookies and trackers by default, safeguarding against invasive advertising networks and cross-site tracking systems. Mullvad Browser enforces a strict no-leakage policy when paired with a VPN. It ensures that no DNS queries or IP information can accidentally expose the user's true location or identity, making it an essential choice for those relying on a VPN for privacy.

The browser's intentional design encourages users to use privacy-enhancing practices, such as disabling cookies entirely when possible or using private browsing sessions for added security. Unlike mainstream browsers, which often default to convenience over safety, Mullvad Browser starts from the principle that privacy should not be optional or an afterthought.

The user experience is intentionally minimalistic. Mullvad Browser does not attempt to compete with flashy interfaces or feature-heavy designs; instead, it focuses entirely on providing a functional and secure browsing environment. This simplicity, while stark, reinforces the browser's purpose: a no-nonsense tool for privacy-conscious individuals. It supports essential features such as tabbed browsing, bookmarks, and a straightforward settings menu, but avoids integration with services or ecosystems that could compromise its integrity.

This dedication to privacy comes with certain trade-offs, however. Mullvad Browser is not built for those seeking convenience features common in mainstream browsers, such as password managers, cloud syncing, or integrated extensions. These omissions are intentional, reflecting Mullvad's philosophy that every additional feature increases the surface area for potential vulnerabilities. As a result, users who are accustomed to such amenities may need to adjust their workflows or rely on external tools.

While Mullvad Browser excels in its role as a privacy-first browser, its reliance on a VPN instead of the Tor network also means that it is best suited for users who already have or are willing to adopt a high-quality VPN. For those who do not pair it with a VPN, the browser's privacy benefits are still significant, but the full extent of its anonymity relies on that partnership. Additionally, like other niche browsers, it may occasionally encounter compatibility issues with Web sites optimized for more mainstream platforms.

Mullvad Browser is not just a product but a statement about the kind of Internet experience its creators believe users deserve: one free from surveillance, tracking, and manipulation. By rejecting the bloated and data-hungry practices of the mainstream, Mullvad Browser creates a streamlined and effective tool for those who prioritize privacy above all else. It reflects a broader philosophy of digital sovereignty, reminding users that they have the right to control their data and their identity in an increasingly monitored world. For those committed to preserving their online anonymity, Mullvad Browser offers an unparalleled combination of simplicity, security, and trustworthiness.

Tor

Tor Browser is a cornerstone of digital privacy and anonymity, offering users unparalleled protection against surveillance, censorship, and tracking. Built on the Tor network, an ingenious system of layered encryption and decentralized routing, the browser allows individuals to access the Internet in a way that obscures their identity and location. Unlike traditional browsers, which transmit data directly to a destination server, Tor routes user traffic through a series of volunteer-operated nodes around the globe. This design effectively masks the user's IP address and encrypts their data multiple times, ensuring that no single entity can trace the entire communication path. The result is a browsing experience that grants individuals a level of anonymity rarely achievable with conventional methods.

At the heart of Tor's appeal is its dedication to user privacy. The browser's core features are specifically designed to thwart tracking and surveillance. By default, it blocks third-party cookies, prevents fingerprinting attempts, and clears all browsing history, cookies, and other session data upon exit. These measures ensure that users leave no trace behind, whether they are accessing sensitive information, bypassing Internet restrictions, or simply seeking an alternative to the pervasive data collection of mainstream browsers.

Tor's NoScript integration adds another layer of protection by disabling potentially harmful scripts unless explicitly allowed by the user, which is especially useful for preventing exploits and mitigating vulnerabilities.

Tor Browser's ability to access the dark Web further underscores its uniqueness. While the dark Web has garnered a reputation for illicit activity, it is also a vital tool for whistleblowers, activists, journalists, and individuals in oppressive regimes, offering them a secure way to communicate and share information.

Tor is more than a browser; it is a lifeline for those seeking to evade censorship and protect their freedom of expression. It also serves as a means of circumventing geo-restrictions, allowing users to access content and services that might otherwise be blocked in their region.

Tor does, however, have its drawbacks. Its reliance on the volunteer-run Tor network can lead to slower browsing speeds, as traffic must pass through multiple nodes before reaching its destination. This is a deliberate trade-off for anonymity, but it can be frustrating for users accustomed to the speed of traditional browsers. Additionally, while Tor is designed to protect against many forms of surveillance, it cannot safeguard against end-user behavior that compromises privacy, such as logging in to accounts or providing personal information. Tor's anonymity also depends on strict adherence to best practices, as combining Tor with non-private applications or services can undermine its protections.

Tor Browser's usability has evolved significantly over the years. Its interface, based on Firefox, is familiar and intuitive, allowing users to navigate with ease despite the complexity of the technology under the hood. While some advanced features and configurations may require technical knowledge, the browser is designed to work securely out of the box, making it accessible even to those without a deep understanding of anonymity tools. Regular updates and contributions from the Tor Project and its community ensure that the browser remains at the forefront of privacy and security.

Tor has, however, faced criticism and challenges from various quarters. Governments and organizations with an interest in surveillance or censorship have sought to block or undermine the Tor network, highlighting its effectiveness as a tool for anonymity. Its association with the dark Web and illicit activity has also led to negative perceptions, despite the browser's vital role in safeguarding human rights and freedom of expression. Additionally, some Web sites and services may block Tor users outright, citing concerns about abuse or fraud originating from anonymized traffic.

Whether used by journalists in repressive regimes, activists seeking to organize securely, or ordinary individuals concerned about their online privacy, Tor stands as a beacon of resistance against the erosion of personal freedoms. Its continued development and widespread adoption demonstrate that there remains a demand for technologies that prioritize user sovereignty, proving that privacy is not just a luxury but a necessity in the modern digital age.

Vivaldi

Vivaldi is a Web browser that stands out for its commitment to customization, functionality, and user-centric design, offering an experience that caters to individuals seeking more control over their online interactions. Created by former Opera Software co-founder Jon von Tetzchner, Vivaldi is designed with the belief that users should have the freedom to tailor their browsing environment to their exact needs, without sacrificing speed, privacy, or security. The browser's philosophy is rooted in empowerment, providing a robust set of tools and features that go far beyond what mainstream browsers typically offer.

Customization lies at the heart of Vivaldi's appeal. From its interface to its functionality, nearly every aspect of the browser can be modified to suit personal preferences. Users can rearrange toolbars, tweak color schemes, and even control the layout of tabs to match their workflow. This unparalleled flexibility extends to features such as tab stacking, which allows users to group multiple tabs for better organization, and tiling, which enables side-by-side viewing of Web sites within the same window. These capabilities make Vivaldi an ideal choice for power users, researchers, and anyone who values efficiency in multitasking.

Beyond customization, Vivaldi is packed with built-in tools that eliminate the need for many third-party extensions. Its integrated notes feature allows users to jot down ideas directly within the browser, complete with support for rich text formatting and screenshots. The browser also includes a full-featured mail client, calendar, and feed reader, transforming it into a comprehensive productivity suite. These additions highlight Vivaldi's commitment to reducing reliance on external services, keeping more of a user's activity within the browser itself.

Privacy is another pillar of Vivaldi's design. The browser does not track user behavior or sell data, a stark contrast to many competitors that rely on advertising and data monetization. It includes built-in ad and tracker blockers, ensuring that users can browse without being followed by invasive tracking technologies.

Vivaldi also supports encrypted syncing of bookmarks, history, passwords, and settings across devices, with data stored securely on Vivaldi servers. Unlike many services, syncing in Vivaldi is end-to-end encrypted, ensuring that even the company cannot access user information.

Vivaldi's performance is strong, thanks to its Chromium-based engine, which ensures compatibility with most modern Web sites and extensions from the Chrome Web Store. Despite its robust feature set, the browser remains responsive and efficient, with resource management that can be tailored to the user's needs.

Features such as lazy loading of tabs and adjustable animation speeds further enhance performance, allowing users to strike the right balance between speed and functionality. In addition, features such as keyboard shortcuts, mouse gestures, and customizable search engines enhance usability, ensuring that users can interact with the browser in ways that feel natural and intuitive. Its regular updates and commitment to user feedback demonstrate a dedication to continuous improvement, with new features and refinements added frequently based on the community's needs.

Vivaldi's wealth of features and customization options may, however, present a steep learning curve for new users or those accustomed to simpler browsers. The sheer volume of settings and tools can feel overwhelming, especially for those who are less tech-savvy or prefer minimalistic interfaces. Additionally, while Vivaldi does an excellent job of integrating a wide range of functionalities, its reliance on the Chromium engine means it is not entirely independent of Google's ecosystem, a point of contention for some privacy-conscious users. Vivaldi also caters to creative workflows and diverse needs with its focus on accessibility and innovation.

Ultimately, Vivaldi is more than a browser—it is a platform for personal expression and productivity, designed for those who demand more from their online tools. Its extensive customization, built-in features, and strong privacy stance make it a standout choice for users who value individuality and control in their digital lives. While its depth and complexity may not appeal to everyone, Vivaldi offers an experience unlike any other, proving that a browser can be as unique as the person using it. In an industry often characterized by homogenization, Vivaldi stands as a testament to the power of choice and innovation, redefining what it means to browse the Web.

PLUGINS: A RESOURCE AND A HIDDEN MENACE

Installed plugins can significantly interfere with privacy, often in ways that users might not anticipate. These software extensions, while designed to enhance the functionality and user experience of Web browsers, can inadvertently or deliberately compromise personal information. The potential privacy risks stem from the very nature of plugins: they are additional pieces of code that integrate into a browser, often requiring permissions to access data and interact with Web content. This integration, while powerful, creates opportunities for data exploitation, tracking, and surveillance.

One of the most significant privacy concerns with plugins is their capacity to collect and transmit user data. Many plugins require access to browsing history, clipboard content, or even sensitive data entered into forms. While this access is often justified as necessary for the plugin's functionality, it also opens the door to misuse. Some plugins are explicitly designed to harvest data, selling it to advertisers or other third parties. Even when the developer's intentions are benign, poor security practices can expose the collected data to breaches or unauthorized access. For instance, plugins that log user activity without proper encryption can inadvertently leak sensitive information if their servers are compromised.

Plugins can also introduce unique fingerprinting risks. Every plugin installed on a browser contributes to the browser's overall configuration, which can be used to identify and track users across the Web. A unique combination of plugins, their versions, and their settings forms part of a digital fingerprint that Web sites and advertisers can exploit. Unlike cookies, which users can clear or block, fingerprinting is a passive method of tracking that does not require user consent and is more difficult to detect or avoid. Thus, each plugin adds to the complexity and traceability of a user's digital profile.

Security vulnerabilities within plugins represent another significant risk to privacy. Many plugins are developed by independent creators or small teams, and not all undergo rigorous testing or regular updates. Outdated plugins may contain exploitable flaws that hackers can leverage to gain access to the browser or even the underlying system. Such vulnerabilities can lead to unauthorized access to personal data, including passwords, financial information, or private communications. Worse still, malicious actors can sometimes distribute compromised versions of legitimate plugins, using them as trojan horses to infiltrate user systems.

The permissions requested by plugins can often exceed what is necessary for their operation, raising red flags about their potential for misuse. Some plugins ask for access to all Web site data, even when their functionality only requires limited interaction with specific sites. This broad level of access can allow plugins to monitor user activity across the Web, capturing details such as search queries, visited pages, and form submissions. Such overreach not only undermines user privacy but also places immense trust in the developer's intentions and security practices, which may not always be warranted.

Plugins can also serve as vectors for invasive advertisements and tracking scripts. Ad-supported plugins, for example, often insert promotional content into Web pages or collect browsing data to serve targeted ads. These practices not only degrade the browsing experience but also compromise privacy by sharing user behavior with third-party networks. Moreover, such plugins can bypass traditional ad-blockers and tracking protections by operating within the browser itself, making them difficult to detect or neutralize.

Another layer of concern arises from the lack of transparency and accountability in the plugin ecosystem. Many users install plugins without thoroughly reviewing their permissions, privacy policies, or developer reputations.

Furthermore, even reputable plugins can be sold or acquired by entities with less scrupulous intentions, turning a once-trustworthy tool into a privacy threat. This scenario has played out repeatedly in the browser ecosystem, with well-regarded plugins suddenly introducing invasive tracking or questionable practices after changing ownership.

In addition to these direct risks, plugins can inadvertently weaken browser-level privacy protections. For instance, a plugin might inadvertently disable features such as strict cookie handling, enhanced tracking prevention, or private browsing mode. Some plugins conflict with browser security settings, introducing gaps that Web sites or malicious actors can exploit. Users often remain unaware of these conflicts, assuming their privacy settings remain intact when, in fact, they have been undermined.

Ultimately, while plugins can greatly enhance the functionality of Web browsers, their potential to interfere with privacy cannot be overlooked. Users must exercise caution when selecting and installing plugins, prioritizing those with transparent privacy policies, minimal permissions, and a track record of responsible development. Regularly reviewing installed plugins, disabling those no longer in use, and staying vigilant about updates are essential practices to mitigate risks. In the broader context, the plugin ecosystem underscores the delicate balance between convenience and security, reminding users that even seemingly innocuous tools can have profound implications for their digital privacy.

Plugins can indeed be useful for protecting one's privacy, provided they are chosen carefully and used correctly. While plugins are often seen as potential privacy risks, there is a category of extensions specifically designed to enhance security, anonymity, and control over personal data. These tools empower users to take active measures against tracking, surveillance, and data exploitation, making them valuable allies in the ongoing battle for online privacy.

One of the most notable ways plugins contribute to privacy protection is by blocking trackers and advertisements. Extensions such as uBlock Origin and Privacy Badger are widely recognized for their ability to prevent third-party trackers from collecting user data. These plugins act as gatekeepers, intercepting tracking scripts embedded in Web sites and blocking them before they can execute. By doing so, they not only improve privacy but also enhance browsing performance by reducing the load caused by ads and unnecessary scripts. Similarly, plugins such as Ghostery provide users with detailed insights into the trackers used by Web sites, offering transparency and control over what is allowed to run.

Another significant category of privacy-enhancing plugins focuses on encrypting Web traffic. Extensions such as HTTPS Everywhere, developed by the Electronic Frontier Foundation (EFF), ensure that users always connect to Web sites using secure HTTPS connections when available. This encryption protects data from being intercepted by malicious actors during transmission, especially when browsing on public Wi-Fi networks. By making secure connections the default, such plugins reduce the risk of sensitive information, such as passwords or financial details, being exposed.

Privacy plugins can also help manage and control cookies, which are a primary tool for tracking user behavior across the Web. Extensions such as Cookie AutoDelete and ClearURLs provide users with the ability to delete cookies automatically after leaving a site or sanitize URLs by removing tracking parameters. These tools work to ensure that cookies and other tracking mechanisms do not accumulate and compromise user privacy over time. They grant users a higher degree of control over their digital footprint, enabling browsing with minimal residual data.

In addition to blocking trackers and managing cookies, certain plugins enhance privacy by mitigating browser fingerprinting. Browser fingerprinting is a sophisticated method of identifying users based on the unique combination of their browser settings, extensions, and hardware configurations.

Plugins such as Trace and CanvasBlocker introduce subtle obfuscations to browsing behavior, making it more difficult for Web sites to build a consistent fingerprint. While no tool can eliminate fingerprinting entirely, these plugins significantly increase the difficulty of accurately identifying users.

For those concerned about surveillance and censorship, plugins designed to anonymize Web activity can be invaluable. Tools such as VPN extensions (e.g., Mullvad or Proton VPN) mask a user's IP address by routing their traffic through remote servers, hiding their location and protecting against monitoring by ISPs or government entities. Similarly, Onion Browser Button and other Tor-related plugins integrate the Tor network into the browsing experience, offering advanced anonymity for sensitive activities.

Password managers, another essential type of plugin, play a pivotal role in maintaining privacy and security. Extensions such as Bitwarden and LastPass securely store and autofill passwords, allowing users to create strong, unique credentials for each Web site without the risk of reusing passwords. By reducing the likelihood of credential theft or phishing attacks, these tools protect users from unauthorized access to their accounts, a critical aspect of maintaining online privacy.

While these privacy-focused plugins provide significant benefits, their effectiveness depends on the user's choices and behavior. It is crucial to select plugins developed by reputable organizations with transparent privacy policies. Plugins that are open source and have a strong track record of regular updates and community involvement tend to be more trustworthy. Users should also be cautious about the number of plugins they install, as each one increases the attack surface and contributes to browser fingerprinting. Regularly auditing installed plugins and removing those that are outdated or unused is an important practice.

Another consideration is compatibility with browser settings and other extensions. Privacy-focused plugins often work best in conjunction with native browser features such as private browsing mode, tracker prevention settings, or built-in ad-blockers. Users should ensure that their plugins complement, rather than conflict with, these native protections to avoid redundancy or interference.

In the broader context, privacy-enhancing plugins serve as a reminder that safeguarding one's digital presence is a shared responsibility between the user and the tools they employ. While no plugin can provide absolute privacy, they offer a practical and accessible means of reducing vulnerabilities and regaining control over personal data. By leveraging the right combination of extensions, users can create a layered defense against the myriad threats that compromise online privacy, transforming their browsers into robust shields in the fight for digital autonomy.

The following subsections provide some examples of privacy-enhancing plugins.

uBlock Origin

uBlock Origin is a highly popular, open-source browser extension designed primarily for blocking ads, trackers, and other potentially intrusive Web elements. It has become a preferred choice among privacy-conscious users and those seeking a cleaner, faster browsing experience. Developed by Raymond Hill, uBlock Origin distinguishes itself from many ad-blockers with its lightweight design, efficiency, and extensive customization options.

One of the most significant strengths of uBlock Origin is its exceptional performance. Unlike some ad-blockers that consume a considerable amount of system resources, uBlock Origin is designed to be highly efficient. It minimizes central processing unit (CPU) and memory usage, ensuring that users can block unwanted elements without sacrificing browser speed or device performance. This efficiency is particularly noticeable when browsing ad-heavy or resource-intensive Web sites, where uBlock Origin can significantly improve page load times.

Another notable feature of uBlock Origin is its robust filtering capabilities. By default, it integrates multiple popular blocklists, such as EasyList, EasyPrivacy, and uBlock's own filter lists. These lists help block ads, tracking scripts, and malware domains right out of the box.

The tool doesn't stop there, however; it offers advanced users the ability to add custom filters or enable additional blocklists tailored to specific needs. This flexibility makes it a powerful tool for users who want granular control over their browsing environment. Privacy is another area where uBlock Origin excels. It blocks tracking scripts and cookies that advertisers use to monitor user behavior, enhancing online anonymity. By disrupting the mechanisms that feed into surveillance, uBlock Origin helps users reclaim control over their digital footprint.

While it has many strengths, uBlock Origin also has some limitations. For one, its extensive features and customization options can be overwhelming for less tech-savvy users. While the default settings work well for most, diving into the advanced options requires a basic understanding of filters, rules, and Web elements. This steep learning curve might deter casual users who prefer a more plug-and-play approach. Another potential downside is the collateral blocking of some non-intrusive or essential Web elements. For instance, certain Web sites might break or lose functionality because crucial scripts are blocked along with the ads.

Although uBlock Origin allows users to whitelist specific sites or elements, identifying and resolving such issues can be cumbersome for inexperienced users. Additionally, the reliance on filter lists can sometimes lead to a reactive rather than proactive approach. As new ad formats and tracking technologies emerge, filter lists need to be updated to address them. While uBlock Origin is quick to adopt changes, there may be a lag between the introduction of new advertising techniques and the availability of updated filters.

In summary, uBlock Origin is a powerful, efficient, and highly customizable ad-blocking extension that excels in enhancing online privacy and improving browsing speed. Its strengths lie in its lightweight design, robust filtering capabilities, and ability to cater to advanced users. Its complexity and occasional over-blocking might, however, pose challenges for less experienced users. Overall, it remains one of the best tools available for those seeking a more private and streamlined Web experience.

Privacy Badger

Privacy Badger is a browser extension developed by EFF that focuses on protecting users' online privacy by blocking trackers and invasive elements on Web sites. Unlike traditional ad-blockers that rely on predefined filter lists, Privacy Badger employs a behavioral approach to identify and block tracking technologies dynamically. This unique methodology sets it apart from many other privacy tools and makes it a valuable option for users concerned about digital surveillance.

One of the key strengths of Privacy Badger is its automated learning mechanism. Rather than depending on static blocklists, the extension observes how Web elements behave during browsing sessions. If Privacy Badger detects that a particular domain is tracking a user across multiple Web sites without consent, it automatically blocks the tracker. This adaptive approach ensures that the extension remains effective against new and evolving tracking techniques, providing a layer of future-proofing that list-based tools might lack.

Another advantage of Privacy Badger is its simplicity. It is designed with non-technical users in mind, offering a user-friendly interface and requiring minimal setup or maintenance. Once installed, it works in the background without requiring manual configuration. This makes it an excellent choice for individuals who want enhanced privacy without dealing with the complexity of custom filters or settings.

Additionally, Privacy Badger visually represents its actions through a system of colored sliders, allowing users to see and adjust the level of blocking for specific domains if desired. Unlike some ad-blocking tools that participate in "acceptable ads" programs or monetize user data, Privacy Badger is entirely non-commercial. Its sole purpose is to protect users from intrusive tracking, ensuring that the tool remains aligned with its mission of safeguarding digital privacy.

Privacy Badger does have its limitations, however. One notable weakness is its comparatively limited functionality as an ad-blocker. While it can block ads that rely on tracking, its primary goal is not to remove advertisements but to stop privacy violations. As a result, users who seek a comprehensive ad-blocking solution might find Privacy Badger lacking in scope. In such cases, combining it with a dedicated ad-blocker such as uBlock Origin may be necessary to achieve a complete browsing experience. Another drawback of Privacy Badger is that its behavioral blocking approach can take time to reach full effectiveness. When installed, it begins observing trackers and only blocks them after identifying suspicious activity across multiple sites. This means that users may initially encounter some level of tracking until the extension has gathered enough data to act. In contrast, filter-based tools provide immediate protection by blocking known trackers from the outset.

Furthermore, while Privacy Badger is effective at addressing privacy concerns, it might not block every invasive element or tracker due to its focus on cross-site tracking. Single-site tracking or less conventional methods might slip through its defenses. This narrower scope could leave some gaps compared to other tools with a broader blocking strategy.

In conclusion, Privacy Badger is a robust and ethical privacy tool that excels in dynamically identifying and blocking trackers without requiring extensive user input. Its strengths lie in its adaptive approach, simplicity, and commitment to user privacy. Its limitations as a comprehensive ad-blocker and its learning curve for effective blocking may, however, make it best suited as a complement to other privacy-enhancing tools. For users who prioritize privacy and ease of use, Privacy Badger is an excellent addition to their digital toolbox.

HTTPS Everywhere

HTTPS Everywhere is a browser extension jointly developed by EFF and the Tor Project. Its primary purpose is to enhance user security and privacy by ensuring that connections to Web sites are encrypted whenever possible. The extension works by rewriting requests to use HTTPS instead of the less secure HTTP, thus protecting users from a range of potential threats, such as eavesdropping, data tampering, and MITM attacks.

One of HTTPS Everywhere's greatest strengths is its simplicity and effectiveness in securing Web traffic. Many Web sites support HTTPS but may not default to it, leaving users vulnerable to interception on unsecured connections. HTTPS Everywhere resolves this issue by automatically redirecting traffic to the HTTPS version of a site whenever it is available. This seamless transition helps protect sensitive information, such as login credentials and financial data, from being exposed to malicious actors on public networks.

Another advantage of HTTPS Everywhere is its extensive coverage of Web sites. It achieves this by relying on a curated set of rulesets that define which domains should be redirected to HTTPS. This database is regularly updated to include new sites, ensuring comprehensive protection for users. Additionally, the extension is lightweight and operates quietly in the background, making it accessible to users with minimal technical expertise.

Beyond its direct security benefits, HTTPS Everywhere also promotes broader adoption of HTTPS across the Web. By encouraging users to default to secure connections, the extension exerts pressure on Web site administrators to implement HTTPS support, contributing to a more secure Internet ecosystem overall.

Despite its strengths, HTTPS Everywhere has notable limitations, particularly in the context of recent technological advancements. The widespread adoption of HTTPS, driven by initiatives such as Google Chrome's "Not Secure" warnings for HTTP sites and the availability of free HTTPS certificates through services such as Let's Encrypt, has rendered the extension less critical for many users. In modern browsers, most Web sites automatically default to HTTPS, reducing the need for a dedicated extension to enforce secure connections.

Another limitation is that HTTPS Everywhere cannot secure connections to Web sites that do not support HTTPS. In such cases, the extension simply allows the connection to proceed over HTTP, albeit with a warning to the user. This means it cannot offer complete protection on the Internet, especially when visiting less secure or outdated Web sites.

Furthermore, the ruleset-based approach of HTTPS Everywhere has its drawbacks. While the extension includes an extensive list of supported sites, it relies on manual updates to maintain its database. If a Web site changes its configuration, or if a new site emerges without being added to the ruleset, HTTPS Everywhere may not function as intended for those cases.

In summary, HTTPS Everywhere has been a pivotal tool in advancing Internet security by making encrypted connections the default wherever possible. Its strengths lie in its simplicity, extensive ruleset coverage, and contribution to promoting HTTPS adoption globally. Its relevance has, however, diminished in the face of widespread HTTPS adoption and browser improvements that natively enforce secure connections. While still useful in certain scenarios, HTTPS Everywhere is increasingly seen as a legacy tool whose functionality is becoming less critical in today's Internet landscape. For users seeking maximum security, combining it with other privacy tools might still provide added value.

Cookie AutoDelete

Cookie AutoDelete is a browser extension designed to enhance user privacy by managing and automatically deleting cookies created during Web-browsing sessions. This tool provides users with greater control over the data that Web sites store on their devices, offering a practical solution for maintaining privacy and preventing tracking. At its core, Cookie AutoDelete works by removing cookies from Web sites that users have visited as soon as they close the corresponding tabs. Unlike default browser behavior, which typically retains cookies until manually cleared or until they expire, this extension ensures that cookies are promptly deleted, minimizing the potential for tracking and data accumulation. Users can configure the extension to maintain certain cookies for trusted sites, offering flexibility without compromising its primary function.

The extension operates through a user-friendly interface, where users can customize their cookie management preferences. They can whitelist or "protect" specific domains, allowing those cookies to persist across sessions, which is particularly useful for Web sites requiring logins or personalized settings. Similarly, users can blacklist domains, ensuring that cookies from those sites are always deleted immediately, even during an active browsing session.

Cookie AutoDelete also supports advanced features such as cleaning other types of browser storage, including local storage, which is often overlooked by traditional cookie management tools. By addressing these less visible forms of storage, the extension provides comprehensive protection against tracking mechanisms that go beyond standard cookies.

A key advantage of Cookie AutoDelete is its adaptability. It allows users to set different behaviors for various browsing modes, such as private or incognito sessions, where it can operate more aggressively to maximize privacy. The extension also integrates with browser permissions, enabling users to define rules for specific scenarios, such as retaining cookies only during a session or deleting them immediately after use.

The impact of Cookie AutoDelete on online privacy is significant. By proactively managing cookies, it helps prevent cross-site tracking, a common method used by advertisers and data brokers to monitor user behavior across different Web sites. This reduction in tracking not only enhances privacy but also improves browsing performance by limiting the storage of unnecessary data.

Cookie AutoDelete does, however, require a degree of user involvement and understanding to function effectively. Misconfiguring the extension—such as accidentally deleting cookies required for authentication—can lead to inconvenience, such as being logged out of frequently used sites. As such, the tool is most effective when users take the time to fine-tune their preferences based on their browsing habits.

In conclusion, Cookie AutoDelete is a powerful and versatile privacy tool for managing cookies and related storage in Web browsers. By offering automated and customizable cookie deletion, it provides users with greater control over their online data, reducing tracking risks and enhancing privacy. While it may require some initial configuration, its benefits make it an invaluable resource for privacy-conscious individuals navigating the modern Web.

Trace

Trace is a privacy-focused browser extension designed to enhance user security and anonymity while navigating the Web. It serves as a comprehensive tool to block tracking technologies, obfuscate identifiable information, and minimize the ability of Web sites and advertisers to monitor user activity. Its multifaceted approach addresses a wide range of tracking methods, making it an effective solution for those seeking to protect their online privacy.

The primary function of Trace is to shield users from various forms of online tracking. It accomplishes this by blocking scripts, trackers, and other elements that collect data about user behavior. By preventing these elements from loading, the extension reduces the amount of information that Web sites can gather about visitors, such as browsing habits, device configurations, and geolocation data. This feature is particularly effective against third-party trackers commonly employed by advertisers and analytics platforms.

Beyond blocking trackers, Trace offers sophisticated techniques to camouflage user activity and thwart fingerprinting, a method used to identify and track users based on their unique device and browser characteristics. Trace manipulates data that Web sites often use to create fingerprints, such as screen resolution, browser headers, and system fonts, introducing subtle variations that make it more difficult to associate specific behaviors with a single user. This approach creates a layer of anonymity, as it prevents Web sites from reliably recognizing repeat visits.

Trace also includes features to mitigate other privacy risks, such as blocking WebRTC IP leaks, which can expose a user's real IP address even when using a VPN. It can disable certain browser features that are prone to abuse, such as hyperlink auditing and the Battery Status API, which Web sites may use to gather additional user data.

Additionally, Trace often comes with options to control referrer headers, preventing Web sites from knowing where a user originated before landing on their page. The extension's interface allows for extensive customization, catering to both novice users seeking simple protection and advanced users requiring fine-grained control. Users can enable or disable specific protections based on their needs, whitelist trusted Web sites, and adjust the intensity of anti-fingerprinting measures. This flexibility ensures that Trace can adapt to a variety of browsing scenarios, from general Web use to high-security contexts.

One of Trace's distinguishing characteristics is its emphasis on providing detailed insights into its functionality. Users can view reports on the trackers and scripts blocked during their sessions, offering transparency and helping them understand the extent of tracking attempts. This educative element encourages awareness about online privacy and the methods used to undermine it.

Like many privacy tools, however, Trace may occasionally interfere with the functionality of certain Web sites, particularly those that rely heavily on third-party scripts for essential features. This potential drawback underscores the importance of its customization options, which allow users to strike a balance between privacy and usability.

In conclusion, Trace is a robust and versatile browser extension that addresses a wide spectrum of online tracking threats. By combining script blocking, anti-fingerprinting measures, and protection against leaks and other vulnerabilities, it empowers users to reclaim control over their digital footprint. While it requires some understanding and configuration to maximize its benefits, Trace stands out as an invaluable tool for anyone prioritizing privacy and security in an increasingly surveilled online environment.

INCOGNITO MODE

Incognito mode, often referred to as private browsing, is a feature in most modern Web browsers that allows users to browse the Internet in a manner that minimizes the storage of their browsing activity on the device they are using. When a user opens an incognito window, the browser creates a temporary browsing session that operates independently of the main session. This temporary session ensures that certain types of data, such as browsing history, cookies, and site data, are not stored on the device once the incognito window is closed.

During an incognito session, the browser does not save visited Web sites to the browsing history, making it impossible for others using the same device to see what Web sites were accessed. Additionally, any cookies that Web sites generate during the session are only stored temporarily and are deleted as soon as the incognito window is closed. This can be particularly useful for avoiding being logged in to accounts or tracked across multiple sessions on shared or public devices. Passwords, search suggestions, and other saved data stored in the browser's autofill database are typically not accessible during an incognito session unless the user actively enables them. This provides an additional layer of privacy by preventing sensitive personal information from being auto-filled in forms or login fields.

It is important to note, however, that incognito mode does not make browsing completely anonymous. While it prevents local storage of browsing data, it does not hide the user's activity from Web sites, ISPs, or network administrators. Incognito mode is often used for a variety of purposes, including shopping for gifts without leaving a digital trail, accessing multiple accounts on the same service simultaneously, or testing how Web sites behave for first-time visitors without the influence of cached data or saved cookies. Despite its benefits, it is not a tool for comprehensive online anonymity, as external entities such as Web sites and ISPs can still track user behavior.

While incognito mode is often perceived as a privacy-enhancing feature, its protection is limited to certain aspects of browsing, and it does not provide comprehensive privacy or anonymity. The primary misconception stems from the belief that incognito mode makes users invisible online, which is not the case. Its limitations highlight why it is not as privacy-oriented as one might think.

First, incognito mode only prevents the browser from storing data locally on the device. This means that browsing history, cookies, and other temporary files are not saved once the incognito session ends. Web sites themselves are still capable of tracking user behavior during an incognito session, however. Even though cookies from the session are deleted afterward, Web sites can use other techniques such as fingerprinting. Browser fingerprinting involves collecting details such as the browser type, operating system, screen resolution, and installed plugins to create a unique profile that can be used to identify users across multiple sessions. This undermines the idea that incognito mode offers true anonymity.

Another significant limitation is that incognito mode does not encrypt traffic or hide the user's IP address. For this reason, incognito mode does not protect against targeted advertising or data collection practices conducted by advertisers, search engines, or social media platforms. Furthermore, while incognito mode isolates its session from the main browsing session on the device, it does not prevent malware, spyware, or keyloggers present on the device from recording user activity. If a device is compromised, using incognito mode will not stop malicious software from capturing sensitive information such as login credentials or financial data entered during the session.

Lastly, incognito mode does not prevent a user's online activity from being monitored if they are logged in to accounts, such as Google or Facebook, while browsing. These platforms can continue to track user behavior within their ecosystems, even in incognito mode, as account login overrides the browser's local privacy settings. In summary, incognito mode provides basic privacy by ensuring that browsing activity is not stored on the device after the session ends, but it falls short of protecting users from external tracking, monitoring, and profiling. It is best viewed as a tool for localized privacy rather than a comprehensive solution for anonymity or security.

PROXY SERVERS

A proxy server is an intermediary system that sits between a user's device and the broader Internet, acting as a gateway for the exchange of requests and responses between the user and the servers they are accessing. When a user connects to the Internet through a proxy server, their Web requests are routed through the proxy, which processes these requests on their behalf. Once the proxy receives the requested data from the target server, it forwards it back to the user.

The primary purpose of a proxy server is to manage, modify, or control Internet traffic to achieve specific goals. One of its key functions is to provide privacy by masking the user's IP address. Instead of the user's real IP address being visible to the destination server, the server only sees the IP address of the proxy server. This helps users maintain a certain level of anonymity, making it more challenging for Web sites or other online entities to track or identify them directly.

Proxy servers are also widely used to improve security. They can act as a buffer or firewall, filtering incoming and outgoing traffic to block malicious content or unauthorized access. By examining the data passing through them, proxy servers can enforce content filtering policies, such as blocking access to specific Web sites or restricting certain types of downloads, making them valuable in corporate or educational environments. Another significant purpose of a proxy server is to enhance performance and efficiency through caching. When multiple users access the same resource, the proxy can store a local copy of frequently requested content. This cached data allows subsequent requests to be served more quickly without needing to fetch the data from the original source server repeatedly, reducing bandwidth usage and improving response times.

Proxy servers also enable users to bypass geographic restrictions or censorship. By connecting to a proxy server in a different location, users can access content that might otherwise be unavailable in their region. This is particularly useful for accessing streaming services, Web sites, or platforms that impose regional restrictions or for navigating around government-imposed Internet blocks. In addition, businesses use proxy servers to monitor employee Internet usage, ensuring that workplace Internet policies are followed. Similarly, organizations may employ proxies to prevent the exposure of sensitive internal systems to the public Internet by routing requests through a controlled intermediary.

While proxy servers offer numerous advantages, they also have limitations and potential risks. The level of privacy and security they provide depends on the type and configuration of the proxy. Some proxies log user activity, which can undermine privacy, while others may introduce latency or reduce connection speeds. Moreover, poorly configured or untrustworthy proxy servers can expose users to data breaches or cyberattacks. In essence, a proxy server is a versatile tool that serves as a mediator between users and the Internet, offering benefits such as improved privacy, security, and performance, while also enabling greater control over Web traffic.

Configuring a proxy server involves setting up the intermediary server to manage and route Internet traffic effectively and then configuring client devices or applications to use it. For example, consider a scenario where a company wants to set up a proxy server to filter Internet traffic and improve security for its employees. The process involves configuring both the proxy server itself and the client devices to connect through it. To begin, the company installs proxy server software, such as Squid, on a dedicated server. Squid is a popular open source proxy server that supports caching and access control. The server should have a reliable network connection and sufficient hardware to handle the expected traffic load. Once the software is installed, the administrator accesses the server's configuration file, typically named `squid.conf`. In this file, the administrator specifies the parameters for the proxy server. The administrator configures the proxy to listen on a specific port, such as 3128, and assigns an IP address for the server to communicate with client devices. Access control settings are then defined, specifying which devices or networks are allowed to connect to the proxy. For example, the administrator might permit traffic only from the company's internal network with a specified range of IP addresses. To enhance security, the proxy is configured to block access to malicious or non-work-related Web sites by defining a blacklist or applying content filtering rules.

Once the server configuration is complete, the proxy service is started, and its operation is tested to ensure it routes traffic as intended. The administrator then configures client devices to use the proxy server. For example, on a Windows computer, this involves navigating to the network settings in the Control Panel or Settings application. The user selects the "Internet Options" or "Network & Internet" setting, depending on the version of Windows. Within the Internet settings, the user accesses the "LAN settings" section and enables the option to use a proxy server. They input the proxy server's IP address and port number (e.g., 192.168.1.100:3128). The configuration is saved, and the browser or application being used is restarted to apply the changes. The same process can be repeated for other operating systems, such as macOS or Linux, with variations in where the proxy settings are located.

After the configuration, all Internet traffic from the client device is routed through the proxy server. The administrator monitors the server's logs to ensure it functions correctly, verifying that it blocks restricted sites and caches frequently accessed content to improve performance. If issues arise, such as connectivity problems or misconfigured rules, the administrator revisits the server settings to make adjustments.

Proxy servers, while highly useful for managing Internet traffic and providing some degree of privacy, come with several limitations that can impact their effectiveness and reliability. One significant limitation is that proxy servers do not provide complete anonymity. While they mask the user's IP address, they do not encrypt the data passing through them by default. This means that any unencrypted data, such as login credentials or sensitive information, can still be intercepted by external parties, especially on unsecured networks. To achieve true privacy, users often need to pair proxies with other tools, such as VPNs or encryption protocols.

Another limitation lies in the potential for proxy servers to store logs of user activity. Many proxies, especially those operated by third parties, may keep records of the Web sites visited and data exchanged. This logging can compromise user privacy, particularly if the proxy operator is untrustworthy or if the logs are accessed by unauthorized entities, such as hackers or government agencies. Users relying on free proxy services are especially vulnerable to this issue, as these services may monetize user data or expose it to risks.

Performance can also be a drawback of using proxy servers. If the proxy server is overloaded with traffic or lacks sufficient processing power and bandwidth, it can slow down Internet connections. This issue is common with free or publicly available proxies, which often serve a large number of users simultaneously.

Furthermore, poorly configured proxies may introduce latency, making it inconvenient for applications requiring real-time data, such as online gaming or video streaming. Proxy servers are also vulnerable to certain security risks.

If a proxy server is compromised, it can become a gateway for cyberattacks. For instance, attackers could use the proxy to intercept and manipulate user traffic, inject malicious code, or launch phishing attacks. This is particularly concerning for proxies that do not support HTTPS, as they leave the data passing through them unencrypted and exposed to threats.

Another limitation is that proxies are not always effective in bypassing sophisticated censorship or geo-restrictions. Many Web sites and services have mechanisms to detect and block traffic coming from known proxy IP addresses. This means users may find themselves unable to access certain content even when using a proxy server. Advanced content platforms and firewalls often employ techniques such as IP blacklisting or behavior-based detection to restrict access from proxies. The maintenance and management of proxy servers can also pose challenges.

Setting up and configuring a proxy server requires technical expertise, particularly when dealing with complex rules for access control, caching, or content filtering. Regular monitoring is essential to ensure the server remains secure and functions correctly, and this can be resource-intensive for organizations or individuals with limited technical capabilities.

Finally, proxy servers are typically limited to handling specific types of traffic, such as Web browsing, and may not work seamlessly with all applications or protocols. This restricts their usefulness in scenarios where broader traffic management or encryption is needed. For example, they may not provide adequate support for securing email communication, P2P file sharing, or other non-HTTP/HTTPS protocols.

In summary, while proxy servers offer valuable functionalities such as traffic management, content filtering, and limited anonymity, their limitations include a lack of encryption, potential privacy concerns from logging, performance issues, vulnerability to security risks, ineffectiveness against advanced detection mechanisms, and the need for technical expertise to manage them effectively. These constraints underscore the importance of understanding the specific use case and risks before relying solely on proxy servers for privacy or security.

HTTPS AND TLS

HTTPS, or Hypertext Transfer Protocol Secure, is an advanced and secure version of HTTP, the Hypertext Transfer Protocol used to transfer data over the Web. HTTP forms the foundation of how Web pages and resources are delivered from servers to browsers, but it transmits data in plain text, leaving it vulnerable to eavesdropping, tampering, and MITM attacks. This lack of inherent security in HTTP can expose sensitive information such as login credentials, credit card numbers, or personal messages to unauthorized parties. In contrast, HTTPS enhances security by incorporating encryption, authentication, and data integrity mechanisms through the use of TLS, a successor to SSL.

When using HTTPS, the communication between the client and server is encrypted, ensuring that even if someone intercepts the transmitted data, it cannot be read without the encryption keys. Encryption safeguards the confidentiality of the information exchanged, which is especially critical for sensitive transactions such as online banking or e-commerce.

Moreover, HTTPS ensures data integrity, which means that the information being transferred cannot be altered or corrupted during transit without detection. This feature guarantees that the data received by the client or server matches what was originally sent, providing an additional layer of trust in the communication.

Authentication is another cornerstone of HTTPS, achieved through digital certificates issued by trusted certificate authorities (CAs). These certificates verify the identity of the Web site's server, protecting users from impersonation attacks where malicious actors attempt to mimic legitimate Web sites.

While HTTP focuses purely on the speed and simplicity of transferring data, HTTPS prioritizes security by adding the TLS handshake process. This handshake involves establishing a secure connection, exchanging encryption keys, and verifying the server's authenticity before any data transfer begins. Consequently, HTTPS introduces a slight overhead in terms of computational resources and time, as the encryption and decryption processes require additional work compared to the straightforward nature of HTTP. Web browsers make this distinction evident to users by displaying visual cues, such as a padlock icon or a green address bar, for HTTPS enabled sites. These indicators serve to reassure users that their connection is secure and that the Web site is authentic. In contrast, visiting an HTTP site might trigger warnings about potential security risks, emphasizing the shift toward a more secure Web environment. Furthermore, search engines and modern platforms favor HTTPS sites in their rankings, incentivizing Web site owners to adopt the protocol.

HTTPS has numerous strengths and weaknesses, which reflect its effectiveness as a secure communication protocol while highlighting some practical challenges. One of the greatest strengths of HTTPS is its ability to ensure the confidentiality of data. By encrypting the information exchanged between a user's browser and a Web server, HTTPS makes it nearly impossible for unauthorized parties to intercept and decipher sensitive information. This encryption is particularly critical for activities such as online banking, e-commerce, and handling personal information, where data breaches could have severe consequences.

In addition, HTTPS guarantees data integrity, which means that any tampering or corruption of data during transmission can be detected. This ensures that users receive the information exactly as it was sent, fostering trust in the system's reliability. Another major strength is its capacity to authenticate Web sites through digital certificates issued by trusted CAs. These certificates verify that a Web site is legitimate, preventing users from falling victim to phishing attacks or impersonation attempts. When users see the padlock icon in their browser's address bar, they are reassured that they are communicating with a verified and secure Web site.

HTTPS also aligns with modern Web standards and practices, with search engines and browsers actively encouraging its use. Many search engines rank HTTPS-enabled Web sites higher, while browsers warn users when they visit non-secure HTTP Web sites. This widespread endorsement has made HTTPS the de facto standard for Web security, enhancing user confidence across the Internet.

HTTPS does, however, have some weaknesses. One of the primary challenges is the computational overhead involved in encrypting and decrypting data, which can slow down the performance of Web servers, especially under heavy traffic. Although advances in hardware and optimization techniques have mitigated this issue to some extent, it remains a factor to consider for large-scale deployments. Another potential weakness lies in the management of digital certificates. Obtaining and maintaining these certificates requires time and resources, as they must be periodically renewed. Organizations must also ensure proper security measures to protect their private keys; if a private key is compromised, the security of the HTTPS connection can be undermined.

Additionally, while HTTPS prevents data interception, it does not safeguard against attacks on the server itself. If a server is poorly configured or vulnerable, attackers may still compromise the system. Lastly, HTTPS is not a cure-all for Web security. It only protects the data in transit, meaning other aspects of a Web site's security infrastructure—such as secure coding practices, robust authentication mechanisms, and regular vulnerability assessments—must also be in place to provide comprehensive protection. Misconfigured implementations of HTTPS, such as using weak encryption algorithms, can introduce vulnerabilities, negating its intended benefits.

REFERENCES

1. Vivaldi Browser [Internet]. [cited 2025 Jan 19]. Vivaldi Browser - The only web browser powerful enough for you! Available from: *https://vivaldi.com*
2. Cookie. In: Wikipedia [Internet]. 2025 [cited 2025 Jan 19]. Available from: *https://en.wikipedia.org/w/index.php?title=Cookie&oldid=1269915638*
3. Cookie-AutoDelete/Cookie-AutoDelete [Internet]. Cookie-AutoDelete; 2025 [cited 2025 Jan 19]. Available from: *https://github.com/Cookie-AutoDelete/Cookie-AutoDelete*
4. Mozilla [Internet]. [cited 2025 Jan 19]. Download the fastest Firefox ever. Available from: *https://www.mozilla.org/en-US/firefox/new/*
5. DuckDuckGo [Internet]. [cited 2025 Jan 19]. DuckDuckGo - Protection. Privacy. Peace of mind.. Available from: *https://duckduckgo.com*
6. Mullvad VPN [Internet]. [cited 2025 Jan 19]. Free the internet. With the Mullvad Browser. Available from: *https://mullvad.net/en/browser*
7. Electronic Frontier Foundation [Internet]. 2011 [cited 2025 Jan 19]. HTTPS Everywhere. Available from: *https://www.eff.org/https-everywhere*
8. LibreWolf Browser [Internet]. [cited 2025 Jan 19]. Available from: *https://librewolf.net/*
9. Electronic Frontier Foundation [Internet]. [cited 2025 Jan 19]. Privacy Badger. Available from: *https://privacybadger.org/*
10. Private browsing. In: Wikipedia [Internet]. 2025 [cited 2025 Jan 19]. Available from: *https://en.wikipedia.org/w/index.php?title=Private_browsing&oldid=1269403698*
11. Proxy server. In: Wikipedia [Internet]. 2025 [cited 2025 Jan 19]. Available from: *https://en.wikipedia.org/w/index.php?title=Proxy_server&oldid=1269616537*

12. Spy pixel. In: Wikipedia [Internet]. 2024 [cited 2025 Jan 19]. Available from: *https://en.wikipedia.org/w/index.php?title=Spy_pixel&oldid=1260838139*

13. Brave [Internet]. [cited 2025 Jan 19]. The browser that puts you first. Available from: *https://brave.com/*

14. The Tor Project | Privacy & Freedom Online [Internet]. [cited 2025 Jan 19]. Available from: *https://torproject.org*

15. Transport Layer Security. In: Wikipedia [Internet]. 2025 [cited 2025 Jan 19]. Available from: *https://en.wikipedia.org/w/index.php?title=Transport_Layer_Security&oldid=1267964057*

16. uBlock Origin [Internet]. [cited 2025 Jan 19]. uBlock Origin - Free, open-source ad content blocker. Available from: *https://ublockorigin.com/*

17. Web beacon. In: Wikipedia [Internet]. 2024 [cited 2025 Jan 19]. Available from: *https://en.wikipedia.org/w/index.php?title=Web_beacon&oldid=1256195382*

18. Which browsers are best for privacy? [Internet]. [cited 2025 Jan 19]. Available from: *https://privacytests.org/index*

CHAPTER 3

CRYPTOGRAPHY

Cryptography, the science and art of securing communication, has a rich and intricate history that spans millennia. Its evolution is deeply intertwined with the development of human society, as the need to protect sensitive information has always been a concern, whether for military, political, or personal purposes. The origins of cryptography can be traced back to ancient civilizations. One of the earliest recorded uses was in ancient Egypt, where scribes used non-standard hieroglyphs to obscure the meaning of texts, primarily for aesthetic or ceremonial reasons. Around the same time, the Mesopotamians employed simple ciphers in clay tablets to protect trade secrets.

Cryptography as a tool for secure communication, however, gained prominence in ancient Greece and Rome. In Greece, the Spartans developed the scytale, a cylindrical tool used for transposition ciphers. A strip of parchment would be wrapped around the scytale, and the message written along its length would appear scrambled unless wrapped around a rod of the same diameter. This device ensured that only intended recipients with the correct tool could decipher the message. In Rome, Julius Caesar popularized the use of substitution ciphers, such as the Caesar cipher, which involved shifting letters by a fixed number of places in the alphabet. Though simple, these methods were effective against the limited literacy and cryptographic knowledge of their time.

As civilizations grew more complex, so did their cryptographic needs. The medieval Islamic Golden Age marked a significant turning point. Scholars such as Al-Kindi advanced the field with the introduction of frequency analysis, a method for breaking substitution ciphers by analyzing the frequency of letters in a language. This mathematical approach was revolutionary and laid the foundation for modern cryptanalysis. During this era, cryptography also began to see applications in diplomacy, as rulers and their envoys needed to exchange sensitive information securely. The Renaissance brought further advancements, particularly in Europe, where the invention of the printing press facilitated the dissemination of knowledge. Cryptographic techniques became more sophisticated, driven by the needs of warring states and emerging nation-states. One notable development was the Vigenère cipher, a polyalphabetic cipher that used a keyword to determine letter shifts. It was deemed unbreakable for centuries and earned the moniker "*le chiffre indéchiffrable*" (the indecipherable cipher).

The nineteenth and early twentieth centuries saw the mechanization of cryptography. The advent of telegraphy and later wireless communication underscored the importance of secure encryption. Machines such as the Enigma, used by Nazi Germany during World War II, represented a quantum leap in cipher complexity. The Allied effort to break the Enigma, led by figures such as Alan Turing, not only shortened the war but also catalyzed the development of early computers. The cracking of the Enigma demonstrated the growing importance of computational power in cryptography and marked the dawn of the modern era.

Post-war cryptography evolved rapidly alongside advances in technology. The Cold War heightened the stakes, with both sides employing increasingly sophisticated methods to protect secrets. This era also saw the rise of cryptography in civilian contexts, particularly with the advent of digital communication. The publication of Claude Shannon's seminal work, *A Mathematical Theory of Communication*, in 1948, established the theoretical underpinnings of modern cryptography, emphasizing concepts such as information entropy and perfect secrecy. The late-twentieth century ushered in the era of public-key cryptography, a transformative concept introduced by Whitfield Diffie and Martin Hellman in 1976. Their work laid the foundation for secure digital communication by enabling two parties to exchange encrypted messages without a pre-shared secret key. Soon after, the RSA algorithm, developed by Rivest, Shamir, and Adleman, provided a practical implementation of public-key cryptography, relying on the computational difficulty of factoring large prime numbers. These innovations paved the way for secure Internet transactions, online banking, and digital signatures.

In the twenty-first century, cryptography has become ubiquitous, underpinning the digital infrastructure of modern society. Advanced algorithms such as elliptic-curve cryptography (ECC) offer greater security with smaller key sizes, making them ideal for resource-constrained devices. Meanwhile, the rise of quantum computing poses new challenges, as it threatens to break many of the cryptographic schemes currently in use. In response, researchers are developing post-quantum cryptography (PQC) to safeguard future communications. Throughout its history, cryptography has been a dynamic field, evolving in response to the ever-changing landscape of communication, computation, and threats. Its journey from simple ciphers to complex algorithms reflects humanity's enduring quest for privacy and security in an interconnected world.

THE FUNDAMENTALS OF CRYPTOGRAPHY

The fundamentals of cryptography form the bedrock upon which secure communication and data protection systems are built. At its core, cryptography is the science of transforming information into a format that ensures confidentiality, integrity, authenticity, and non-repudiation. These principles, collectively referred to as the objectives of cryptography, are achieved through the interplay of mathematical theories, algorithms, and protocols. Understanding the fundamentals requires an exploration of these objectives, the types of cryptographic techniques, and the essential concepts that govern their design and implementation.

The primary objective of cryptography is to maintain confidentiality, ensuring that information is accessible only to authorized parties. This is achieved through encryption, the process of converting plaintext (readable data) into ciphertext (encoded data). Decryption reverses this process, restoring the original plaintext. Encryption is based on mathematical functions that make it computationally infeasible for unauthorized individuals to decipher the ciphertext without a key. Integrity is another cornerstone of cryptography, ensuring that data has not been tampered with during transmission or storage. Techniques such as cryptographic hash functions are used to create fixed-length digests of data. Any alteration to the original data results in a completely different hash value, making it easy to detect modifications.

Cryptography also guarantees authenticity, which involves verifying the identity of the entities involved in communication. Digital signatures, which rely on asymmetric key cryptography, are a powerful tool for ensuring that a message or document genuinely originates from a claimed sender. Additionally, cryptographic protocols such as certificates, issued by trusted CAs, facilitate secure authentication in digital environments. Non-repudiation is closely linked to authenticity. It prevents individuals from denying their involvement in a transaction or communication. Digital signatures play a dual role here by proving both the origin and the signer's acknowledgment of the content, thus establishing accountability.

Cryptographic techniques are broadly classified into two categories: symmetric key and asymmetric key cryptography. Symmetric key cryptography uses the same key for both encryption and decryption. Examples include the Data Encryption Standard (DES) and its successor, the Advanced Encryption Standard (AES). While symmetric encryption is efficient and fast, it suffers from key distribution challenges, as the same key must be securely shared between parties beforehand. Asymmetric key cryptography, also known as public-key cryptography, resolves the key distribution problem. It employs a pair of keys: a public key for encryption and a private key for decryption. The RSA algorithm and ECC are prominent examples of this approach. Although asymmetric cryptography is computationally more intensive than its symmetric counterpart, it is indispensable for secure key exchange, digital signatures, and secure Web communications.

The effectiveness of cryptographic systems relies heavily on key management. A cryptographic key is a string of bits used by an algorithm to transform plaintext into ciphertext and vice versa. Key generation, storage, distribution, and rotation are critical processes in maintaining the strength of a cryptographic system. Compromised keys render even the most advanced algorithms useless, highlighting the importance of secure key management practices. The strength of cryptographic systems also depends on the complexity of the underlying mathematical problems. For example, the security of RSA relies on the difficulty of factoring large integers, while ECC depends on the computational hardness of solving the discrete logarithm problem in elliptic curve groups. Advances in mathematics and computational power, such as the emergence of quantum computing, pose a threat to these traditional cryptographic systems.

Another fundamental concept in cryptography is cryptographic protocols, which are structured sets of rules for secure communication. Protocols such as TLS ensure the secure exchange of information over the Internet, while blockchain protocols leverage cryptography to enable decentralized, tamper-proof ledgers. Finally, cryptography operates within the broader framework of cryptographic standards and policies. Organizations such as the National Institute of Standards and Technology (NIST) and the International Organization for Standardization (ISO) establish guidelines for the development and implementation of cryptographic systems, ensuring they meet global security requirements.

The fundamentals of cryptography are more than just technical constructs; they embody principles of trust and protection that are vital in a digital age. By safeguarding the integrity of information and the privacy of individuals, cryptography underpins the secure functioning of societies and economies, making it an indispensable field in the modern world.

KEY CRYPTOGRAPHIC ALGORITHMS

Key cryptographic algorithms are the core tools that enable secure communication, data protection, and authentication in modern cryptography. These algorithms are the mechanisms by which plaintext is transformed into ciphertext and vice versa, ensuring the confidentiality, integrity, and authenticity of information. Each algorithm is designed with a specific purpose, strength, and use case in mind, and they can be broadly categorized into symmetric key algorithms, asymmetric key algorithms, and hash functions. Understanding these algorithms and their roles offers insight into how cryptographic systems operate in practice.

Symmetric key algorithms rely on a single, shared secret key for both encryption and decryption. They are efficient and fast, making them ideal for encrypting large amounts of data. One of the earliest widely used symmetric algorithms was DES, developed in the 1970s. DES operates on 64-bit blocks of data using a 56-bit key and employs a series of substitution and permutation operations to encrypt the data. Advances in computational power, however, rendered DES insecure due to its relatively short key length, leading to its replacement by AES. AES, standardized in 2001, is the gold standard for symmetric encryption today. It uses key sizes of 128, 192, or 256 bits and operates on 128-bit data blocks. Its strength lies in its combination of substitution, permutation, and key schedule processes, which ensure robust security against brute-force attacks and cryptanalysis. AES is widely implemented in applications ranging from securing Internet traffic to encrypting sensitive files. Other notable symmetric algorithms include Triple DES (3DES), which extends DES by applying the algorithm three times with different keys, and ChaCha20, a modern stream cipher known for its speed and suitability for mobile devices and constrained environments. Despite their efficiency, symmetric algorithms require secure key distribution, which can be challenging in large or decentralized systems.

Asymmetric key algorithms, also known as public-key algorithms, address the limitations of key distribution in symmetric cryptography. These algorithms use a pair of mathematically related keys: a public key for encryption and a private key for decryption. One of the most influential asymmetric algorithms is the RSA algorithm, named after its inventors Rivest, Shamir, and Adleman. RSA relies on the difficulty of factoring large composite numbers into their prime factors, a problem that remains computationally infeasible for sufficiently large keys. RSA is widely used for secure key exchange, digital signatures, and certificate-based authentication. Another significant asymmetric algorithm is ECC, which achieves equivalent security to RSA with much smaller key sizes. ECC is based on the mathematics of elliptic curves over finite fields, and its efficiency makes it particularly well suited for resource-constrained environments such as mobile devices and IoT systems. Algorithms such as the Elliptic Curve Digital Signature Algorithm (ECDSA) and Elliptic Curve Diffie-Hellman (ECDH) are built on ECC principles and are commonly used for digital signatures and secure key exchange, respectively. The Diffie-Hellman key exchange protocol, introduced in 1976, was the first widely adopted public-key algorithm. It allows two parties to establish a shared secret over an insecure channel without prior knowledge of each other's keys. Although it does not provide encryption or authentication on its own, it remains a foundational element of modern cryptographic protocols.

Hash functions, while not encryption algorithms, are an integral part of cryptographic systems. A hash function takes an input and produces a fixed-size output, known as a hash or digest, that uniquely represents the input. Hash functions are used for data integrity verification, password hashing, and digital signatures. A good hash function is one-way (it cannot be reversed) and collision-resistant (it is computationally infeasible to find two different inputs with the same hash). Prominent cryptographic hash functions include SHA-2 and its successor, SHA-3, which are part of the Secure Hash Algorithm family. These functions are designed to provide robust security against attacks, such as pre-image and collision attacks. Earlier algorithms such as MD5 and SHA-1 have been deprecated due to vulnerabilities discovered through cryptanalysis, highlighting the importance of the continuous evaluation and evolution of cryptographic algorithms.

In addition to these categories, hybrid cryptographic systems combine symmetric and asymmetric algorithms to leverage the strengths of both. For example, a system might use RSA or ECC to securely exchange a symmetric key, which is then used for encrypting large datasets. This approach optimizes both security and performance. The security of cryptographic algorithms is also closely tied to the size of their keys and the computational assumptions underlying their design. As computational power increases and new technologies such as quantum computing emerge, algorithms must adapt. For instance, post-quantum cryptographic algorithms are being developed to withstand attacks from quantum computers, which could potentially break traditional asymmetric algorithms such as RSA and ECC.

Key cryptographic algorithms are the engines that drive the secure exchange and protection of information in the digital age. Their development and deployment reflect the intricate balance between mathematical innovation, computational efficiency, and the ever-evolving landscape of security threats. By understanding these algorithms and their applications, we gain a deeper appreciation for the foundational role cryptography plays in modern technology.

CRYPTOGRAPHIC PROTOCOLS

Cryptographic protocols are structured sets of rules and procedures designed to ensure secure communication, authentication, and data integrity across networks and systems. They serve as the backbone of modern digital security, enabling individuals and organizations to exchange sensitive information safely over potentially insecure channels. These protocols integrate various cryptographic algorithms, principles, and mechanisms to address specific security objectives such as confidentiality, integrity, authenticity, and non-repudiation. At their core, cryptographic protocols are built to address a range of challenges posed by digital communication.

One fundamental objective is secure data transmission, which involves protecting information from being intercepted or altered by unauthorized parties. Protocols such as TLS and its predecessor, SSL, are widely used to secure Internet communications. TLS establishes a secure channel between clients and servers through a handshake process, where cryptographic keys are negotiated using algorithms such as RSA or Diffie-Hellman. Once the connection is established, symmetric encryption algorithms such as AES are used to encrypt the data exchanged, ensuring both security and performance.

Another key function of cryptographic protocols is authentication, which verifies the identity of users, devices, or systems. Protocols such as Kerberos achieve this by employing a trusted third party (the key distribution center, or KDC) to authenticate users and grant them secure access to resources. Authentication protocols often rely on digital certificates, which are issued by CAs in systems such as public key infrastructure (PKI). Certificates validate the ownership of public keys, enabling trust between parties without prior direct interaction. Key exchange protocols are a crucial subset of cryptographic protocols that facilitate the secure sharing of cryptographic keys between parties. The Diffie-Hellman key exchange, for example, enables two parties to establish a shared secret key over an insecure channel without transmitting the key itself. This foundational protocol has been extended into variations such as ECDH, which provides enhanced security with smaller key sizes, making it well suited for modern applications.

Cryptographic protocols also play a vital role in ensuring message integrity and authenticity. Protocols such as hash-based message authentication code (HMAC) combine a cryptographic hash function with a secret key to produce a unique code for each message. This code is verified by the recipient to ensure that the message has not been tampered with and originates from the claimed sender. Similarly, digital signature protocols, which use asymmetric cryptography, enable verification of the sender's identity and message authenticity. Standards such as the Digital Signature Algorithm (DSA) and Elliptic Curve Digital Signature Algorithm (ECDSA) are widely employed for this purpose.

In addition to securing communication, cryptographic protocols underpin more specialized functions, such as secure payment systems, digital voting, and blockchain technology. Secure electronic transaction (SET) protocols were among the earliest cryptographic systems designed to facilitate secure online payments by encrypting credit card details and authenticating both buyers and sellers. Blockchain protocols, exemplified by Bitcoin and Ethereum, use cryptographic primitives such as hash functions, digital signatures, and Merkle trees to create decentralized, tamper-proof ledgers. These protocols rely on consensus mechanisms, such as proof of work or proof of stake, to validate transactions and maintain the integrity of the blockchain.

The design of cryptographic protocols also addresses challenges related to secure multi-party computation (MPC) and zero-knowledge proofs (ZKPs). In secure MPC, protocols enable multiple parties to jointly compute a function over their inputs while keeping those inputs private. ZKP protocols allow one party to prove knowledge of a secret without revealing the secret itself. These advanced cryptographic techniques have applications in privacy-preserving authentication, secure voting systems, and confidential data analysis.

The robustness of cryptographic protocols depends on their adherence to rigorous security models and standards. Protocols are often evaluated against potential vulnerabilities, such as MITM attacks, replay attacks, and cryptographic flaws. Standards organizations, including ISO and the Internet Engineering Task Force (IETF), play a critical role in establishing best practices and protocols, such as IPSec for secure Internet communication and OAuth for secure user authentication and authorization.

Cryptographic protocols are an essential component of the digital ecosystem, enabling trust and security in an increasingly interconnected world. Their development and refinement reflect a continuous effort to balance the demands of functionality, performance, and resistance to emerging threats. By integrating mathematical rigor with practical implementation, cryptographic protocols remain a cornerstone of cybersecurity, safeguarding the integrity and privacy of global digital interactions.

APPLICATIONS OF CRYPTOGRAPHY

Cryptography plays a foundational role in securing and enabling countless applications across various domains in our interconnected world. Its principles and techniques provide the backbone for protecting sensitive information, ensuring secure communication, verifying identities, and enabling trust in digital interactions. As technology has evolved, the applications of cryptography have expanded far beyond their original military and governmental uses, becoming essential in everyday life, business, and emerging technologies.

One of the most prominent applications of cryptography is in secure communication. From personal messaging apps to large-scale corporate networks, cryptographic protocols ensure that conversations remain private and inaccessible to unauthorized parties. Protocols such as TLS and Secure/Multipurpose Internet Mail Extensions (S/MIME) enable the encryption of Internet traffic and emails, preventing eavesdropping and data breaches. Messaging platforms such as WhatsApp and Signal utilize E2EE, ensuring that only the intended sender and receiver can read the exchanged messages, even if the messages pass through intermediate servers.

Cryptography is also critical in securing financial transactions and online payments. Every time a credit card is swiped or a digital payment is made, cryptographic algorithms ensure that the transaction data is encrypted and authenticated. Systems such as EMV (which stands for Europay, Mastercard,

Visa) use public-key cryptography to prevent fraud in chip-based cards. Cryptographic protocols such as SET and modern payment gateways such as PayPal and Apple Pay rely on encryption and digital signatures to safeguard transaction integrity and prevent unauthorized access to financial data.

In the realm of identity verification and access control, cryptography underpins systems that authenticate users and devices. Digital certificates, issued through PKI, validate identities in online transactions and secure Web sites through HTTPS. MFA systems use cryptographic tokens, such as one-time passwords (OTPs) generated by algorithms such as HMAC-based one-time password (HOTP) and time-based one-time password (TOTP), to enhance security. Biometric systems also employ cryptographic techniques to securely store and verify unique identifiers such as fingerprints and facial scans.

Cryptography has become indispensable in protecting data at rest and in transit. Encryption algorithms such as AES are used to safeguard data stored on devices, servers, and cloud platforms, ensuring that even if the storage medium is compromised, the data remains unintelligible. VPNs use cryptographic protocols such as IPSec to encrypt data traveling over public networks, enabling secure remote access and protecting users' online privacy.

Emerging technologies such as blockchain and cryptocurrencies owe their existence to cryptographic innovations. Cryptography ensures the immutability, security, and decentralization of blockchain systems. Techniques such as cryptographic hash functions, digital signatures, and Merkle trees enable tamper-proof records and secure transactions. Cryptocurrencies such as Bitcoin and Ethereum utilize cryptographic principles to create decentralized financial systems, where users can transfer value without intermediaries while ensuring transparency and security.

Cryptography also plays a critical role in safeguarding national security and military operations. Governments use advanced cryptographic systems to protect classified communications, conduct secure diplomatic exchanges, and prevent adversaries from intercepting sensitive information. Military-grade encryption, such as the Suite B cryptographic standards developed by the National Security Agency (NSA), ensures the confidentiality and integrity of operations.

In the healthcare sector, cryptography ensures the security and privacy of sensitive medical data. As patient records become digitized and healthcare systems interconnected, encryption protects data stored in electronic health records (EHRs) and secures the transmission of sensitive information between providers. Cryptographic techniques are also used to maintain the confidentiality of genomic data and to secure medical devices against cyber threats.

Another vital application of cryptography is in intellectual property (IP) protection and digital rights management (DRM). Cryptographic algorithms prevent unauthorized copying and distribution of copyrighted content such as software, music, and movies. Encryption and watermarking techniques ensure that content creators retain control over how their work is accessed and used.

Emerging fields such as IoT and smart technologies rely heavily on cryptography to address security challenges. IoT devices often operate in distributed environments, making them vulnerable to attacks. Cryptographic protocols ensure secure device-to-device communication, authentication, and data integrity. Lightweight encryption algorithms tailored for resource-constrained IoT devices, such as ChaCha20, are increasingly being implemented to safeguard smart homes, vehicles, and industrial systems.

In the context of secure voting systems, cryptography provides mechanisms for verifiable and tamper-proof electronic elections. Cryptographic techniques such as E2EE, secure MPC, and ZKPs enable the creation of systems where votes can be cast, transmitted, and counted securely while maintaining voter privacy.

In academia and research, cryptography is used to enable privacy-preserving data analysis and computation. Techniques such as homomorphic encryption allow computations to be performed on encrypted data without decrypting it, preserving privacy in sensitive applications such as genomic analysis, financial modeling, and machine learning (ML).

Cryptography is deeply embedded in every aspect of the digital age, underpinning the security and trust required for communication, commerce, and innovation. Its applications are vast and ever-expanding, adapting to the evolving challenges of a connected world. As technology continues to progress, cryptography remains a critical enabler of secure and reliable systems, safeguarding the foundations of our digital lives.

CRYPTOGRAPHIC ATTACKS AND DEFENSES

Cryptographic attacks and defenses represent the ongoing battle between those seeking to compromise security systems and those working to protect them. Cryptographic systems, while designed to provide robust security, are not immune to vulnerabilities. Understanding the methods attackers use to exploit these vulnerabilities, and the corresponding defenses developed to counteract them, is crucial for building resilient cryptographic solutions.

Cryptographic attacks target the fundamental principles of security: confidentiality, integrity, authenticity, and non-repudiation. Attackers often seek to decrypt sensitive information, forge digital signatures, impersonate authorized users, or tamper with data. To achieve these goals, they employ various techniques that exploit weaknesses in algorithms, protocols, or their implementation.

One of the most basic types of attack is the brute-force attack, where an attacker systematically tries all possible keys until the correct one is found. The feasibility of this attack depends on the key length and computational resources available. For example, symmetric encryption algorithms such as DES with a 56-bit key have been rendered insecure due to the relatively small number of possible keys. Modern defenses against brute-force attacks involve using longer keys, as seen in AES, which supports key lengths of 128, 192, and 256 bits, making exhaustive search impractical.

Another category of attack is the ciphertext-only attack, where the attacker has access only to the encrypted data and tries to deduce the plaintext or the encryption key. More sophisticated variants include known-plaintext attacks, where the attacker knows some plaintext-ciphertext pairs, and chosen-plaintext attacks, where the attacker can encrypt plaintext messages of their choice. The latter is particularly relevant in adaptive environments where attackers can influence input data.

Cryptanalysis is a broader approach that seeks to exploit weaknesses in the design of cryptographic algorithms. Techniques such as linear cryptanalysis and differential cryptanalysis analyze patterns in the encryption process to extract information about the key. These methods were instrumental in demonstrating the vulnerabilities of older algorithms such as DES and have driven the development of more secure systems, such as AES, which are designed to withstand such analysis.

A specific form of cryptanalytic attack is the side-channel attack, which targets the implementation of cryptographic algorithms rather than the algorithms themselves. These attacks exploit information leaked during the computation process, such as timing, power consumption, or electromagnetic emissions. For example, a timing attack might measure the time taken to execute cryptographic operations to infer key bits. Defenses against side-channel attacks include implementing constant-time algorithms, adding noise to measurements, and using hardware-level protections.

MITM attacks are another prevalent threat, particularly in communication systems. In an MITM attack, the attacker intercepts and potentially alters communication between two parties without their knowledge. Protocols such as TLS incorporate defenses against MITM attacks by using public-key cryptography for secure key exchange and ensuring that server certificates are verified.

Replay attacks involve intercepting and re-sending legitimate messages to trick systems into accepting them as valid. Cryptographic protocols defend against these attacks by incorporating time-sensitive elements, such as timestamps, and one-time-use values, such as nonces, to ensure that messages cannot be reused.

Hash functions are also targets of cryptographic attacks. In a collision attack, the attacker seeks to find two different inputs that produce the same hash output. This type of attack undermines the integrity of systems relying on hashes, such as digital signatures and certificates. The discovery of vulnerabilities in MD5 and SHA-1 due to collision attacks has led to their deprecation in favor of more secure algorithms such as SHA-2 and SHA-3. Defenses against collision attacks include using cryptographic hash functions with larger output sizes and stronger collision resistance.

Password attacks are another common threat in cryptographic systems, particularly when passwords are used as keys or authentication credentials. Techniques such as dictionary attacks and rainbow table attacks exploit weak or commonly used passwords. To mitigate these threats, systems employ password-hashing algorithms such as bcrypt, Argon2, or Password-Based Key Derivation Function 2 (PBKDF2), which include salting and iterative hashing to make attacks computationally expensive.

Public-key cryptography introduces its own set of vulnerabilities. For example, the security of RSA relies on the difficulty of factoring large integers, and ECC depends on the discrete logarithm problem over elliptic curves. Advances in computational methods or algorithms, such as quantum computing, threaten to break these cryptographic assumptions. Quantum computers, for instance, could use Shor's algorithm to efficiently solve problems that underpin RSA and ECC. In response, researchers are developing post-quantum cryptographic algorithms that rely on mathematical problems believed to be resistant to quantum attacks, such as lattice-based and code-based cryptography.

Protocol-level vulnerabilities also present opportunities for cryptographic attacks. Flaws in the design or implementation of protocols can lead to exploits such as the POODLE attack on SSL or the Heartbleed vulnerability in OpenSSL. Addressing these weaknesses requires rigorous protocol analysis, thorough implementation testing, and regular updates to fix discovered flaws.

Cryptographic defenses go beyond algorithmic design to include best practices for implementation and usage. These practices involve secure key management, such as using hardware security modules (HSMs) for key storage, employing MFA, and regularly rotating cryptographic keys. Ensuring that software libraries are up to date and free of known vulnerabilities is another critical aspect of defense.

Education and awareness are also vital. Developers and users must understand the limitations of cryptographic systems and avoid common pitfalls, such as using outdated algorithms, reusing keys, or failing to verify certificates.

In conclusion, cryptographic attacks and defenses represent a dynamic and evolving field within cybersecurity. As attackers develop new techniques to exploit weaknesses, cryptographers respond with innovations to strengthen systems and protocols. This constant interplay drives the evolution of cryptography, ensuring that it remains a critical enabler of secure and trusted digital interactions. By staying ahead of potential threats and adopting robust defenses, organizations and individuals can protect their information and maintain the integrity of their systems in an increasingly hostile digital environment.

LEGAL AND ETHICAL CONSIDERATIONS

The field of cryptography is deeply intertwined with legal and ethical considerations that shape its development, deployment, and use. These considerations arise from the dual nature of cryptography: while it serves as a powerful tool to protect privacy, ensure data security, and enable trust in digital interactions, it can also be misused to conceal illicit activities, evade regulation, or create barriers to lawful access. Balancing these competing interests is a complex challenge that involves governments, private organizations, and individuals.

One of the most significant legal considerations surrounding cryptography is the question of privacy versus state security. Cryptographic systems enable individuals and organizations to protect their communications and data from unauthorized access, supporting the fundamental right to privacy enshrined in international human rights frameworks such as the Universal Declaration of Human Rights. This same privacy can, however, hinder law enforcement and intelligence agencies in their efforts to combat crime, terrorism, and cyber threats. Governments have historically sought ways to regulate or gain access to encrypted communications, leading to heated debates about the limits of privacy and the role of the state.

For example, the use of strong encryption in consumer devices, such as smartphones, has led to high-profile standoffs between technology companies and governments. In the 2016 case involving Apple and the FBI, the U.S. government sought assistance in unlocking an encrypted iPhone used by a suspect in a terrorism investigation. Apple refused, citing concerns that creating a backdoor could compromise the security of all its users. This case exemplifies the broader tension between the need for robust encryption to protect users and the desire for government access to encrypted data in specific circumstances.

The issue of encryption backdoors highlights another legal and ethical challenge: the potential for such mechanisms to be exploited by malicious actors. While governments may advocate for lawful access systems to aid investigations, security experts argue that introducing backdoors inherently weakens the overall security of cryptographic systems. If a backdoor exists, it can be discovered or exploited by cybercriminals, foreign governments, or other unauthorized entities, undermining the very protections that encryption seeks to provide.

Cryptography is also subject to legal restrictions in many jurisdictions, particularly regarding its export, import, and use. Historically, cryptographic technology has been classified as a dual-use good, meaning it can be used for both civilian and military purposes. This classification has led to stringent export controls, such as those outlined in the Wassenaar Arrangement, an international agreement governing the export of dual-use technologies. For many years, the U.S. government imposed strict controls on the export of strong encryption, treating it as a munition. These restrictions were relaxed in the late 1990s following pressure from technology companies and advocacy groups, but export controls on cryptography remain an important legal consideration for multinational organizations.

Another significant legal concern is the use of cryptography in criminal activities. Encrypted messaging applications, secure communication tools, and anonymization technologies such as Tor are frequently used by criminal organizations to evade surveillance and law enforcement. This has led to calls for greater regulation of encryption technologies and mandatory decryption capabilities in certain cases. Such measures must, however, be carefully designed to avoid infringing on the rights of legitimate users or stifling innovation in the technology sector.

Cryptography also raises ethical questions about its use in surveillance and data collection. Governments and corporations alike deploy cryptographic technologies to secure their systems, but they may also use them to collect and analyze vast amounts of data about individuals. Ethical concerns arise when these practices infringe on personal freedoms, lack transparency, or are conducted without adequate oversight. For example, the widespread use of encryption by government surveillance agencies, as revealed by whistleblower Edward Snowden, sparked global debates about the ethics of mass surveillance and the balance between national security and individual privacy.

Additionally, the deployment of cryptographic technologies in developing and emerging economies raises ethical concerns about accessibility and equity. While encryption is essential for securing financial transactions, protecting healthcare data, and enabling digital education, the high costs of implementing advanced cryptographic solutions can exclude under-resourced communities. Ethical considerations must account for the need to make cryptographic technologies affordable and accessible to all, ensuring that their benefits are distributed equitably.

In the corporate world, cryptography is critical for securing IP, safeguarding customer data, and ensuring compliance with legal and regulatory requirements. Businesses must, however, navigate ethical dilemmas when their cryptographic practices conflict with public interest or transparency. For instance, while companies may encrypt user data to enhance security, they must also balance this with their legal obligations to cooperate with investigations and avoid shielding illegal activities.

Cryptographic technologies also play a role in emerging ethical debates around artificial intelligence (AI), blockchain, and quantum computing. For example, blockchain systems rely heavily on cryptographic principles to ensure data integrity and immutability, but their decentralized nature raises questions about accountability and governance. Similarly, quantum computing threatens to render many existing cryptographic systems obsolete, creating an urgent need for PQC to ensure continued security.

To address these complex legal and ethical challenges, policymakers, technologists, and ethicists must collaborate to establish frameworks that promote responsible use of cryptography. This involves enacting laws that protect privacy while enabling legitimate law enforcement access, fostering international cooperation to regulate the export and use of cryptographic technologies, and ensuring that cryptographic innovations align with ethical principles of fairness, accountability, and transparency.

In conclusion, the legal and ethical considerations of cryptography are as multifaceted as the technology itself. Cryptography is both a shield that protects our digital lives and a tool that can be wielded for questionable purposes. Balancing the competing demands of privacy, security, innovation, and accountability requires ongoing dialogue and careful policy-making. As cryptographic technologies continue to evolve, so too must the legal and ethical frameworks that govern their use, ensuring that they serve as instruments of progress and trust in the digital age.

THE FUTURE OF CRYPTOGRAPHY

The future of cryptography is a dynamic and rapidly evolving landscape shaped by technological advancements, emerging threats, and the growing complexity of our interconnected world. As the backbone of digital security, cryptography will continue to play a critical role in safeguarding data, enabling secure communication, and maintaining trust in an increasingly digital society. The field does, however, face significant challenges and transformative opportunities that will shape its trajectory in the years to come.

One of the most profound influences on the future of cryptography is the advent of quantum computing. While classical computers rely on bits, quantum computers use qubits, which leverage quantum mechanical properties to perform computations that are infeasible for traditional systems. To address this looming challenge, researchers are actively developing PQC, also known as quantum-resistant cryptography. These new cryptographic algorithms are designed to resist attacks from both classical and quantum computers. Lattice-based cryptography, code-based cryptography, multivariate polynomial cryptography, and hash-based cryptography are among the leading candidates for post-quantum standards. NIST has been spearheading efforts to standardize PQC algorithms, with several finalists already identified. The transition to quantum-resistant cryptography is expected to be a complex and gradual process, requiring widespread updates to existing systems and protocols.

Beyond the quantum threat, the future of cryptography will also be shaped by the rise of AI and ML. These technologies are dual-use in nature, offering both opportunities and challenges for cryptographic systems. On the one hand, AI can enhance cryptography by automating the detection of vulnerabilities, optimizing algorithms, and predicting potential attack vectors. On the other hand, adversaries can use AI to conduct more sophisticated attacks, such as identifying weaknesses in cryptographic implementations or generating realistic phishing attacks that bypass traditional defenses. The interplay between cryptography and AI will likely lead to a new era of adaptive and intelligent security systems.

Another critical trend in cryptography is the growing importance of privacy-enhancing technologies (PETs). As data privacy becomes a paramount concern for individuals, businesses, and governments, cryptographic techniques such as ZKPs, homomorphic encryption, and secure MPC are gaining traction. These technologies enable secure computation and verification without revealing sensitive information, making them invaluable for applications such as digital identity verification, secure voting systems, and privacy-preserving ML. ZKPs, in particular, are expected to play a central role in the future of blockchain and decentralized finance (DeFi), enabling transactions and smart contracts that are both secure and private.

IoT and the proliferation of connected devices will further drive the evolution of cryptography. IoT devices, ranging from smart home appliances to industrial sensors, often operate in resource-constrained environments with limited processing power and memory. This necessitates the development of lightweight cryptographic algorithms that can provide robust security without overwhelming device capabilities. Additionally, as IoT ecosystems grow, ensuring secure communication and data integrity across vast, decentralized networks will require innovative cryptographic protocols and frameworks.

The future of cryptography is also closely tied to the advancement of blockchain technology and decentralized systems. Blockchain relies heavily on cryptographic primitives to ensure data integrity, consensus, and immutability. As the technology matures, there will be a growing demand for more efficient and scalable cryptographic solutions to support large-scale applications, such as supply chain management, digital identity, and DeFi. New cryptographic techniques, such as verifiable delay functions (VDFs) and threshold cryptography, are already being explored to enhance the scalability and security of blockchain systems.

As cryptography evolves, the need for standardization and interoperability will become increasingly important. The global nature of digital communication and commerce necessitates cryptographic standards that can be widely adopted and trusted across borders. Efforts by organizations such as NIST, ISO, and IETF will play a crucial role in establishing frameworks that ensure compatibility and security in diverse environments. Education and workforce development will be essential to the future of cryptography. As the field becomes more complex, there will be a growing need for skilled professionals who can design, implement, and analyze cryptographic systems. Academic institutions, industry leaders, and governments will need to invest in training programs and initiatives to cultivate the next generation of cryptographers and security experts.

The future of cryptography is marked by both unprecedented challenges and remarkable opportunities. Quantum computing, AI, and IoT will push the boundaries of what cryptographic systems can achieve, while PETs and blockchain innovations promise to redefine the digital landscape. At the same time, the field must navigate a complex web of legal, ethical, and practical considerations to ensure that cryptography continues to serve as a force for security, trust, and progress in the digital age. As we move forward, the adaptability and resilience of cryptographic systems will be critical to addressing the ever-changing threat landscape and realizing the full potential of our interconnected world.

OPEN-SOURCE SOFTWARE RELATED TO CRYPTOGRAPHY

Open-source software related to cryptography provides powerful tools for secure communication, data protection, and encryption. Many of these tools are user-friendly and accessible to common users. The following subsections describe some of the most useful open-source cryptographic software solutions for different purposes.

VeraCrypt

VeraCrypt is a highly regarded open-source disk encryption software that builds upon its predecessor, TrueCrypt, and addresses many of the security concerns associated with it. For users prioritizing data security, VeraCrypt has become a trusted tool for encrypting sensitive information, thanks to its robust encryption algorithms, cross-platform compatibility, and user-friendly design.

One of VeraCrypt's standout features is its exceptional commitment to security. It employs strong encryption standards, including AES, Serpent, and Twofish, and allows users to implement cascading combinations of these algorithms for enhanced protection. The software also strengthens the algorithms with unique security configurations, such as increased iteration counts, which make brute-force attacks significantly more difficult. This added layer of complexity, while slightly impacting performance during volume creation and mounting, reflects VeraCrypt's prioritization of security over speed.

Another key feature is its ability to create encrypted volumes within files or on entire partitions and storage devices. VeraCrypt can encrypt system partitions, enabling full-disk encryption for protecting operating systems against unauthorized access. Its "hidden volume" functionality is particularly noteworthy, as it allows users to create a secondary, hidden encrypted volume within a primary one. This offers plausible deniability, as the existence of the hidden volume is virtually undetectable without the correct credentials.

VeraCrypt is also lauded for its cross-platform compatibility. It supports major operating systems, including Windows, macOS, and Linux, allowing users to create and access encrypted volumes across different platforms seamlessly. Additionally, the software is free and open source, fostering transparency and trust within the security community. The open-source nature of VeraCrypt means that its code can be audited and verified for vulnerabilities, which enhances its credibility among privacy-conscious users.

VeraCrypt does have some limitations, however. Its reliance on strong encryption algorithms and higher iteration counts can lead to slower performance compared to other encryption tools, particularly during initial setup or when accessing encrypted data. While this trade-off is acceptable for many users seeking high levels of security, it may not be ideal for those requiring real-time performance or handling large files frequently.

The user interface, while functional, could also benefit from a more modern and intuitive design. For beginners unfamiliar with encryption software, the setup process and terminology may appear daunting. Although the software provides extensive documentation and guides, new users may face a learning curve before fully understanding its features and configurations.

In terms of security, VeraCrypt is not without its critics. While the project has undergone security audits that validated its robustness, some experts have pointed out that no software can be entirely immune to vulnerabilities. Regular updates and community engagement help mitigate these concerns, but users must remain vigilant in keeping their systems and the software itself up to date.

In conclusion, VeraCrypt stands out as a powerful and reliable encryption tool suitable for both casual users and professionals with stringent security requirements. Its strong encryption algorithms, cross-platform functionality, and open-source transparency make it a preferred choice for protecting sensitive data. While it does have its trade-offs in terms of performance and user interface, these are minor compared to the level of security and flexibility it provides. For those willing to invest time in understanding its features, VeraCrypt is a top-tier solution for ensuring data confidentiality in an increasingly digital world.

GnuPG

GNU Privacy Guard (GnuPG) is a widely used and highly respected open-source tool for secure communication and data encryption. As a free implementation of the OpenPGP standard, GnuPG allows users to encrypt and sign their data and communications, making it a go-to option for anyone looking to ensure the confidentiality, integrity, and authenticity of their messages and files. Over time, it has become one of the most trusted encryption tools available, widely adopted in both personal and professional settings.

At its core, GnuPG offers strong encryption capabilities using a combination of asymmetric encryption (public and private keys) and symmetric encryption (shared secret keys). The system is based on the OpenPGP standard, which is well established and widely used, meaning that GnuPG users can securely exchange encrypted data with anyone who also uses OpenPGP-compatible software. The use of asymmetric encryption allows for secure key distribution, where a public key can be freely shared to encrypt data, while the private key, kept secret, is used to decrypt it. This fundamental feature allows GnuPG to facilitate encrypted email communication, file encryption, and digital signatures, providing a broad range of security functions.

One of GnuPG's most notable features is its ability to sign messages and files, which helps to verify the authenticity of the sender and ensure that the data has not been tampered with. Digital signatures are integral to establishing trust, and GnuPG provides a reliable way to authenticate identities. The software also supports keyring management, allowing users to store and manage multiple keys, including their own private key and the public keys of others with whom they wish to communicate securely. This ability to manage keys effectively is crucial for maintaining a secure and trusted network of communications, especially in environments where secure exchanges are frequent.

GnuPG is compatible with a wide range of platforms, including Linux, Windows, and macOS, and can be integrated with various email clients and applications. On Linux systems, it's often used in conjunction with other tools, such as Thunderbird and Enigmail, to provide seamless email encryption. For Windows and macOS users, there are also graphical front-end interfaces, such as Gpg4win and GPGTools, that make it easier to use GnuPG without relying solely on command-line operations. While the command-line interface (CLI) is extremely powerful and flexible, it can be intimidating for those who are not familiar with terminal-based software, making the graphical frontends a valuable addition for less experienced users.

The software's open-source nature is another of its key strengths. By being open source, GnuPG allows anyone to examine its code for vulnerabilities, suggest improvements, and contribute to its development. This transparency has earned GnuPG the trust of privacy advocates, security experts, and governments around the world. Security audits are regularly conducted, helping to identify and resolve potential weaknesses and ensuring that the software remains secure over time. Like all open-source projects, however, it also faces the possibility of vulnerabilities being discovered, though the large, active community surrounding GnuPG helps to address such issues quickly.

Despite its many strengths, GnuPG does come with some challenges. For one, the software is quite complex, and new users may find the learning curve to be steep. Understanding key management, encryption processes, and the importance of protecting private keys can be daunting for those who are not already familiar with cryptography and security concepts. While the graphical interfaces help to some extent, the tool remains highly technical, and some users may find it difficult to navigate, particularly when troubleshooting issues or dealing with key management. The documentation is extensive and helpful, but still assumes a certain level of familiarity with cryptographic concepts.

Additionally, while GnuPG provides excellent encryption and decryption capabilities, it can be cumbersome for those who need to quickly encrypt and decrypt large numbers of files or messages. Batch processing and automated encryption tasks can be utilized, but it often requires writing scripts or additional configuration, which might be more advanced than what a casual user is prepared to handle.

Another area of concern is key management. While GnuPG allows for a high level of control over key creation, expiration dates, revocation certificates, and key signatures, poor management of keys can lead to security vulnerabilities. Losing a private key or failing to revoke a compromised key can have serious consequences and thus requires careful attention from the user.

In conclusion, GnuPG is a powerful, flexible, and widely trusted tool for encryption and secure communication. It offers strong encryption standards, digital signatures, and key management capabilities, making it an ideal choice for anyone who needs to protect sensitive data. The open-source nature of GnuPG enhances its credibility and trustworthiness in the privacy and security community, ensuring that it remains a reliable choice for safeguarding communications. While it can be difficult to use for beginners due to its complexity and reliance on command line operations, those who take the time to learn how to use it will find a robust tool that offers substantial control over encryption. Overall, GnuPG is a cornerstone of modern cryptographic practices and continues to be an essential tool for anyone serious about protecting their privacy.

Cryptomator

Cryptomator is an open-source encryption tool designed to provide an easy and secure way to encrypt files stored in cloud services. As cloud storage has become increasingly ubiquitous for both personal and professional use, ensuring that sensitive data stored remotely remains protected has never been more important. Cryptomator stands out as an excellent solution for encrypting files before they are uploaded to services such as Dropbox, Google Drive, and OneDrive, ensuring that only the user has access to the decrypted versions of their files.

One of Cryptomator's most significant advantages is its simplicity and user-friendly design. The application is focused on providing encryption without requiring deep technical knowledge from its users. It achieves this by encrypting files locally on the user's machine before they are uploaded to the cloud, thus guaranteeing that files are protected from unauthorized access even if the cloud provider's servers are compromised. The software encrypts files at the file level, meaning each individual file is encrypted separately, rather than creating a single large encrypted container. This approach provides better flexibility when accessing encrypted files from different devices or environments, as users can decrypt only the files they need, rather than having to mount a large encrypted volume.

Cryptomator uses AES-256 encryption, which is widely recognized as a secure and efficient encryption algorithm. AES-256 is known for its strength, and its use in Cryptomator ensures that files are protected with state-of-the-art cryptographic security. Additionally, Cryptomator implements transparent encryption, meaning that the encryption process is automatic and invisible to the user. Once configured, users can simply interact with their cloud-stored files as if they were unencrypted, with Cryptomator automatically handling the encryption and decryption in the background. This ease of use makes Cryptomator particularly attractive for users who want strong security without dealing with the complexities often associated with encryption software.

The software supports a wide range of cloud services, including popular options such as Dropbox, Google Drive, and OneDrive. Cryptomator integrates smoothly with the file system, creating a virtual drive that users can interact with as though it were a regular folder on their computer. Once the user enters their password, Cryptomator mounts this encrypted vault, allowing them to access their files in their decrypted form. When files are saved or modified, Cryptomator automatically encrypts the changes and uploads them back to the cloud. This seamless integration is crucial for those who use cloud storage as a primary method for file management but still require the protection of their sensitive data.

Another notable feature of Cryptomator is its cross-platform compatibility. The software is available for Windows, macOS, Linux, and mobile devices, including iOS and Android. This ensures that users can access and manage their encrypted files across different devices without compromising security. Cryptomator's mobile apps are particularly useful for people who need to access encrypted data on the go. The mobile apps function similarly to the desktop versions, making it easy for users to access, upload, or modify encrypted files while ensuring the data remains protected at all times.

While Cryptomator's ease of use and strong security make it a highly effective encryption solution, it does have certain limitations. One potential drawback is that Cryptomator is designed specifically for encrypting individual files in cloud storage, rather than entire disk or partition encryption. This means it cannot be used as a full-disk encryption solution, which may be necessary for users who require system-wide protection. Users seeking more comprehensive security solutions, such as for encrypting entire drives or operating systems, may need to look for alternatives that offer full-disk encryption.

Another limitation is that Cryptomator does not support the encryption of file names. While the contents of the files are securely encrypted, the file names, folder structure, and metadata (such as creation date and size) remain visible to anyone who has access to the cloud storage. This means that while the content of the files is secure, some information about the files is exposed. For users who require complete anonymity, including obfuscation of file names and metadata, this could be a significant concern.

Furthermore, while the software is designed to be simple and intuitive, users who are unfamiliar with cloud storage encryption might initially be uncertain about how to configure their vaults or manage encryption keys. Cryptomator does provide helpful guides and documentation, but novice users may still face a bit of a learning curve when first setting up their vaults. Fortunately, the software is very reliable once configured properly, and the cryptographic processes run seamlessly in the background.

In terms of performance, Cryptomator performs well in most scenarios. It encrypts files in real time and synchronizes them with cloud storage without causing significant delays or noticeable lag. The performance can be impacted, however, when working with extremely large files or large numbers of small files, as each individual file is encrypted separately. While this approach enhances security and flexibility, it may slightly reduce performance compared to encryption tools that work with larger container files.

One of Cryptomator's greatest strengths is its commitment to openness and transparency. Being open-source software, Cryptomator allows anyone to audit the source code for potential vulnerabilities, ensuring that the software is secure and free from backdoors. Additionally, its open-source nature means it benefits from community-driven development and continuous improvements. This fosters trust among privacy-conscious users, as they can independently verify the software's security features.

Cryptomator is an excellent tool for anyone seeking a straightforward, secure solution for encrypting their files in the cloud. Its AES 256 encryption, transparent encryption model, and seamless cloud storage integration make it one of the most effective encryption tools for protecting sensitive data while taking advantage of cloud services. Cryptomator's cross-platform support and ease of use further enhance its appeal to a wide range of users, from casual consumers to more security-conscious professionals. It is, however, important to keep in mind its limitations, particularly in terms of its inability to encrypt file names and the fact that it is not a full-disk encryption solution. For users who need to encrypt specific files rather than entire disks, and for whom ease of use and strong encryption are priorities, Cryptomator stands out as an exceptional choice in the field of cloud storage encryption.

AxCrypt 1.0

AxCrypt is a robust and user-friendly file encryption software that has gained popularity for its simplicity and effectiveness in protecting sensitive data. Developed as a commercial product with a free version offering essential features, AxCrypt is widely used by individuals and businesses alike to secure files stored locally or in the cloud. What sets AxCrypt apart from many other encryption tools is its focus on ease of use, combined with strong encryption standards, making it a suitable choice for both novice users and those with more advanced security needs. It is important to note, however, that while AxCrypt version 1 was fully open-source, the release of version 2 transitioned the software to a proprietary, commercial model with a restricted free tier, changing its standing within the purely open-source community.

One of the standout features of AxCrypt is its seamless integration with the Windows operating system. The software is designed to work directly within the Windows File Explorer, making it exceptionally easy for users to encrypt, decrypt, and manage their files. With just a right-click, users can encrypt files, and the encryption process is straightforward, requiring little to no setup. The integration into the operating system ensures that AxCrypt feels like a natural part of the user's environment, allowing encryption and decryption to occur quickly and efficiently. For users on Windows, this convenience is one of AxCrypt's greatest strengths, as it eliminates the need to open a separate application to perform encryption tasks.

AxCrypt uses the AES-128 encryption standard, which, while not as strong as AES-256, is still widely considered secure for most use cases. The AES encryption algorithm is one of the most trusted and commonly used cryptographic standards in the world, providing a high level of security. AxCrypt also offers the option of password protection, where users are required to input a password in order to access encrypted files. This ensures that only authorized users can decrypt and view the contents of the file. Additionally, AxCrypt supports the use of password management features, such as the ability to store passwords securely, and it includes a keyfile option for those who prefer MFA.

One of AxCrypt's notable strengths is its ability to create encrypted archives or containers, allowing users to bundle multiple files into a single encrypted package. This is useful when users need to encrypt large numbers of files or when working with files that need to be transferred securely. The ability to protect multiple files within one archive simplifies file management, especially when working with cloud storage or file-sharing services. Additionally, AxCrypt supports cloud storage services such as Dropbox, Google Drive, and OneDrive, making it easier for users to protect files stored in the cloud. This integration allows users to keep their encrypted files on these services while maintaining control over their security.

AxCrypt also provides a feature called "secure file sharing," which allows users to securely share encrypted files with others. This feature is particularly beneficial for businesses or individuals who need to send confidential files over the Internet. By sending encrypted files, users can ensure that the contents remain private, even if the files are intercepted during transmission. The recipient, who must have AxCrypt installed, can decrypt the files using a password, thus ensuring secure and efficient file sharing.

For those who prefer to use mobile devices, AxCrypt offers mobile applications for both iOS and Android, allowing users to view and manage their encrypted files while on the go. The mobile apps function similarly to the desktop version, enabling users to decrypt files, store them securely, and manage their encrypted content. This cross-platform compatibility ensures that users can maintain a high level of security even when using devices other than their primary computers. The mobile apps are a great addition for users who need access to their encrypted files while traveling or when working remotely.

While AxCrypt excels in simplicity and ease of use, it does have some limitations. For one, the free version of AxCrypt is relatively limited in its features. While it provides basic file encryption functionality, it lacks access to some advanced features, such as file compression, the ability to encrypt folders, and cloud-based collaboration tools. These features are only available in the premium version, which requires a subscription. As a result, users seeking more robust file management and encryption options may find the free version insufficient for their needs. The subscription cost may be a concern for some, particularly those who only require basic encryption functionalities.

Additionally, while AES-128 encryption is secure, it is not as strong as AES-256 encryption, which some users may prefer for the highest levels of data security. While AES-128 is still considered highly secure for most applications, users who require top-tier encryption may find this a limiting factor. Moreover, the absence of some advanced encryption features, such as the ability to create secure container files or encrypt entire drives, means that AxCrypt is better suited for individual file encryption rather than full-disk encryption.

Another drawback is that AxCrypt is primarily designed for Windows, with the mobile apps providing a secondary option for other platforms. While there is a version available for macOS, it is not as widely adopted or feature-rich as the Windows version. This may present an issue for users who rely heavily on macOS or other operating systems, as they may not have access to the same level of functionality that Windows users do.

The user interface of AxCrypt, while simple and intuitive, can occasionally feel limited. Some users may find the software's feature set too basic, especially compared to more comprehensive encryption tools. The lack of advanced options, such as file name encryption or custom encryption settings, may also be a downside for those with more specialized needs. For individuals who want a more customizable encryption solution or a full suite of advanced security features, AxCrypt may feel restrictive.

AxCrypt is a reliable and easy-to-use encryption tool that strikes a balance between simplicity and security. It is an excellent choice for individuals or businesses that need a straightforward solution to protect files and ensure secure file sharing, especially when using cloud storage services. The software's AES-128 encryption, seamless integration with Windows, and mobile app support make it a practical solution for everyday file encryption needs. While it may not be the most advanced or feature-rich option available, AxCrypt is a great entry-level tool for users for whom ease of use and efficient file protection are priorities. Those who require more advanced features or higher levels of encryption, however, may need to consider other encryption tools that provide greater flexibility and stronger security measures.

KeePass

KeePass is a highly regarded open-source password manager designed to securely store and manage passwords. Over the years, it has earned a reputation for its robust security features, flexibility, and wide range of customization options, making it a popular choice for individuals and businesses alike. KeePass offers a reliable solution for managing and protecting sensitive data, particularly passwords, in an increasingly digital world where online security is paramount.

At its core, KeePass uses AES-256 encryption to protect password databases, which is widely regarded as one of the strongest encryption algorithms available. This provides a high level of security, ensuring that passwords and other sensitive information stored within the database are well protected. Users create a master password to access their password database, and KeePass ensures that this password is never stored in plain text. The application also supports the use of keyfiles, which add an additional layer of security by requiring a physical file to unlock the database in addition to the master password. This MFA approach makes KeePass an excellent choice for users who want to ensure that their passwords are protected by more than just a single factor.

One of KeePass's major strengths is its versatility. The software allows users to store not only passwords but also other sensitive information, such as PINs, credit card numbers, license keys, and other private data, in securely encrypted fields. Each entry can be organized into customizable categories, making it easy to organize and manage the stored data. KeePass also supports the creation of strong, unique passwords for each entry using its built-in password generator. This feature is invaluable for ensuring that passwords are not reused, which is a common vulnerability in digital security. The ability to generate strong, random passwords helps to mitigate the risk of brute-force attacks and reduces the likelihood of a successful password-cracking attempt.

KeePass is highly flexible in terms of storage options, allowing users to save their password database locally on their computer, on an external drive, or in a cloud storage service. This makes it easy to access passwords from different devices while maintaining security. When using cloud storage, users can sync their database across multiple devices, allowing for convenient access to passwords from anywhere, as long as the proper decryption credentials are available. This flexibility is crucial for users who need to access their passwords from multiple locations or on multiple devices, ensuring that they always have secure access to their accounts.

The application also includes several useful features for enhancing user experience and security. KeePass supports auto-type functionality, which allows users to automatically fill in passwords on login forms for Web sites and applications. This eliminates the need to manually enter passwords, making the login process faster and reducing the risk of keylogging or phishing attacks. Additionally, KeePass supports the ability to store and generate OTPs and integrates with popular two-factor authentication (2FA) systems such as TOTP. This integration strengthens the security of accounts that require additional authentication steps beyond just a password.

For those who prefer a more visual or user-friendly interface, KeePass provides customizable themes and support for plugins, allowing users to enhance the functionality and appearance of the software. This level of customization ensures that KeePass can cater to a wide range of user preferences, whether they are seeking simplicity or more advanced features. The large number of plugins available further extends the software's capabilities, adding everything from advanced search tools to the ability to integrate with other password managers and security applications.

KeePass is available for Windows, with unofficial ports for macOS, Linux, and mobile devices. While the Windows version is the most feature-complete, users on other platforms can still access KeePass through third-party applications. For example, on mobile devices, applications such as Keepass2Android and KeePass Touch allow users to securely access their KeePass databases. While these apps work well and provide a high degree of compatibility, they may not have the full feature set of the Windows version, and the integration can sometimes be a bit clunkier than native applications. Still, the availability of these third-party apps is a big advantage, as it enables users to access their stored passwords on a variety of devices.

Despite its many advantages, KeePass does have certain limitations that users should be aware of. One of the main drawbacks is the lack of a cloud-based solution built directly into the application. While KeePass allows users to store their database files in the cloud, this requires manual setup, and the syncing process is not as seamless as it would be in a cloud-native password manager such as LastPass or 1Password. Users must rely on third-party cloud services such as Google Drive, Dropbox, or OneDrive to sync their KeePass database across devices. This setup may be confusing for less tech-savvy users, especially those who are not familiar with managing cloud-based storage or dealing with synchronization issues. For those who prioritize security and want to have more control over where their data is stored, however, this lack of built-in cloud syncing may be seen as a benefit.

Another potential issue is KeePass's reliance on a master password to access the password database. While this is a standard security feature, it also means that if a user forgets their master password, they will be unable to access their password database unless they have a backup keyfile or another recovery method set up. This can be a risk for users who do not take proper precautions, such as using a secure password manager to store their master password or setting up a password recovery plan. Additionally, while KeePass allows for keyfile-based authentication, this feature requires additional setup, and users may find it cumbersome to configure initially.

The user interface of KeePass is functional but can feel somewhat outdated compared to more modern password managers. While it is highly customizable, some users may find the design to be less visually appealing or more complex to navigate than the sleek, minimalistic interfaces of other password managers. For users who prioritize functionality and security over aesthetics, however, this may not be a significant concern.

KeePass is a powerful and highly secure password manager that provides exceptional protection for sensitive data. Its use of AES-256 encryption, MFA support, and flexible storage options make it an excellent choice for users who need to store and manage passwords securely. The software's open-source nature adds to its credibility, ensuring transparency and trust in its security practices. While KeePass's interface may not be as polished as some other password managers, and its cloud syncing process may require extra setup, its customization options, robust security features, and cross-platform compatibility make it a versatile and highly recommended tool for anyone serious about password security. For users who value control over their data and prefer a more hands-on approach to password management, KeePass remains one of the best options available.

Bitwarden

Bitwarden is a popular open-source password manager that has gained widespread recognition for its ease of use, security features, and affordability. As online security becomes increasingly critical, password managers such as Bitwarden offer users a reliable and effective way to store, manage, and generate secure passwords. By using strong encryption and offering seamless syncing across multiple devices, Bitwarden has positioned itself as one of the most accessible and secure options for individuals and businesses seeking to protect their passwords and other sensitive data.

One of Bitwarden's most appealing features is its robust and transparent security model. The software uses AES-256-bit encryption, which is one of the most secure and widely trusted encryption standards in the industry. This ensures that all stored passwords and other sensitive information are encrypted on the user's device before being uploaded to Bitwarden's cloud servers. The encryption process is entirely client-side, meaning that only the user, with their master password, can decrypt the data. Bitwarden's zero-knowledge architecture guarantees that the company has no access to the user's data, further enhancing privacy and security. In addition to the AES-256 encryption standard, Bitwarden also uses PBKDF2 to strengthen password protection by making brute-force attacks more difficult.

A key selling point of Bitwarden is its open-source nature. As an open-source project, Bitwarden allows anyone to examine its code, ensuring transparency and enabling independent security audits. This openness has earned it the trust of security experts and privacy advocates, who value the ability to verify that the software is free from vulnerabilities and backdoors. Open-source software also benefits from the contributions of the community, allowing for continuous improvement and faster identification of any potential issues.

Bitwarden offers a variety of features that make it highly useful for both individual and business users. One of its primary functions is the secure storage of passwords, which are organized within a password vault. Users can store not only passwords but also other sensitive data, such as credit card information, secure notes, and identity details. The vault can be accessed from various devices, including desktop computers, smartphones, and tablets, with seamless syncing across all platforms. This cross-platform support is one of Bitwarden's most valuable aspects, as it allows users to securely access their data wherever they are, with no need to worry about keeping their passwords in sync across different devices manually. Bitwarden is available on a wide range of platforms, including Windows, macOS, Linux, iOS, and Android, as well as in browser extensions for Chrome, Firefox, Safari, Edge, and other popular Web browsers.

The password generation feature of Bitwarden is another important tool for users who want to ensure that their passwords are secure. The built-in password generator allows users to create strong, unique passwords for each of their accounts, mitigating the risks of password reuse, which is a common vulnerability in digital security. The password generator can be customized to meet specific requirements, such as password length, character types, and complexity, making it highly adaptable to the user's needs. This feature is particularly useful for people who struggle with coming up with secure passwords on their own or who want to automate the process of securing their accounts.

Bitwarden also provides secure sharing options, which are useful for individuals or teams who need to share login credentials. The ability to share encrypted passwords securely without exposing them in plain text is invaluable for business environments, collaborative projects, or even families. Passwords can be shared with others using Bitwarden's "organization" feature, which enables teams to manage shared credentials in a secure and controlled manner. The sharing of sensitive data within organizations is protected by encryption, and users can set permissions to control who has access to what data, ensuring that only authorized individuals can view or edit the information.

The free version of Bitwarden offers a generous set of features, including unlimited password storage, secure password generation, and cross-platform syncing. This makes Bitwarden an excellent option for individuals looking for a cost-effective way to secure their passwords. For users who need additional features, however, Bitwarden offers premium subscriptions that provide added functionality, including advanced 2FA options, encrypted file storage, emergency access, and the ability to generate additional vault items. The premium subscription is reasonably priced, which makes it an affordable option for users who require additional security or functionality. Additionally, Bitwarden offers a family plan and business-oriented plans that provide more robust features, such as team sharing, custom password policies, and more granular control over permissions.

For users who prioritize privacy, Bitwarden offers self-hosting options, which allow individuals or organizations to host their own Bitwarden instance on their own servers. This gives users full control over their data and ensures that sensitive information is not stored on Bitwarden's cloud servers. The self-hosting option will be especially appealing to businesses or privacy-conscious users who want to have complete control over their password management system and avoid reliance on third-party cloud providers.

In terms of performance, Bitwarden is a lightweight and fast application that performs well across different platforms and devices. The desktop and mobile apps are responsive and easy to navigate, with a clean and intuitive interface that simplifies the process of managing passwords and other data. The browser extensions are equally user-friendly, allowing users to fill in login credentials automatically when visiting Web sites, making logging in faster and more convenient. Bitwarden's syncing process is reliable and ensures that data is always up to date across all devices.

While Bitwarden has many strengths, there are some potential drawbacks to consider. One of the main criticisms is that the user interface, although functional, is not as polished as some of the more premium password managers. Although the design is clean and user-friendly, it may not have the same level of sophistication or customization options as other password managers, such as 1Password and Dashlane. Some users may find the interface less visually appealing or feature-rich compared to these alternatives. Additionally, while Bitwarden's free version provides a solid set of features, users who want advanced features, such as more control over 2FA options and file attachments, need to upgrade to the premium plan. The price for the premium plan is low, but some users may prefer a completely free solution.

Another limitation is that Bitwarden, like many password managers, relies on a master password to unlock the vault. While this is a standard and necessary security measure, it also means that if a user forgets their master password, they could potentially lose access to their entire vault. While Bitwarden offers some recovery options, such as email-based recovery, these methods may not be foolproof in all cases. Users should take precautions to ensure that their master password is both strong and memorable or use a secure method to store it.

In conclusion, Bitwarden is an excellent password manager that combines strong security features, flexibility, and affordability. Its open-source nature, AES-256 encryption, and cross-platform support make it a trusted solution for individuals and businesses seeking to manage passwords securely. The free version offers a generous range of features, and the premium subscription provides even more advanced options at an affordable price. Bitwarden's emphasis on transparency, privacy, and security has made it a go-to choice for users who want a reliable password manager that offers both ease of use and strong protection for their sensitive data. While it may not be as feature-rich or visually polished as some competitors, Bitwarden's combination of functionality, affordability, and security makes it a top choice for anyone looking to safeguard their passwords and online accounts.

Signal

Signal is a leading secure messaging application that has garnered significant attention and praise for its dedication to privacy, robust encryption protocols, and user-friendly design. Developed by the Signal Foundation, a nonprofit organization committed to advancing private communication, Signal stands out as a top choice for individuals and organizations seeking to protect their conversations from prying eyes. Its open-source nature, straightforward interface, and commitment to user privacy make it a standout in the world of secure communication tools.

At the heart of Signal's appeal is its E2EE, which ensures that messages, calls, and media shared through the app are accessible only to the intended recipients. Signal employs the Signal Protocol, an encryption framework that has become the gold standard in secure communication. This protocol is widely respected in the cryptography community and is used by other major platforms, such as WhatsApp and Facebook Messenger. Signal sets itself apart, however, by implementing the protocol in its purest form, without compromising user privacy for commercial interests or metadata collection.

One of Signal's most significant strengths is its strict adherence to privacy principles. The app collects virtually no user data, retaining only the bare minimum necessary for functionality—such as a user's phone number. Unlike many competitors, Signal does not store message metadata, such as who communicated with whom and when. This commitment to privacy is further bolstered by features such as disappearing messages, which allow users to set a timer for messages to delete automatically after a specified period. This adds an extra layer of security, particularly for sensitive or ephemeral conversations.

Signal is also open source, meaning its source code is publicly available for scrutiny by security experts and the general public. This transparency builds trust, as anyone can verify that the app operates as claimed and that there are no hidden vulnerabilities or backdoors. The open-source nature of Signal ensures continuous improvements and fosters a collaborative approach to security. It stands as a stark contrast to proprietary messaging apps, where users must rely solely on the developers' claims regarding security and privacy.

The app is feature-rich, offering not just secure text messaging but also encrypted voice and video calls. Signal's call quality is generally excellent, even in areas with weak network connections, thanks to its use of efficient codecs and data compression. Group messaging and calling are also supported, making Signal a viable alternative to mainstream communication platforms for both personal and professional use. Users can create groups, share media files, and even set up group video calls, all with the same level of security provided for one-on-one communication.

Signal's interface is simple and intuitive, making it accessible to users of all technical skill levels. The clean design emphasizes ease of use without compromising on functionality. Setting up the app is straightforward: users register with their phone number, and no additional credentials or accounts are required. The app is available for Android, iOS, Windows, macOS, and Linux, ensuring compatibility across a wide range of devices. Signal also offers a desktop client that syncs seamlessly with the mobile app, allowing users to access their messages across multiple platforms.

A standout feature of Signal is its support for rich media sharing. Users can send photos, videos, documents, and voice messages with the same E2EE that protects text messages and calls. Signal also offers additional privacy-enhancing features, such as the ability to blur faces in images before sending them, which is particularly useful for protecting the identities of individuals in sensitive situations.

Signal's commitment to privacy extends beyond encryption. The app recently introduced features such as PINs for account recovery, ensuring that even if someone gains access to a user's phone number, they cannot take over the account without the PIN. Signal also has a "sealed sender" feature, which minimizes metadata exposure by concealing information about the sender during message transmission. These innovative privacy measures demonstrate Signal's proactive approach to safeguarding user data.

Signal is not without its limitations, however. One of the most frequently cited drawbacks is its reliance on phone numbers for user identification. While this simplifies the registration process, it also raises privacy concerns for users who prefer to keep their phone numbers private. Signal has made some strides in addressing this issue by exploring alternatives, such as usernames, but phone numbers remain the primary identifier for now. Additionally, while Signal supports syncing across devices, it currently lacks the ability to use the app independently on multiple devices simultaneously (e.g., two phones), which can be inconvenient for users with multiple devices.

Another limitation is Signal's relatively small user base compared to mainstream messaging platforms such as WhatsApp. While Signal has experienced significant growth in recent years, particularly following high-profile endorsements and concerns over the privacy policies of other platforms, its adoption remains limited in certain regions and demographics. This can make it challenging for users to fully transition to Signal if their contacts do not also use the app.

From a usability perspective, while Signal's design is clean and functional, some users may find its feature set less extensive compared to other messaging apps. For example, it lacks certain advanced customization options and entertainment-focused features, such as stickers and GIF libraries, that are common in other apps. While these omissions are deliberate to maintain simplicity and focus on security, they may deter users who prioritize these features in their communication tools.

Despite these limitations, Signal's strengths far outweigh its shortcomings. The app is supported entirely by donations and grants, allowing it to remain independent of commercial interests and free from the data monetization practices common in the tech industry. This financial model ensures that Signal's primary focus remains on user privacy and security.

Signal is a highly secure, transparent, and reliable messaging platform that sets the standard for private communication. Its robust encryption, open-source nature, and privacy-focused features make it an ideal choice for users who value their digital security. While its reliance on phone numbers and relatively limited feature set may pose minor challenges, Signal's unwavering commitment to privacy and its user-first approach make it a top recommendation for anyone seeking a secure alternative to mainstream messaging apps. Whether for personal use or professional communication, Signal is a trustworthy and dependable tool in the fight for digital privacy.

Wire

Wire is a secure communication platform that blends privacy, functionality, and a sleek design to deliver a comprehensive messaging and collaboration solution. Known for its strong encryption standards, multi-platform support, and user-centric approach, Wire has become a trusted choice for individuals, teams, and organizations seeking a secure alternative to mainstream messaging and collaboration tools. Wire's ability to balance robust security with modern features makes it particularly appealing to both privacy-conscious users and enterprises prioritizing data protection.

The cornerstone of Wire's appeal is its E2EE, which protects all messages, calls, files, and other communications from being intercepted or accessed by unauthorized parties. Wire employs the Proteus protocol, an adaptation of the Signal Protocol, which is widely recognized for its security and reliability. This ensures that all communications are encrypted on the sender's device and remain inaccessible to Wire's servers or any third parties. Even metadata exposure is minimized, with the platform employing various techniques to obfuscate user interactions and preserve privacy. This level of encryption is applied by default, ensuring that users are protected without requiring additional configuration.

Wire takes pride in its open-source nature, a feature that enhances trust and transparency. The platform's source code is publicly available and undergoes regular independent audits, allowing security experts to verify its claims and identify potential vulnerabilities. This openness ensures that Wire remains accountable to its users and continuously evolves in response to emerging security challenges. The platform's commitment to transparency is a key factor in its credibility, distinguishing it from closed-source competitors that rely on proprietary protocols.

Wire is designed with versatility in mind, offering a broad range of features to support secure communication and collaboration. In addition to secure text messaging, Wire supports high-quality voice and video calls, group chats, and file sharing. These capabilities make it a viable solution for both personal and professional use. The platform is particularly well suited for remote teams and businesses, offering tools such as conference calling, screen sharing, and group management features. These enterprise-grade functionalities are complemented by the same level of security applied to individual communications, ensuring that sensitive business data remains protected.

The platform's interface is modern, intuitive, and aesthetically pleasing. Wire combines functionality with a clean, minimalist design that makes it easy to navigate for users of all technical skill levels. The application is available across multiple platforms, including Windows, macOS, Linux, iOS, and Android, with seamless synchronization across devices. This cross-platform compatibility ensures that users can access their accounts and communicate securely regardless of their preferred operating system. Wire also offers a Web version, adding another layer of flexibility for users who may not want to install dedicated software on their devices.

One of Wire's standout features is its strong support for team collaboration. The platform allows organizations to create multiple workspaces, each with its own set of users and permissions. This is particularly useful for businesses that manage multiple projects or departments. Wire enables the secure sharing of files, links, and multimedia content within these workspaces, fostering seamless collaboration while maintaining data security. Additionally, the platform supports guest accounts, allowing external collaborators to participate in discussions without compromising the organization's overall security framework.

For enterprises, Wire offers tailored solutions that include additional features such as centralized management, compliance tools, and integration options. Wire's business-oriented plans are designed to meet regulatory requirements, such as the General Data Protection Regulation (GDPR) and

HIPAA, making it an attractive choice for industries with strict data protection standards. Organizations can deploy Wire on their own servers or within their private cloud environments, further enhancing control over sensitive information. This flexibility is particularly appealing to companies seeking to align their communication tools with their internal security policies.

Wire also addresses the increasing demand for ephemeral communication. The platform includes features such as timed messages, which automatically delete after a set period. This functionality is particularly valuable for users or organizations dealing with sensitive information that does not need to be retained. Additionally, Wire provides users with detailed controls over their data, allowing them to manage message history and delete messages or conversations as needed.

Despite its many advantages, Wire is not without its limitations. One of the most notable challenges is its relatively small user base compared to larger platforms such as WhatsApp and Microsoft Teams. While Wire is well suited for secure internal communications, users may find it difficult to convince their external contacts to adopt the platform. This limits its utility for personal use in cases where friends, family, or collaborators are not already using the app.

Another potential drawback is the cost associated with some of Wire's advanced features. While the platform offers a free version for individuals, its business and enterprise plans come with subscription fees. These plans provide valuable tools and additional functionality, but smaller organizations or casual users may find the pricing a barrier, especially when compared to other free or low-cost alternatives. For those for whom security and compliance are priorities, however, the cost is often justified by the enhanced protection and control Wire offers.

Wire's reliance on phone numbers or email addresses for user registration is another area of concern for privacy-conscious users who prefer anonymous communication. While these identifiers are necessary for account creation and syncing across devices, they may deter individuals who value complete anonymity. The company has worked to mitigate this concern by implementing robust encryption and data minimization practices, but it remains a consideration for certain users.

Wire is a powerful and secure communication platform that excels in providing encrypted messaging and collaboration tools for individuals and organizations alike. Its strong focus on privacy, combined with a user-friendly design and comprehensive feature set, makes it a compelling choice for anyone seeking a secure alternative to mainstream communication apps. While its smaller user base and cost for advanced features may present challenges, Wire's commitment to transparency, open-source development, and enterprise-grade security ensures that it remains a leading option for those who prioritize data protection and secure communication. Whether for personal use, team collaboration, or enterprise deployment, Wire offers a reliable and robust solution for modern communication needs.

Proton Mail

Proton Mail is a highly secure email service that has become synonymous with privacy and encrypted communication. Developed by scientists from CERN and MIT in 2014 and headquartered in Switzerland, Proton Mail emphasizes user security and privacy above all else. With a focus on E2EE, a strong legal framework under Swiss privacy laws, and an intuitive user interface, Proton Mail has established itself as a premier option for individuals and organizations seeking a secure alternative to mainstream email providers.

At the core of Proton Mail's appeal is its commitment to E2EE. Emails sent between Proton Mail users are encrypted in such a way that only the sender and recipient can access their content. This encryption is client-side, meaning messages are encrypted on the sender's device and can only be decrypted by the intended recipient. Proton Mail's zero-access architecture ensures that even the company itself cannot read user emails. For emails sent to non-Proton Mail users, the service allows encryption with a password and optional expiration dates, ensuring that sensitive information remains protected.

Proton Mail uses AES, RSA, and OpenPGP standards to secure its communications. These encryption protocols are well established and widely trusted within the cybersecurity community. Additionally, Proton Mail's commitment to open-source development adds a layer of transparency and trust. Its codebase is publicly available, allowing independent security experts to review and verify the service's encryption methods. This openness aligns with Proton Mail's philosophy of fostering trust through accountability and continuous improvement.

One of the most significant advantages of Proton Mail is its location in Switzerland, a country known for its strong privacy laws. Swiss law provides robust protections against government surveillance and third-party data requests. Any access to user data requires a Swiss court order, and because

Proton Mail does not retain unencrypted emails or IP logs, the amount of information available is minimal. This legal framework ensures that user data is far less vulnerable to breaches or unwarranted access compared to services operating in jurisdictions with weaker privacy protections.

Proton Mail's user interface is clean, modern, and easy to use, making it accessible to users of all technical skill levels. The service is available through webmail, as well as Android and iOS apps, ensuring seamless access across devices. The layout is intuitive, featuring familiar email management tools such as folders, labels, and a robust search function. While security is Proton Mail's priority, the platform does not sacrifice usability, offering a straightforward experience comparable to mainstream email providers such as Gmail or Outlook.

A notable feature of Proton Mail is its integration with Proton services, including Proton Drive, Proton VPN, and Proton Calendar. This ecosystem allows users to maintain a high level of privacy across multiple aspects of their digital lives. For instance, users can benefit from secure cloud storage, anonymous Web browsing, and encrypted scheduling, all managed from a unified account. This comprehensive approach to privacy makes Proton Mail an appealing choice for users seeking a holistic solution.

Proton Mail also offers features tailored to different user needs. Its free tier provides a generous allotment, including 1 GB of storage, a single email address, and essential encryption tools. For those requiring additional functionality, such as more storage, custom domains, or priority customer support, Proton Mail offers reasonably priced paid plans. These plans cater to both individual users and businesses, with advanced options such as multiple users, professional domains, and enhanced collaboration tools.

For businesses, Proton Mail's enterprise features are particularly compelling. The ability to host encrypted email on a custom domain, manage user permissions, and integrate with other Proton services ensures that organizations can maintain robust privacy standards without compromising efficiency. Businesses that handle sensitive data, such as those in healthcare, law, and finance, often find Proton Mail an attractive alternative to conventional providers.

Privacy-conscious users will appreciate Proton Mail's dedication to minimizing data collection. The service does not track user behavior or display targeted advertisements. Instead, it relies on subscription fees for revenue, allowing it to remain independent of data monetization practices. Proton

Mail's adherence to this model ensures that users are not subjected to invasive profiling or data sharing.

Proton Mail is not without its limitations, however. One common criticism is the storage capacity of the free plan, which may be insufficient for users accustomed to the large quotas offered by services such as Gmail. While this can be resolved by upgrading to a paid plan, it may deter some users who rely heavily on free services. Another potential drawback is the relatively high cost of premium plans compared to non-secure email providers, although the added security features and peace of mind often justify the expense for privacy-focused users.

Another limitation is Proton Mail's occasional compatibility issues with non-Proton Mail users. While the service allows encrypted communication with external recipients via password-protected messages, this process can be cumbersome for recipients unfamiliar with secure email practices. Similarly, some advanced features available in other email clients, such as seamless integration with third-party tools or expansive add-ons, may not yet be fully realized within Proton Mail's ecosystem.

Proton Mail's spam filtering, while effective, can also be overly aggressive at times, leading to false positives. While users have control over their spam settings, the need to manually adjust filters may be inconvenient for those accustomed to less intrusive systems.

Proton Mail is an exceptional email provider that prioritizes security, privacy, and transparency. Its robust encryption protocols, zero-access architecture, and alignment with Swiss privacy laws make it a leading choice for individuals and organizations that value confidentiality. While its storage limits and premium pricing may pose challenges for some, Proton Mail's commitment to user privacy and its expanding suite of services provide substantial value. For anyone seeking a secure, user-friendly, and ethical alternative to mainstream email services, Proton Mail is a top-tier option. Whether for personal communication, professional use, or integration into a broader privacy-focused workflow, Proton Mail offers an unparalleled combination of security and functionality.

OnionShare

OnionShare is an innovative open-source tool designed to facilitate anonymous and secure file sharing, Web site hosting, and even messaging, using the Tor network. Its unique approach to privacy and security has made it a favorite among users who require anonymity or need to share sensitive information without compromising confidentiality. By leveraging the Tor network, OnionShare ensures that user activities remain private and resistant to surveillance or interception, setting it apart from traditional file-sharing services.

OnionShare uses Tor's onion services to create temporary, private Web servers directly on a user's computer. When a user shares a file, OnionShare generates a unique, non-guessable `.onion` URL that recipients can use to download the file. This URL does not reveal any identifying information about the sender or their location, as it operates entirely within the Tor ecosystem. Furthermore, no third-party servers are involved in the process, ensuring that files remain accessible only to those with the unique URL and access to the Tor network.

One of OnionShare's most appealing features is its simplicity. Despite its reliance on advanced technologies such as Tor, the tool is designed with user-friendliness in mind. Its clean, straightforward interface makes it accessible to individuals with varying levels of technical expertise. To share a file, users simply drag and drop the file into the application, click "Start Sharing," and share the resulting URL with the intended recipient. The recipient then uses Tor Browser to access and download the file securely. This ease of use is a significant advantage, particularly for individuals who are new to privacy tools.

OnionShare also offers robust security features. Files shared through the platform are not stored on any central server; they remain on the sender's device until the recipient downloads them. Once the sharing session is complete, the temporary onion service is closed, and the link becomes invalid. This ensures that files are only accessible for the duration of the sharing session. Additionally, OnionShare supports optional password protection for the shared link, adding another layer of security against unauthorized access.

Beyond file sharing, OnionShare has expanded its functionality to include anonymous Web site hosting and secure messaging. These features allow users to host static Web sites or communicate securely without revealing their identities. The anonymous Web site hosting feature is particularly useful for activists, journalists, or whistleblowers who need to publish sensitive information without exposing themselves to potential risks. The secure messaging feature operates similarly to private chats, with the same level of anonymity and encryption provided by the Tor network.

OnionShare's reliance on the Tor network is both its strength and its limitation. While Tor provides unparalleled anonymity, it also requires that both the sender and recipient have access to the network. This dependency may pose a barrier for users in regions where Tor is blocked or where Internet access is heavily censored. Additionally, downloading and setting up Tor Browser may be an extra step for recipients unfamiliar with the technology, potentially complicating the process.

Another limitation of OnionShare is its dependency on the sender's device and Internet connection. Since files are hosted directly from the sender's computer, the sender must remain online for the duration of the sharing session. If the connection is interrupted or the device goes offline, the sharing session ends, and the file becomes inaccessible. This contrasts with centralized file-sharing services, which store files on cloud servers for on-demand access.

While OnionShare excels at providing secure, anonymous file sharing, it is not a comprehensive replacement for more feature-rich file-sharing platforms. For example, it lacks the ability to share extremely large files efficiently, as upload and download speeds are constrained by the Tor network and the sender's Internet connection. Additionally, its focus on anonymity and security means it does not offer features such as file versioning, collaboration tools, or integration with other productivity applications.

In terms of usability, while OnionShare's interface is straightforward, its reliance on Tor can present a learning curve for users unfamiliar with privacy tools. Setting up Tor Browser, understanding `.onion` URLs, and ensuring secure sharing practices may require additional effort, especially for less tech-savvy users. The software does, however, include clear documentation and community support, which helps mitigate these challenges.

OnionShare is a powerful and unique tool for those who prioritize privacy and anonymity in file sharing, Web site hosting, and messaging. Its use of Tor's onion services ensures a high level of security and confidentiality, making it an excellent choice for activists, journalists, whistleblowers, and privacy-conscious individuals. While it has some limitations, such as dependency on Tor and the need for the sender to remain online, its strengths in protecting user anonymity and avoiding centralized servers are unparalleled. For users who value these attributes and are willing to navigate the nuances of the Tor network, OnionShare is an invaluable resource in the realm of secure communication and information sharing.

Magic Wormhole

Magic Wormhole is an open-source tool that simplifies the process of securely transferring files, folders, and even text snippets between devices. Known for its innovative approach to secure communication, Magic Wormhole is designed to address a common problem: how to send files quickly, directly, and securely without requiring complex setups or intermediaries. Developed with simplicity and security in mind, it offers a compelling alternative to traditional file-sharing methods.

At the heart of Magic Wormhole is its novel approach to establishing a secure connection between two devices. Instead of relying on accounts, passwords, or extensive configuration, the tool generates short, human-readable "wormhole code" that serves as a unique identifier for the transfer session. This code is ephemeral and random, typically consisting of a combination of words and numbers, such as "7-purple-swordfish." The sender shares this code with the recipient, who enters it into their Magic Wormhole client to establish the connection. Once the code is entered, the file transfer begins directly between the devices, bypassing third-party servers.

Magic Wormhole uses strong encryption to ensure the security of the transfer. The connection is secured using the SPAKE2 protocol, a modern cryptographic technique that prevents eavesdropping or MITM attacks. Even if someone intercepts the wormhole code, they would need additional information to decrypt the data, making the transfer highly secure. This encryption occurs from end to end, ensuring that no one except the intended recipient can access the content of the transfer.

One of Magic Wormhole's key strengths is its simplicity. Unlike many file-sharing tools that require users to create accounts, configure settings, or upload files to a server, Magic Wormhole operates entirely without overhead. It requires only that both devices have the Magic Wormhole software installed and that the sender and recipient share the wormhole code in real time. This makes it particularly appealing for quick, ad hoc transfers where ease of use and immediacy are essential.

The tool is also highly versatile. It supports a wide range of operating systems, including Windows, macOS, Linux, and even some mobile platforms, provided they have the necessary Python environment. Magic Wormhole is a command-line application, which may initially seem daunting to non-technical users, but its straightforward syntax and minimal commands make it accessible with minimal learning. For users seeking a graphical interface, there are third-party projects that provide graphical user interfaces (GUIs) built on Magic Wormhole's core functionality.

One of Magic Wormhole's standout features is its direct P2P architecture. Files are not uploaded to a cloud server or stored on an intermediary platform; they travel directly from the sender's device to the recipient's device. This ensures both privacy and efficiency, as the transfer speed is determined by the users' Internet connections rather than server limitations. Additionally, Magic Wormhole does not retain any data after the transfer is complete, further enhancing its privacy credentials.

The reliance on P2P communication, however, does introduce certain limitations. Both the sender and recipient must be online simultaneously for the transfer to occur, and they need to share the wormhole code in real time. This can be a constraint in scenarios where asynchronous file sharing is preferred. Additionally, the direct transfer method may struggle with very large files, as performance can be impacted by bandwidth and connection stability.

Another limitation is the lack of built-in user interfaces. While the command-line approach is efficient and lightweight, it may not appeal to users accustomed to graphical interfaces or those unfamiliar with terminal commands. The open-source community has addressed this gap to some extent by developing third-party GUIs, but these are not officially supported by the Magic Wormhole project.

Magic Wormhole is particularly useful for developers, system administrators, and privacy-conscious users who value security and efficiency. It is also a great option for scenarios where quick, one-off transfers are required, such as sharing a file with a colleague during a meeting or sending sensitive documents to a client without relying on email or cloud storage. Its ephemeral nature and lack of data retention make it ideal for confidential exchanges. The open-source nature of Magic Wormhole is another major advantage.

Despite its niche appeal, Magic Wormhole's lack of mainstream adoption can be a hurdle. The sender and recipient both need to have the software installed and be familiar with its operation, which can be a barrier for non-technical users or in environments where installation permissions are restricted. Moreover, while the project is robust and well maintained, it does not have the extensive marketing or user-friendly ecosystems of commercial alternatives.

Magic Wormhole is an exceptional tool for secure, efficient, and straightforward file transfers. Its reliance on ephemeral wormhole codes,

E2EE, and direct P2P communication makes it one of the most secure options available for transferring data between devices. While its CLI and real-time dependency may limit its appeal to a broader audience, it is an indispensable tool for those who value security, privacy, and simplicity. Whether used for small, confidential exchanges or as part of a privacy-conscious workflow, Magic Wormhole exemplifies the power and utility of well-designed open-source software.

REFERENCES

1. Advanced Encryption Standard. In: Wikipedia [Internet]. 2024 [cited 2025 Jan 21]. Available from: *https://en.wikipedia.org/w/index.php?title=Advanced_Encryption_Standard&oldid=1264219392*
2. Authentication. In: Wikipedia [Internet]. 2025 [cited 2025 Jan 21]. Available from: *https://en.wikipedia.org/w/index.php?title=Authentication&oldid=1268193078*
3. Cipher. In: Wikipedia [Internet]. 2024 [cited 2025 Jan 21]. Available from: *https://en.wikipedia.org/w/index.php?title=Cipher&oldid=1258577625*
4. Computational hardness assumption. In: Wikipedia [Internet]. 2024 [cited 2025 Jan 21]. Available from: *https://en.wikipedia.org/w/index.php?title=Computational_hardness_assumption&oldid=1264743869*
5. Confidentiality. In: Wikipedia [Internet]. 2024 [cited 2025 Jan 21]. Available from: *https://en.wikipedia.org/w/index.php?title=Confidentiality&oldid=1256344993*
6. Cryptography. In: Wikipedia [Internet]. 2025 [cited 2025 Jan 21]. Available from: *https://en.wikipedia.org/w/index.php?title=Cryptography&oldid=1270632731*
7. Data Encryption Standard. In: Wikipedia [Internet]. 2025 [cited 2025 Jan 21]. Available from: *https://en.wikipedia.org/w/index.php?title=Data_Encryption_Standard&oldid=1267271546*
8. Data integrity. In: Wikipedia [Internet]. 2024 [cited 2025 Jan 21]. Available from: *https://en.wikipedia.org/w/index.php?title=Data_integrity&oldid=1211946886*

9. Diffie-Hellman key exchange. In: Wikipedia [Internet]. 2025 [cited 2025 Jan 21]. Available from: *https://en.wikipedia.org/w/index.php?title=Diffie%E2%80%93Hellman_key_exchange&oldid=1270557009*

10. E-commerce. In: Wikipedia [Internet]. 2024 [cited 2025 Jan 21]. Available from: *https://en.wikipedia.org/w/index.php?title=E-commerce&oldid=1264953436*

11. Elliptic-curve cryptography. In: Wikipedia [Internet]. 2024 [cited 2025 Jan 21]. Available from: *https://en.wikipedia.org/w/index.php?title=Elliptic-curve_cryptography&oldid=1259065219*

12. Encryption. In: Wikipedia [Internet]. 2025 [cited 2025 Jan 21]. Available from: *https://en.wikipedia.org/w/index.php?title=Encryption&oldid=1270292539*

13. Integer factorization. In: Wikipedia [Internet]. 2024 [cited 2025 Jan 21]. Available from: *https://en.wikipedia.org/w/index.php?title=Integer_factorization&oldid=1263211531*

14. Key (cryptography). In: Wikipedia [Internet]. 2024 [cited 2025 Jan 21]. Available from: *https://en.wikipedia.org/w/index.php?title=Key_(cryptography)&oldid=1260085944*

15. Non-repudiation. In: Wikipedia [Internet]. 2024 [cited 2025 Jan 21]. Available from: *https://en.wikipedia.org/w/index.php?title=Non-repudiation&oldid=1266502104*

16. Post-quantum cryptography. In: Wikipedia [Internet]. 2025 [cited 2025 Jan 21]. Available from: *https://en.wikipedia.org/w/index.php?title=Post-quantum_cryptography&oldid=1270468790*

17. RSA (cryptosystem). In: Wikipedia [Internet]. 2025 [cited 2025 Jan 21]. Available from: *https://en.wikipedia.org/w/index.php?title=RSA_(cryptosystem)&oldid=1267990112*

CHAPTER 4

Open-Source Software

The open-source movement is a transformative approach to software development and distribution that emphasizes transparency, collaboration, and community-driven innovation. It revolves around the idea that the source code of software should be made freely available for anyone to view, modify, and share. This philosophy contrasts with proprietary software models, where the code is typically locked and controlled by the vendor. The open-source movement encourages the collective contribution of developers worldwide, allowing for the rapid improvement of software and ensuring that it can be adapted to diverse needs. By fostering an inclusive environment, open-source projects empower individuals and organizations to create, improve, and customize software without the restrictions of traditional licensing models. Over time, the movement has gained significant momentum, not only influencing the software industry but also shaping broader trends in areas such as hardware design, education, and even governance. Through its emphasis on accessibility and cooperation, the open-source movement has contributed to the creation of some of the most widely used technologies today.

HISTORY

The history of open-source software is deeply intertwined with the evolution of the computing industry, driven by a series of technological, social, and philosophical developments that have reshaped the way software is created, shared, and distributed. The roots of open-source software can be traced back to the early days of computing in the mid-20th century, when software was often shared freely among researchers, developers, and academic institutions. During this period, software was generally seen as a tool to enable hardware to function, and its distribution was often unencumbered by commercial interests.

One of the earliest and most significant milestones in the development of open-source software occurred in the 1950s and 1960s. During this time, software was typically written by engineers and scientists at universities and research institutions, with the expectation that it would be freely shared. These early programmers believed that collaboration and the free exchange of knowledge would lead to the betterment of the field as a whole. This spirit of cooperation and knowledge-sharing can be seen in projects such as the development of early programming languages, operating systems, and mathematical tools that were distributed openly within academic circles.

In the 1970s, a key turning point in the history of open-source software occurred with the rise of the Unix operating system. Unix, developed at AT&T's Bell Labs by Ken Thompson, Dennis Ritchie, and others, was notable for its simplicity, portability, and modular design. The operating system was widely adopted in academic and research institutions, and the Unix community embraced a culture of sharing code and collaborating on improvements. The open nature of Unix's development was crucial in establishing the foundational principles of open-source software, as it allowed others to study, modify, and build upon the code.

Despite these early successes, the 1980s marked a pivotal shift toward proprietary software. The emergence of personal computing, combined with the rise of corporate companies, began to change the way software was distributed. In this new environment, software became a commodity, and licensing models were developed to restrict access to source code. This shift was further catalyzed by the legal and commercial strategies that companies employed to protect their IP, leading to the rise of closed-source software and the formalization of software patents.

The open-source movement did not fade entirely in the face of this commercialization. In the mid-1980s, Richard Stallman, a software programmer at the Massachusetts Institute of Technology (MIT), launched a campaign to preserve software freedom. Stallman's frustration with proprietary software and the restrictive licensing practices led him to found the Free Software Foundation (FSF) in 1985. The FSF advocated for the concept of "free software," which emphasized the user's freedom to run, modify, and distribute software. Stallman's crowning achievement was the creation of the GNU General Public License (GPL) in 1989, a licensing model that ensured the protection of these freedoms. The GNU project, initiated by Stallman, also sought to create a complete, free Unix-like operating system. While the GNU operating system itself was never fully realized, it laid the groundwork for what would eventually become one of the most successful open-source projects in history: Linux.

In 1991, Finnish computer science student Linus Torvalds released the first version of the Linux kernel, an operating system kernel that was designed to be compatible with the GNU operating system. Torvalds' decision to release the Linux kernel under the GPL was a pivotal moment for the open-source movement. By embracing the principles of open-source licensing and releasing his code freely, Torvalds created a powerful platform for collaboration and development. The combination of the Linux kernel with the tools from the GNU project resulted in the creation of a fully open-source operating system that was capable of running on a variety of hardware platforms. As Linux grew in popularity, it became a symbol of the success of the open-source model, demonstrating that freely available software could be competitive with proprietary offerings.

The 1990s also saw the rise of other important open-source projects, such as the Apache HTTP Server, which became the dominant Web server software. The release of Netscape's source code in 1998, which eventually led to the creation of the Mozilla Foundation and the Firefox browser, further solidified open-source software's place in the mainstream.

The early 2000s marked a period of growth and maturation for the open-source movement. Companies such as Red Hat, a leading provider of Linux-based enterprise solutions, began to profit from the support and services surrounding open-source software. The open-source business model, which emphasized providing services, support, and customization for open-source software, proved to be a viable and sustainable alternative to the traditional proprietary software model. Additionally, the growing success of open-source projects such as the Apache Software Foundation and the Mozilla Foundation further demonstrated the power of collaborative development.

One of the most significant developments in the 2000s was the rise of open-source software in enterprise environments. Major corporations such as IBM, Oracle, and Google began to embrace open-source solutions, often contributing to or supporting existing projects. This shift was driven by the realization that open-source software could offer greater flexibility, security, and cost savings than proprietary alternatives. The success of open-source projects such as the MySQL database, the Apache Web server, and the Eclipse development environment paved the way for open-source software to be used in mission-critical applications.

The growth of the open-source movement continued into the 2010s and beyond. The proliferation of platforms such as GitHub, which enabled developers to collaborate and share code more easily than ever before, helped to further expand the reach of open-source software. The rise of cloud computing also played a role in the expansion of open-source technologies, as companies sought to build scalable and cost-effective solutions using open-source tools and frameworks.

Today, open-source software is ubiquitous, and its influence extends far beyond the realm of software development. Open-source principles have been adopted in areas such as hardware design, education, and even governance. Technologies such as Kubernetes, Docker, and TensorFlow have become essential tools in fields such as cloud computing and ML, while open-source software is used in everything from smartphones to supercomputers. Major corporations, including Google, Microsoft, and Facebook, have embraced open-source software, contributing to projects and creating their own open-source initiatives.

The history of open-source software is a testament to the power of collaboration, transparency, and community-driven innovation. From its humble beginnings in academic research to its current status as a dominant force in the tech industry, open-source software has fundamentally changed the way software is developed, distributed, and used. Its impact on technology and society continues to grow, and its legacy will likely shape the future of computing for generations to come.

PHILOSOPHY

Open-source software is founded on principles of freedom, collaboration, transparency, and accessibility. At its core, the open-source movement challenges traditional notions of software ownership and distribution, advocating for a world where software is not a commodity to be bought and sold but a collective resource that can be shared, modified, and improved by anyone. This philosophy has not only shaped the way software is created but also influenced broader discussions on IP, ethics, and the role of community in technological development.

One of the central tenets of the open-source philosophy is the idea of software freedom. Pioneered by Richard Stallman and the FSF in the 1980s, software freedom emphasizes the rights of users to run, modify, and distribute software without restrictions. This perspective challenges the proprietary software model, in which the source code is kept secret and users are subject to licensing agreements that limit their ability to modify or share the software. According to Stallman, software freedom is not just a technical issue but a social and ethical one. The FSF's GNU GPL, introduced in 1989, was designed to ensure that software under this license could never be proprietary and that users would always have the right to access and modify the code. This philosophy regards the act of modifying and sharing software as an expression of freedom, creativity, and collective empowerment.

The open-source movement also embraces the concept of collaboration. Rather than viewing software development as the work of a single company or individual, open-source software is seen as a community-driven effort. Developers and users from around the world can contribute to a project, offering improvements, bug fixes, and new features. This collaborative nature fosters a sense of shared ownership and responsibility for the software. Open-source projects are often developed in public repositories, where anyone can view the code, propose changes, and participate in discussions. The result is a dynamic ecosystem in which innovation is driven by the collective efforts of a diverse and global community of contributors, rather than by a centralized authority.

Transparency is another key element of the open-source philosophy. Unlike proprietary software, where the inner workings of a program are hidden from the user, open-source software allows anyone to examine the source code. This transparency builds trust among users, as they can inspect the software for security vulnerabilities, understand how it operates, and ensure that it aligns with their values. The idea that software should be open and visible to all reflects a broader commitment to openness and accountability in technology. Transparency also facilitates learning and knowledge-sharing, as developers and users alike can study the code to understand how it works and contribute to its improvement.

A foundational concept within the open-source philosophy is the belief in accessibility—not just in terms of free availability, but also in creating software that is accessible to all people, regardless of their technical skill level. Open-source projects often prioritize user-friendliness, ensuring that people with varying levels of expertise can use, modify, and benefit from the software.

This accessibility extends beyond just the software itself to include documentation, community support, and resources that help users and developers engage with the project. The open-source movement has been instrumental in democratizing technology, making it possible for people from diverse backgrounds to participate in and benefit from the technological advancements that shape our world.

The community-driven nature of open-source software also extends to its governance model. Open-source projects typically operate with a more decentralized and meritocratic approach than traditional corporate-controlled software. In many open-source projects, decisions about the direction of development are made through consensus or by elected maintainers, rather than by a single corporate entity. This approach allows for more democratic decision-making, where the best ideas can rise to the top based on merit and the collective needs of the community. As a result, the open-source community is often seen as a model of collaboration and shared responsibility, where people come together to work on problems that benefit everyone, rather than focusing on personal profit.

Another important aspect of the open-source philosophy is its approach to innovation. Open-source software encourages rapid iteration and experimentation, allowing developers to quickly prototype, test, and refine new ideas. Because the code is open and accessible, innovation is not stifled by commercial interests or corporate gatekeepers. Developers are free to experiment and build upon existing projects, which accelerates the pace of technological progress. Open-source projects often serve as a breeding ground for new ideas and technologies, as they provide a platform for experimentation without the restrictions imposed by proprietary licenses. Many groundbreaking technologies, such as the Linux operating system, the Apache Web server, and the Kubernetes container orchestration system, have emerged from the open-source ecosystem.

The open-source philosophy also intersects with broader ethical concerns, particularly around issues of privacy, security, and control. Many open-source advocates view proprietary software as a tool for surveillance and control, as it often collects user data and restricts users' ability to protect their privacy. Open-source software, by contrast, is seen as a way to reclaim control over technology and protect users from exploitation. The transparency and freedom of open-source code allow users to take charge of their digital lives, making choices that align with their values and ensuring that their software works for them, rather than the other way around. This ethical dimension of open-source software has made it a powerful force in movements advocating for digital rights, net neutrality, and privacy protection.

Finally, the sustainability of open-source software has become a growing concern in recent years. While the open-source model has proven to be highly effective in fostering innovation, it has also raised questions about how open-source projects can be sustained over the long term. Many open-source projects are developed by volunteers who donate their time and expertise without monetary compensation. As open-source software becomes more integral to business and enterprise environments, there has been an increasing recognition that financial and organizational support is necessary to maintain and grow these projects. In response, a variety of new business models have emerged to support open-source sustainability, including support subscriptions, donations, and even corporate sponsorships.

The philosophy of open-source software is a vision of a more open, collaborative, and ethical technology landscape. It challenges traditional notions of ownership and control, advocating for freedom, transparency, and community-driven innovation. By prioritizing accessibility, collaboration, and shared responsibility, open-source software has transformed the way technology is developed and used, empowering individuals and communities to shape their digital futures. As the open-source movement continues to evolve, its philosophy remains a powerful force for change, inspiring new generations of developers and users to work together toward a more open and equitable digital world.

THE IMPACT ON SOFTWARE AND TECHNOLOGY

The impact of the open-source movement on technology and software has been profound, reshaping the way software is developed, distributed, and used. The open-source philosophy, which advocates for transparency, collaboration, and accessibility, has transformed both the software industry and the broader technological landscape. From the inception of open-source software in the late-twentieth century to its widespread adoption in the twenty-first century, its influence has been felt in numerous aspects of technology, including software development practices, the rise of new technologies, and the way businesses approach innovation and sustainability.

One of the most significant impacts of the open-source movement has been the democratization of software development. By making source code freely available to anyone, open-source software allows developers from around the world to collaborate, contribute, and improve software without the barriers imposed by proprietary licensing. This has led to an explosion of innovation, as developers are no longer constrained by the limitations of commercial software models. Open-source projects are typically developed in public repositories, where anyone can view the code, suggest changes, and contribute to its improvement. This openness has fostered a global community of developers, many of whom collaborate across geographic and organizational boundaries to create software that meets the needs of users worldwide.

The rise of open-source software has also had a profound impact on the software development process itself. In contrast to the closed, proprietary development models, open-source software is developed in an iterative, transparent, and community-driven manner. This has led to new development practices, such as continuous integration and continuous delivery (CI/CD), which allow software to be rapidly tested and deployed. Open-source projects are often characterized by frequent updates, bug fixes, and new features, as developers work together to improve the software over time. This collaborative development model has not only accelerated the pace of innovation but also created a more inclusive and diverse environment for developers to contribute to projects, leading to the creation of software that is more robust, secure, and adaptable.

Furthermore, open-source software has played a crucial role in shaping the infrastructure of the modern Internet. Many of the key technologies that underpin the Internet, such as Web servers, databases, and content management systems, are open source. Projects such as the Apache HTTP Server, the MySQL database, and the WordPress content management system have been fundamental in enabling the rapid growth of the Internet, making it easier and more affordable for organizations to establish an online presence. The open-source nature of these technologies has allowed them to evolve and improve over time, with a global community of developers contributing to their continued development.

Another major impact of open-source software has been its disruption of the software licensing model. In the proprietary software model, software is treated as a product to be sold, with users typically paying for licenses to use the software. Open-source software, on the other hand, challenges this notion by making the source code freely available. While open-source software is often free to use, businesses can still generate revenue through support services, custom development, and consulting. This has led to the rise of the open-source business model, where companies such as Red Hat, Canonical, and MongoDB offer paid services and enterprise-grade solutions built around open-source technologies. These companies demonstrate that it is possible to generate revenue from open-source software without sacrificing its core principles of openness and freedom.

The open-source movement has also influenced the adoption of new technologies and the creation of new paradigms. One of the most notable examples is the rise of containerization and cloud computing. Technologies such as Docker and Kubernetes, both open-source projects, have revolutionized the way applications are deployed and scaled in cloud environments. Docker allows developers to package applications and their dependencies into lightweight containers that can be easily deployed across different environments, while Kubernetes provides a powerful platform for orchestrating and managing containerized applications at scale. These open-source projects have become essential tools in modern DevOps practices and have played a major role in the proliferation of cloud-based infrastructure. The success of these technologies highlights the importance of open-source contributions to the development of cutting-edge technologies.

Open-source software has also had a significant impact on security and privacy. In contrast to proprietary software, where the source code is closed and its vulnerabilities are often hidden from users, open-source software allows anyone to inspect the code and identify potential security issues. This transparency has led to a culture of rigorous peer review, where developers from around the world work together to identify and fix security flaws. Open-source software is often more secure than proprietary alternatives because it benefits from the contributions of a large and diverse community of developers who actively monitor and improve the software. Additionally, many open-source projects prioritize user privacy and security, giving users more control over their data and ensuring that their software is not tracking or exploiting them.

The open-source movement has also reshaped the business landscape, particularly in the tech industry. In the past, companies relied on proprietary software to gain a competitive edge and create differentiation in the market. Today, many of the most successful companies in the tech industry, such as Google, Microsoft, and Facebook, contribute to open-source projects and leverage open-source software in their products and services. These companies have realized that open-source software can drive innovation, reduce costs, and provide a more flexible and customizable solution than proprietary software. The widespread adoption of open-source technologies by large corporations has helped to legitimize the open-source model and has led to greater collaboration between the private and public sectors.

Furthermore, open-source software has had a profound impact on education and learning. By providing free access to high-quality software, open-source projects have made it easier for students, educators, and researchers to access the tools they need to study and develop new technologies. Open-source software has also become a key part of computer science curricula in universities around the world, as it allows students to learn by examining real-world code and contributing to active projects. This has led to a new generation of developers who are well versed in open-source principles and practices, and who are more likely to contribute to the continued growth of the open-source ecosystem.

In the realm of hardware, open-source principles have inspired the development of open hardware projects, such as the Arduino microcontroller and the Raspberry Pi. These projects have made hardware development more accessible to a wider audience, empowering individuals and small organizations to create custom hardware solutions without the need for expensive proprietary components. The success of open hardware has further demonstrated the potential of open-source principles to transform industries beyond software. The impact of open-source software on technology and software has been nothing short of revolutionary.

SOFTWARE ROBUSTNESS AND PRIVACY

The impact of open-source software on security, software robustness, and privacy has also been profound, sparking debates over both its advantages and challenges. Open-source software is often praised for its transparency, which allows for greater scrutiny and peer review, but it also raises concerns about security vulnerabilities, maintenance issues, and the potential for exploitation by malicious actors. The balance between openness and security, the robustness of software developed collaboratively, and the privacy implications of open-source solutions are central to discussions about the role of open source in modern computing.

One of the most widely cited advantages of open-source software in security is its transparency and auditability. Because open-source code is publicly accessible, it can be reviewed, tested, and audited by anyone, including security researchers and independent experts. This level of scrutiny makes it easier to identify and fix security vulnerabilities, reducing the risk of undiscovered backdoors or hidden exploits. Unlike proprietary software, where security flaws may go unnoticed or unreported for long periods, open-source projects benefit from a global community that actively monitors code for weaknesses. This process has been instrumental in identifying and mitigating security issues in widely used open-source software, such as the Linux kernel, OpenSSL, and Apache Web servers. Many security professionals argue that the open-source model fosters greater trust, as users can independently verify that there are no hidden data collection mechanisms or deliberate weaknesses in the software.

The openness of open-source software, however, also presents significant security risks, particularly in the form of supply chain attacks. Because open-source projects often rely on contributions from a diverse and decentralized community, attackers can attempt to introduce malicious code into widely used dependencies. This can be done by taking control of abandoned projects, injecting malicious commits into repositories, or exploiting package managers to distribute compromised software. High-profile incidents, such as the SolarWinds attack and the Log4j vulnerability, have demonstrated how attackers can exploit weaknesses in open-source dependencies to compromise millions of systems worldwide. These security risks have led to increasing calls for better governance, stricter code review policies, and automated tools to detect vulnerabilities in open-source projects.

Another critical issue is the sustainability of security maintenance in open-source projects. While large, well-funded open-source projects often have dedicated security teams, many smaller but widely used projects rely on volunteer developers who may not have the time or resources to prioritize security. This has led to cases where essential software components remain vulnerable for long periods because no one is actively maintaining them. The OpenSSL Heartbleed vulnerability, which exposed millions of Internet users to data leaks in 2014, was a result of an underfunded and understaffed project despite its widespread use. In response, initiatives such as the Open Source Security Foundation (OpenSSF) and Google's Open Source Security Team have sought to provide funding, security audits, and best practices for securing open-source projects. Nevertheless, ensuring long-term security maintenance for the vast ecosystem of open-source software remains a challenge.

Open-source software also plays a crucial role in software robustness and reliability. Because open-source projects often involve contributions from a global community of developers, they tend to evolve rapidly, with frequent updates, bug fixes, and performance improvements. The iterative development model of open-source software encourages constant refinement, leading to more stable and reliable code over time. Many of the most robust and resilient software systems today, such as the Linux operating system, the Apache Web server, and PostgreSQL, are open-source projects that have been continuously improved through years of community-driven development. Additionally, because open-source software allows for public scrutiny, it is often more resistant to vendor lock-in and sudden discontinuation, providing long-term reliability for users.

Despite these advantages, the fragmentation of open-source software can sometimes hinder robustness. Because open-source projects are often forked or modified by different communities, different versions of the same software may develop independently, leading to inconsistencies and compatibility issues. This can make it difficult to ensure that security patches and updates are applied uniformly across all versions of a project. For example, in the case of Linux distributions, different package maintainers may apply security fixes at different rates, potentially leaving some users exposed to vulnerabilities longer than others. Standardizing best practices for software maintenance and patch distribution remains an ongoing challenge in the open-source ecosystem.

Privacy is another area where open-source software has had a major impact, offering users alternatives to proprietary software that may engage in data collection and surveillance. Open-source projects such as Tor, Signal, and Nextcloud have provided privacy-focused alternatives to mainstream applications, allowing users to maintain greater control over their data. The ability to inspect and verify source code ensures that these applications do not include hidden trackers, spyware, or unauthorized data-sharing mechanisms. This has made open-source software particularly attractive to activists, journalists, and organizations concerned with digital rights and online privacy.

The privacy implications of open-source software are not always straightforward, however. While open-source projects generally offer greater transparency, they may still rely on external dependencies, APIs, or cloud services that can introduce privacy risks. Additionally, the decentralized nature of open-source development means that privacy-focused features may not always be prioritized or implemented consistently across different projects. Some open-source applications may also lack user-friendly privacy settings, requiring technical expertise to configure them properly for optimal privacy protection. For instance, while open-source operating systems such as Linux offer advanced privacy options, configuring them for maximum privacy often requires specific knowledge of security settings, encryption tools, and firewall configurations.

Another controversy surrounding privacy and open-source software is the increasing corporate influence on major open-source projects. While corporate companies have contributed significantly to open-source development, their involvement has raised concerns about whether they prioritize user privacy. Some critics argue that these corporations use open-source contributions as a way to gain trust while embedding features that benefit their business models, such as telemetry data collection or integration with proprietary cloud services. The debate over whether corporate-backed open-source projects can truly uphold strong privacy protections continues to be a point of contention in the community.

The future of security, software robustness, and privacy in open-source software will likely involve a combination of improved governance, better funding models, and increased automation in security auditing. Initiatives such as software bills of materials (SBOMs), automated vulnerability scanners, and ML-based security analysis tools are being developed to help identify and mitigate risks in open-source projects. Additionally, there is a growing push for regulatory frameworks that encourage open-source security best practices while ensuring that companies using open-source software contribute back to its maintenance and security.

Open-source software has had a transformative impact on security, robustness, and privacy, offering transparency, reliability, and privacy-focused alternatives to proprietary solutions. It does, however, also face significant challenges, including security vulnerabilities, underfunded maintenance, supply chain risks, and corporate influence. As the open-source ecosystem continues to grow, addressing these challenges will be crucial to ensuring that open-source software remains a secure, reliable, and privacy-conscious foundation for modern technology. The ongoing evolution of open-source security practices and governance models will determine whether the movement can maintain its commitment to openness while effectively addressing the complex demands of security and privacy in an increasingly digital world.

COMMUNITY-DRIVEN DEVELOPMENT

The role of community in the open-source movement is fundamental, shaping its philosophy, development model, and long-term sustainability. Unlike proprietary software, which is typically created and maintained by a centralized organization, open-source software thrives on collaboration, where a diverse group of individuals and organizations contribute to a shared codebase. This collective effort has led to some of the most successful and widely used software projects in the world, including the Linux operating system, the Apache Web server, and the Python programming language. The open-source community not only drives innovation but also fosters a culture of knowledge sharing, inclusivity, and mutual support. While the community aspect of open source is often seen as its greatest strength, it also presents challenges related to governance, contributor burnout, and maintaining long-term engagement.

Contributors include independent developers, hobbyists, researchers, corporate employees, and nonprofit organizations. By allowing anyone to contribute, open-source projects benefit from diverse perspectives and expertise, leading to continuous improvements in functionality, security, and performance. This decentralized approach enables rapid innovation, as developers can independently experiment with new ideas, propose enhancements, and submit bug fixes without waiting for approval from a single authority.

The open-source community also plays a crucial role in peer review and quality control. Because the source code is openly accessible, contributions undergo rigorous review by other developers before being merged into the main project. This peer review process ensures that new code meets quality standards, follows best practices, and does not introduce security vulnerabilities. Many open-source projects have structured contribution guidelines and maintainers who oversee code reviews to maintain the integrity of the software. The distributed nature of this review system often results in higher code quality compared to proprietary software, where security audits and bug detection are limited to internal teams.

Another key aspect of the open-source community is its culture of knowledge sharing and mentorship. Many open-source projects encourage new developers to participate by providing documentation, tutorials, and mentorship programs. Platforms such as GitHub, GitLab, and Bitbucket make it easier for newcomers to explore projects, understand codebases, and contribute. This culture of knowledge exchange has helped open-source software become a training ground for developers, allowing them to improve their skills, gain experience with real-world projects, and build professional networks.

Despite its strengths, the open-source community also faces significant challenges, particularly in governance and decision-making. Because open-source projects involve contributors from different backgrounds and organizations, disagreements over project direction, leadership, and priorities can arise. Some projects are governed by a *benevolent dictator* model, where a single individual—often the project's original creator—makes final decisions. Examples include Linus Torvalds for the Linux kernel and Guido van Rossum for Python (before stepping down in 2018). Other projects use a *meritocratic* model, where contributors with a strong track record gain more influence over decision-making. Some large projects, such as Kubernetes and the Apache Foundation, have adopted democratic governance models with formal committees, steering groups, and voting processes. Governance disputes have, however, sometimes led to community fractures and project forks, such as the split between OpenOffice and LibreOffice or MySQL and MariaDB.

Another major challenge in open-source communities is contributor burnout and sustainability. Many open-source projects rely on unpaid or underpaid developers who contribute their time voluntarily. While some contributors work for companies that support open-source development, many are independent developers who juggle open-source contributions with full-time jobs or personal commitments. Maintaining popular open-source projects can be demanding, with developers facing constant bug reports, feature requests, and security vulnerabilities. This has led to cases where maintainers step away from projects due to stress and exhaustion. The lack of financial support for maintainers has been a growing concern, with initiatives such as GitHub Sponsors, Open Collective, and Software Freedom Conservancy (SFC) aiming to provide funding for open-source contributors.

The role of corporate participation in open-source communities is another complex issue. While open source was originally driven by independent developers and academic institutions, major technology companies now play a significant role in open-source development. Many corporations contribute to open-source projects, hire developers to work on open-source software, and release their own open-source tools. This has led to faster development and greater adoption of open-source software, but it has also raised concerns about whether corporate interests align with the values of the broader community. Some community members worry that large corporations may prioritize features that benefit their business models rather than the needs of independent users. In some cases, corporations have taken control of open-source projects and later changed their licensing terms, leading to accusations of "open-washing"—the practice of adopting open-source principles for marketing purposes while maintaining proprietary control.

The open-source community also plays a vital role in advocacy and ethical discussions about software freedom. Organizations such as FSF and the Open Source Initiative (OSI) work to promote the principles of open-source software, defend user freedoms, and prevent restrictive licensing practices. Community-driven movements have pushed back against DRM, software patents, and proprietary standards that limit user control over technology. Additionally, ethical discussions about open-source licensing have emerged, with some developers proposing ethical source licenses that restrict the use of software for unethical purposes, such as surveillance or military applications. These debates highlight the evolving nature of community values within the open-source movement.

Looking ahead, the future of open-source communities will likely involve improving governance models, securing sustainable funding, and balancing corporate involvement with community interests. New funding mechanisms, such as corporate sponsorships, crowdfunding, and public grants, are emerging to support open-source contributors. Efforts to improve community governance and reduce maintainer burnout are gaining traction, with more projects adopting structured leadership models and mentorship programs. Additionally, as open-source software continues to grow in importance, there is a growing recognition that governments, corporations, and nonprofit organizations must work together to ensure the long-term health of open-source communities.

The role of community in the open-source movement is central to its success, enabling collaboration, peer review, knowledge sharing, and innovation. Open-source communities, however, also face challenges related to governance, sustainability, contributor burnout, and corporate influence. As open-source software becomes more critical to modern technology, ensuring that these communities remain vibrant, inclusive, and well supported will be essential for the continued growth and success of the open-source movement.

GNU/LINUX: THE OPEN-SOURCE OPERATING SYSTEM

Linux is one of the most significant achievements of the open-source movement, serving as both a technological cornerstone and a symbol of the power of collaborative development. Since its inception in 1991 by Linus Torvalds,

Linux has grown from a small personal project into a global phenomenon, powering everything from smartphones and supercomputers to Web servers and embedded devices. Its open-source nature, flexibility, and reliability have made it the backbone of modern computing, challenging proprietary operating systems and redefining software development paradigms. Over the decades, Linux has fostered an extensive ecosystem of distributions, communities, and corporate contributions, making it one of the most influential software projects in history.

The origins of Linux can be traced back to Unix, an operating system developed in the late 1960s and early 1970s at AT&T's Bell Labs. Unix became widely used in academia and industry, but its proprietary nature led to restrictions on modifications and distribution. In response, the GNU Project, founded by Richard Stallman in 1983, aimed to create a completely free and open-source Unix-like operating system. By the late 1980s, the GNU Project had developed many essential components, but it lacked a fully functional kernel. In 1991, Linus Torvalds, then a student at the University of Helsinki, created the Linux kernel as a hobby project, releasing it under an open-source license. When combined with GNU utilities, Linux became a fully functional operating system, often referred to as GNU/Linux.

One of the defining moments in Linux's history came in 1992, when Torvalds re-licensed the Linux kernel under the GNU GPL. This decision ensured that Linux would remain free and open source, allowing anyone to modify it, distribute it, and contribute to its development. The GPL's copyleft provisions required that any derivative works also be open source, fostering a culture of transparency and collaboration that would define Linux's evolution.

As Linux matured, it quickly gained traction among hobbyists, researchers, and system administrators who were drawn to its stability, performance, and flexibility. The late 1990s and early 2000s saw the rise of Linux distributions, which packaged the Linux kernel with software, drivers, and user-friendly tools. Early distributions such as Slackware and Debian laid the groundwork for later user-friendly versions, such as Red Hat, SUSE, and Ubuntu. These distributions catered to different needs, ranging from enterprise deployments to desktop computing, expanding Linux's reach beyond technical users.

One of Linux's most significant contributions to computing has been its dominance in the server and cloud computing markets. Unlike proprietary operating systems, Linux provided a cost-effective, highly customizable alternative for Web hosting and enterprise environments. The emergence of

LAMP (which stands for Linux, Apache, MySQL, PHP/Python/Perl) as the preferred stack for Web development cemented Linux's role as the foundation of the modern Internet. Companies such as Google, Facebook, Amazon, and Twitter built their infrastructures on Linux, leveraging its scalability and security.

The rise of corporate support for Linux marked a turning point in its mainstream adoption. By the early 2000s, major technology companies began contributing to Linux development. Red Hat pioneered the enterprise Linux model, offering commercial support and certification for its distribution while maintaining open-source principles. IBM invested heavily in Linux, making it a key component of its enterprise strategy. By the 2010s, Microsoft had embraced Linux as well, integrating it into its cloud services and even joining the Linux Foundation.

Another major milestone in Linux's evolution was its dominance in mobile computing. In 2008, Google released Android, a Linux-based operating system that would go on to become the most widely used operating system in the world. Unlike traditional Linux distributions, Android modified the Linux kernel to support mobile hardware and introduced a unique application framework. While some purists argue that Android's closed-source components diverge from Linux's original philosophy, its widespread adoption underscores Linux's versatility and impact on consumer technology.

Linux has also played a crucial role in supercomputing and embedded systems. The vast majority of the world's top supercomputers run Linux due to its ability to handle massive parallel processing workloads. Linux is also the preferred choice for embedded systems, from smart TVs and networking devices to automotive software and industrial automation.

Despite its success, Linux has faced challenges, particularly in desktop adoption. While distributions such as Ubuntu and Fedora have made Linux more user-friendly, Windows and macOS continue to dominate the desktop market due to factors such as hardware compatibility, software availability, and user familiarity. Linux-based alternatives, such as ChromeOS and SteamOS, have, however, gained traction in specific markets, offering lightweight and gaming-focused experiences.

The governance and development model of Linux is another key aspect of its success. Unlike proprietary operating systems controlled by a single company, Linux development is decentralized, with contributions from thousands of developers worldwide. The Linux kernel is maintained by a core team of developers, with Linus Torvalds acting as the final arbiter of changes ("benevolent dictator for life"). The Linux Foundation, a nonprofit organization, supports Linux development by funding key projects, organizing collaboration among companies, and maintaining industry standards.

One of the most debated topics in Linux development is the role of corporate influence. While companies such as Google, Intel, IBM, and Red Hat have significantly contributed to Linux, some community members worry about potential conflicts between corporate priorities and open-source values. The systemd controversy, where a modern init system replaced traditional Unix-like startup processes, highlighted tensions between developers favoring innovation and those prioritizing Unix traditions.

Security is another area where Linux has had a profound impact. Unlike proprietary operating systems that rely on closed-source security patches, Linux benefits from public code review and rapid community-driven security updates. Linux is not immune to security threats, however, as demonstrated by vulnerabilities such as Heartbleed and Spectre/Meltdown. The open-source model enables faster detection and remediation of security flaws, but it also raises concerns about who is responsible for the long-term maintenance of critical components.

Looking to the future, Linux will continue to be a driving force in computing. The cloud-native movement, powered by technologies such as Kubernetes and containers, is built on Linux. The expansion of Linux into AI, ML, and edge computing will further solidify its role in emerging technologies. Additionally, the rise of open-source hardware projects such as RISC-V suggests that Linux's principles of openness may extend beyond software into computing architectures.

Linux is far more than an operating system—it is a testament to the power of collaborative, open-source development. Its impact on servers, mobile computing, cloud infrastructure, and supercomputing is unparalleled, and its governance model continues to inspire new generations of developers. While challenges such as desktop adoption, corporate influence, and security management persist, Linux remains a cornerstone of modern computing, embodying the ideals of freedom, transparency, and innovation that define the open-source movement.

GITHUB

GitHub has become the dominant platform for collaborative software development, version control, and project management. Since its launch in 2008, GitHub has revolutionized how developers contribute to open-source projects by providing an intuitive interface for Git, a powerful version control system created by Linus Torvalds. Over the years, GitHub has grown from a simple code-hosting service into a comprehensive ecosystem that integrates issue tracking, pull requests, continuous integration, and automation tools. Its influence on the open-source community, software development practices, and even corporate software strategies is immense. GitHub's rise has, however, also brought challenges and controversies, particularly regarding its acquisition by Microsoft, its policies on open-source licensing, and its role in shaping the future of open-source collaboration.

At its core, GitHub is a repository hosting platform that allows developers to store, manage, and share their code using Git. Unlike traditional software development environments, where version control was often confined to internal teams, GitHub enables distributed collaboration by allowing developers from around the world to contribute to a shared codebase. This model has significantly accelerated open-source software development, making it easier for developers to propose changes, review contributions, and merge improvements into projects efficiently. GitHub's interface and workflow—based on pull requests, branches, and issue tracking—have set a de facto standard for modern open-source development.

One of GitHub's most significant contributions to the open-source movement is its role in fostering community-driven development. The platform enables developers to "fork" projects, allowing them to create their own versions of existing repositories while preserving links to the original project. This makes it easy to experiment with changes, propose improvements, and contribute back to the original codebase. GitHub also provides collaboration tools such as discussions, wikis, and actions for automating workflows, which enhance community engagement. These features have made GitHub the go-to platform for open-source maintainers, independent developers, and corporate-backed projects alike.

GitHub's impact on the visibility and discoverability of open-source projects has been profound. The platform allows developers to browse, search, and contribute to millions of public repositories, making it easier to find and engage with projects that align with their interests or expertise. The introduction of GitHub Stars, trending repositories, and project insights has helped open-source projects gain exposure and attract contributors. Additionally, GitHub's integration with package managers, CI/CD tools, and cloud platforms has further solidified its role in the open-source ecosystem.

GitHub's centralized dominance over the open-source ecosystem has, however, raised concerns about the risks of over-reliance on a single platform. While Git itself is a decentralized version control system, GitHub operates as a proprietary, cloud-hosted service, meaning that developers depend on GitHub's infrastructure and policies to maintain their projects. This became particularly controversial in 2018 when Microsoft acquired GitHub, leading to fears that the company might exert excessive influence over the open-source ecosystem. While Microsoft has since made significant contributions to open-source software and maintained GitHub's commitment to open development, some developers remain skeptical of a large corporation controlling such a critical part of the open-source infrastructure.

One of the most debated issues surrounding GitHub is its handling of software licensing and content moderation. GitHub provides tools for developers to apply open-source licenses to their projects, but the platform has also faced criticism for inconsistencies in enforcing these licenses. For example, while GitHub hosts projects under a variety of open-source licenses, it has also faced demands to take action against repositories that violate IP laws, national regulations, or ethical concerns. The most notable controversy arose in 2019 when GitHub, in compliance with U.S. trade sanctions, restricted access to developers in Iran, Crimea, and other sanctioned regions. This decision highlighted the tension between GitHub's global role as an open-source platform and its obligations as a U.S.-based corporation subject to government regulations.

Another major shift in GitHub's strategy came with the introduction of GitHub Copilot, an AI-powered code-generation tool developed in collaboration with OpenAI. Copilot uses ML models trained on vast amounts of public code from GitHub repositories to suggest code snippets and entire functions to developers in real time. While Copilot has been praised for increasing developer productivity, it has also raised legal and ethical questions about whether AI-generated code violates open-source licenses. Some developers have argued that GitHub is profiting from open-source code without adequately crediting contributors or ensuring that AI-generated code complies with licensing terms.

GitHub has also introduced initiatives to support open-source maintainers and funding mechanisms. Programs such as GitHub Sponsors allow developers to receive financial support for their contributions, addressing one of the longstanding challenges of open-source sustainability. Additionally, GitHub has invested in security initiatives such as GitHub security advisories, Dependabot alerts, and code scanning to improve the security of open-source software and protect against vulnerabilities.

Despite these advancements, GitHub faces competition from alternative platforms, such as GitLab, Bitbucket, and self-hosted Git solutions such as Gitea. Some open-source projects, particularly those concerned about corporate control, have moved away from GitHub in favor of decentralized or self-hosted alternatives. The rise of decentralized code-hosting solutions and federated platforms such as Forgejo signals a growing demand for open-source infrastructure that is not controlled by a single entity.

Looking to the future, GitHub's role in open-source development is likely to continue evolving. As the platform expands its AI-powered tools, strengthens security measures, and introduces new collaboration features, it will remain a central hub for software development. Ongoing debates about license enforcement, AI ethics, and corporate influence, however, will shape how the open-source community interacts with GitHub. While it remains the dominant platform for hosting and managing open-source projects, developers and organizations may seek greater control over their repositories by exploring federated or decentralized alternatives.

LEGAL FRAMEWORK

The legal framework of the open-source movement is one of its most defining aspects, as it establishes the principles governing the creation, distribution, modification, and usage of open-source software. Unlike proprietary software, where the source code is kept secret and users are bound by restrictive licensing agreements, open-source software is released under licenses that explicitly allow users to access, modify, and share the code freely. This legal foundation has enabled the widespread adoption and collaborative development of open-source software, but it has also led to complex legal debates regarding IP, licensing compatibility, enforcement, and corporate influence.

At the heart of open-source software lies *licensing*, which dictates how software can be used, modified, and distributed. Open-source licenses grant users freedoms that proprietary software does not, but they also impose certain conditions to ensure that these freedoms are preserved. Open-source licenses generally fall into two main categories: permissive licenses and copyleft licenses.

Permissive licenses, such as the MIT License, the Apache License 2.0, and the BSD License, allow software to be freely modified and redistributed with minimal restrictions. These licenses enable developers to incorporate open-source code into both open- and closed-source projects without requiring them to release their own modifications under an open-source license. This makes permissive licenses attractive to businesses and commercial software developers, as they can integrate open-source components into proprietary products without legal complications.

In contrast, *copyleft licenses*, such as the GNU GPL and the Affero General Public License (AGPL), require that any modified versions of the software must also be released under the same open-source license. This ensures that the freedoms granted by open-source software remain intact even as the software evolves. The GPL, created by FSF under the leadership of Richard Stallman, is one of the most influential copyleft licenses. It mandates that any derivative works or redistributions of GPL-licensed software must also be open source, preventing companies from taking open-source code and making it proprietary. The AGPL extends these requirements to software-as-a-service (SaaS) applications, ensuring that even Web-based services using AGPL-licensed code must release their modifications.

The distinction between permissive and copyleft licenses has led to ongoing debates within the open-source community. Some developers prefer permissive licenses because they maximize adoption and allow open-source code to be used in commercial products, thereby increasing its real-world impact. Others argue that copyleft licenses better protect the principles of software freedom, preventing corporations from exploiting open-source contributions without giving back to the community.

One of the most significant legal challenges in open-source software is license compatibility. Because different open-source licenses impose different conditions, combining code from multiple projects with incompatible licenses can create legal conflicts. For example, software licensed under the GPL cannot be easily combined with code licensed under the Apache License 2.0 due to differences in their legal requirements. This has led to efforts by organizations such as OSI and FSF to clarify license compatibility issues and guide developers in choosing appropriate licenses.

Another important aspect of the legal framework of open-source software is IP and copyright law. Open-source software relies on traditional copyright law to enforce licensing terms, even though it grants users more freedoms than proprietary software. When a developer contributes code to an open-source project, they typically retain copyright over their contribution but grant others a license to use it under the project's open-source terms. Some projects, however, require contributors to sign a Contributor License Agreement (CLA), which transfers or licenses their copyright to the project maintainers or an overseeing foundation. This practice is common in corporate-backed open-source projects, as it helps centralize legal control over the software and streamline licensing decisions.

Patent law also plays a crucial role in open-source software. Some companies have used software patents to claim ownership over fundamental programming techniques and algorithms, leading to legal disputes that threaten open-source projects. To mitigate this risk, several open-source licenses, such as the Apache License 2.0, include explicit patent clauses that grant users protection from patent claims by contributors. Additionally, initiatives such as the Open Invention Network (OIN) have been established to create patent pools that protect open-source projects from litigation by patent trolls or proprietary software vendors.

Despite the legal protections offered by open-source licenses, license enforcement remains a complex issue. Some companies and developers have violated open-source licenses by using open-source software in proprietary products without complying with licensing terms. In response, organizations such as SFC and FSF have taken legal action to enforce compliance with open-source licenses, particularly the GPL. Lawsuits related to open-source licensing violations have set important precedents, reinforcing the legal validity of open-source licenses and ensuring that companies respect the terms under which they use open-source software.

Another emerging legal issue is the role of governments and regulation in open-source software. Governments worldwide are increasingly adopting open-source software for public infrastructure, and some jurisdictions are considering policies that require public software projects to be open source. Regulatory concerns, such as data protection laws (e.g., GDPR in Europe) and cybersecurity policies, however, may lead to the introduction of new legal requirements for open-source projects. Ensuring compliance with these regulations while maintaining the openness and collaborative nature of open-source software presents an ongoing legal challenge.

Looking ahead, the legal framework of open-source software will likely continue evolving in response to new challenges such as AI-generated code, open-source software liability, and the intersection of open source with emerging technologies. The rise of AI-powered code generation tools such as GitHub Copilot has raised legal questions about whether AI-generated code can be subject to open-source licenses and whether such tools inadvertently reproduce copyrighted code. Additionally, as open-source software becomes more embedded in critical infrastructure, discussions about software liability and accountability for security vulnerabilities are becoming more prominent.

The legal framework of the open-source movement is essential for defining how open-source software is developed, distributed, and used. Open-source licenses, copyright law, patent protections, and enforcement mechanisms ensure that open-source software remains accessible and sustainable. Legal challenges such as license compatibility, corporate influence, and government regulation, however, continue to shape the landscape. As open-source software becomes increasingly integral to the global technology ecosystem, maintaining a robust and adaptable legal framework will be crucial for preserving the principles of openness, collaboration, and innovation.

THE BUSINESS OF OPEN SOURCE

The business of open source has evolved significantly over the past few decades, transforming from a niche philosophy into a dominant force in the software industry. Initially, open-source software was often perceived as a threat to traditional proprietary business models, but today it is an integral part of commercial software development. Companies of all sizes have embraced open source not only as a means of reducing costs but also as a strategic advantage for innovation, collaboration, and market dominance. The business landscape of open-source software now includes a variety of revenue models, challenges, and ethical considerations, making it one of the most dynamic sectors in the software economy.

One of the earliest misconceptions about open-source software was that it could not be monetized. Because open-source licenses generally allow users to access, modify, and redistribute software freely, businesses initially struggled to see how they could generate revenue without selling proprietary licenses. Companies quickly realized, however, that while the software itself may be free, there are numerous ways to build profitable businesses around open-source products and services. Over time, different business models emerged, each leveraging the strengths of open-source development while creating sustainable revenue streams.

One of the most common business models in open source is the support and services model. Companies such as Red Hat, Canonical (the maker of Ubuntu), and SUSE have built successful businesses by offering enterprise support, consulting, and maintenance services for their open-source software. While the core software is free to use, enterprises pay for technical support, security patches, performance optimizations, and guaranteed service-level agreements (SLAs). This model works particularly well for large organizations that rely on open-source software for critical infrastructure but need professional support to ensure stability and security.

Another widely used model is the open-core model, where companies offer a free, open-source version of their software while keeping certain advanced features proprietary. This approach allows businesses to attract users with a free version and then monetize premium features targeted at enterprises. The open-core model has, however, been controversial within the open-source community, as some argue that it undermines the spirit of free and open collaboration by withholding key functionalities behind paywalls.

The rise of cloud computing has given birth to the hosted services model, where companies offer open-source software as a managed service, charging customers for cloud hosting, maintenance, and scaling. This model has been particularly lucrative for companies such as MongoDB, Databricks (built on Apache Spark), and Automattic (the company behind WordPress.com). Cloud providers such as AWS, Google Cloud, and Microsoft Azure have also profited by offering managed versions of popular open-source databases, AI frameworks, and developer tools. This has, however, led to tensions between cloud providers and open-source software creators, as companies that develop and maintain open-source projects often receive little direct financial benefit while cloud giants generate significant revenue from hosting those same projects.

In response to concerns about cloud providers monetizing open-source projects without contributing back, some companies have adopted alternative licensing models to protect their business interests. Licenses such as the Server

Side Public License (SSPL), introduced by MongoDB, and the Business Source License (BSL), used by MariaDB and CockroachDB, impose restrictions on how cloud providers can commercialize the software while allowing general open-source use. These licensing changes have sparked debate within the open-source community, with some arguing that they go against the principles of open-source freedom, while others see them as necessary adaptations to ensure sustainable funding.

A growing trend in the open-source business ecosystem is corporate sponsorship and funding initiatives. Organizations such as OpenSSF, GitHub Sponsors, Open Collective, and the Linux Foundation provide financial support to maintainers and contributors who work on critical open-source infrastructure. Many large tech companies now recognize the importance of financially supporting the open-source projects they depend on and have created funding programs to help sustain them. Google's Open Source Maintenance Crew and Microsoft's investments in Linux and GitHub reflect how major corporations are integrating open-source sustainability into their business strategies.

Despite the success of many open-source business models, the movement still faces significant challenges related to sustainability and fair compensation for developers. While large corporations profit from open-source software, individual maintainers and small teams often struggle to receive financial support for their work. This has led to cases where vital open-source projects suffer from contributor burnout, lack of updates, and security vulnerabilities due to insufficient funding. The debate over how to fairly compensate open-source maintainers has led to discussions about whether companies that rely on open-source software should be required to contribute back, either financially or through development efforts.

Another challenge is the competition between open-source and proprietary business models. While open-source software has disrupted many traditional software markets, some companies have responded by offering proprietary alternatives with enhanced features, ease of use, and dedicated customer support. This is particularly evident in enterprise software, where companies such as Oracle and Microsoft continue to dominate with proprietary databases and cloud services despite competition from open-source alternatives. Some businesses that start as open-source companies eventually shift toward proprietary models as they scale, leading to conflicts within their original communities.

Looking ahead, the future of open-source business models will likely involve a mix of subscription-based monetization, ethical licensing, and collaborative funding mechanisms. More companies are experimenting with hybrid approaches that balance open-source transparency with sustainable revenue generation. There is also a growing recognition that governments and public institutions should play a role in funding and maintaining critical open-source infrastructure, as demonstrated by initiatives such as the European Commission's funding for open-source security projects.

The business of open source has matured from a radical experiment into a mainstream economic force that underpins much of the modern technology landscape. While open-source software presents challenges in terms of monetization, sustainability, and competition with proprietary models, it has also created innovative business opportunities that continue to reshape the industry. As companies, developers, and communities work to refine the balance between openness and profitability, the future of open-source business models will likely evolve to ensure both financial sustainability and the continued growth of collaborative software development.

ETHICAL IMPLICATIONS

The ethical and social implications of the open-source movement are profound, influencing how technology is developed, shared, and controlled in society. Open-source software embodies values such as transparency, collaboration, and freedom, challenging proprietary models that restrict access to knowledge and technology. By allowing anyone to view, modify, and distribute code, open source promotes inclusivity and democratizes software development. It also raises ethical dilemmas, however, related to digital equity, security, labor exploitation, and the responsibilities of developers in shaping technology's impact on society. As open-source software continues to power critical infrastructure, AI, and digital governance, its ethical and social dimensions have become more relevant than ever.

One of the core ethical principles of open source is accessibility and inclusivity. Unlike proprietary software, which often requires costly licenses or subscriptions, open-source software is freely available to individuals, organizations, and governments, regardless of economic status. This fosters digital inclusion, enabling people in developing regions to access high-quality software without financial barriers. Open source has been instrumental in education, providing free alternatives to expensive software for students and researchers. Projects such as Linux, LibreOffice, and Open Educational Resources (OER) have expanded access to technology and knowledge worldwide. Digital inclusivity, however, also depends on other factors, such as Internet access, hardware affordability, and digital literacy, meaning that open-source software alone cannot fully address the digital divide.

Transparency is another fundamental ethical aspect of open-source software. In a world where proprietary software operates as a "black box," hiding its internal mechanisms, open-source code offers a level of scrutiny that enhances trust and accountability. This is especially important for government software, security tools, and AI algorithms, where transparency can help prevent misuse, discrimination, and bias. Open-source initiatives such as OpenAI's early models, the open government movement, and public health informatics demonstrate the power of transparent software in promoting ethical decision-making. Transparency does not, however, automatically guarantee ethical behavior—users still need the technical knowledge to audit and verify code, and bad actors can also exploit openly available code for malicious purposes.

The ethical dimension of privacy and surveillance is another key issue. Open-source software provides an alternative to corporate-controlled digital ecosystems that often collect and monetize user data. Privacy-focused projects such as Signal (for secure messaging), Tor (for anonymous browsing), and Nextcloud (for self-hosted cloud storage) empower users with greater control over their personal information. Unlike proprietary platforms, which often track users and exploit data for advertising, open-source alternatives allow individuals and organizations to retain control over their digital footprint. Not all open-source projects prioritize privacy, however, and some may still integrate telemetry, cloud-based tracking, or dependencies on proprietary services, raising concerns about how ethical principles are implemented in practice.

Security is both an ethical and a social issue in open-source development. The principle of "many eyes make all bugs shallow" suggests that open-source code is more secure because vulnerabilities can be identified and fixed by the community. This model assumes, however, that enough skilled contributors are reviewing the code, which is not always the case. The Heartbleed vulnerability in OpenSSL and the Log4Shell exploit revealed that even widely used open-source projects could suffer from critical security flaws that go undetected for years. Ethical questions arise when organizations rely on open-source software without contributing to its maintenance, leaving unpaid developers to bear the responsibility for security and bug fixes. The open source sustainability crisis highlights this issue, as many essential projects depend on volunteer labor with little financial support.

Another ethical dilemma is the exploitation of unpaid labor in open-source development. While open source is built on voluntary collaboration, the increasing reliance of corporations on unpaid contributions raises concerns about fairness and labor rights. Large companies benefit from free labor while profiting from open-source software, often without financially supporting maintainers or contributors. This imbalance has led to burnout among maintainers, some of whom have publicly protested by deliberately sabotaging their projects or restricting corporate use. The "licensing backlash," where developers introduce ethical licenses to prevent misuse by corporations or unethical organizations, reflects growing frustration with the commodification of open-source work.

The ethical debate around open-source licensing and responsible use has intensified in recent years. The traditional open-source ethos emphasizes freedom, allowing anyone to use the software for any purpose. Some developers, however, argue that this principle enables unethical actors, including oppressive governments, surveillance agencies, and military organizations, to exploit open-source software for harmful purposes. In response, some projects have adopted ethical licensing models, such as the Hippocratic License, which restricts use by organizations that violate human rights. This shift challenges the traditional definition of open source as "free for all," raising questions about whether ethical restrictions align with or contradict open-source principles.

The role of open source in social activism and digital rights is another important ethical consideration. Open-source tools have been crucial in journalism, whistleblowing, and human rights advocacy, providing secure platforms for communication and information-sharing. Projects such as SecureDrop (for whistleblowers), OSM (for humanitarian mapping), and Mastodon (for decentralized social media) have empowered activists, dissidents, and marginalized communities. Open-source technology can, however, also be weaponized by bad actors, from cybercriminals using encryption tools to extremist groups leveraging decentralized platforms. This raises difficult ethical questions about how open-source software should be regulated without undermining freedom and innovation.

AI and ML introduce new ethical concerns in open-source development. Open-source AI models, such as GPT and Stable Diffusion, have democratized access to AI tools but also raise concerns about bias, misinformation, and potential misuse. Unlike proprietary AI models, which may have internal ethical review processes, open-source AI lacks centralized oversight, making it easier for unethical applications to emerge. The balance between openness and responsibility remains a major ethical challenge in AI-driven open-source projects.

Looking to the future, the ethical and social implications of open-source software will continue to evolve. As governments, corporations, and individuals rely increasingly on open-source technologies, discussions about fair compensation, ethical licensing, security responsibility, and digital rights will become more pressing. The open-source movement's original vision of freedom, transparency, and community collaboration remains relevant, but it must adapt to new realities where ethical dilemmas and power imbalances complicate its implementation.

The open-source movement has profound ethical and social implications, shaping digital access, privacy, security, and labor rights in the modern world. While open source promotes inclusivity and transparency, it also faces challenges related to sustainability, responsible use, and the exploitation of unpaid labor. As the movement continues to grow, maintaining a balance between openness and ethical responsibility will be essential to ensuring that open-source software remains a force for positive change in society.

FUTURE DEVELOPMENT

The future of the open-source movement promises to be as transformative as its past, with emerging trends, challenges, and opportunities that will shape its evolution in the coming decades. As technology continues to advance, open-source software is expected to play an even more central role in driving innovation, expanding accessibility, and influencing industries beyond traditional software development. With increasing adoption by enterprises, deeper integration with AI and cloud computing, and the ongoing need for sustainability, the movement is poised to redefine the way technology is built, shared, and maintained.

One of the most significant factors shaping the future of open source is its growing integration with AI and ML. AI has become one of the most critical areas of technological advancement, and many of the leading AI frameworks—such as TensorFlow, PyTorch, and Hugging Face's Transformers—are open-source projects. This trend is expected to accelerate as AI research and development continue to evolve. Open-source AI tools foster collaboration among researchers, allowing for transparency, reproducibility, and faster innovation. AI also presents challenges for the open-source model, however, particularly regarding ethical concerns, bias, and data privacy. The open-source community will likely play a crucial role in establishing standards and best practices for responsible AI development, ensuring that AI technologies remain transparent, auditable, and accessible to a broad range of users.

Another key area of future development is the expansion of open-source principles into new domains. While open-source software has already made significant inroads into hardware, education, and government, the movement is now influencing areas such as biotechnology, robotics, and even space exploration. Open-source hardware initiatives, such as RISC-V (an open-source processor architecture), are challenging traditional hardware monopolies by providing more accessible and customizable alternatives. Similarly, projects such as Open Insulin and OpenBCI are applying open-source methodologies to biomedical research, enabling greater collaboration and innovation in the life sciences. The application of open-source principles to these emerging fields will likely create new opportunities for knowledge-sharing, cost reduction, and decentralized development.

The evolution of cloud computing and open-source infrastructure will also be a defining factor in the future of the open-source movement. Open-source technologies such as Kubernetes, Docker, and OpenStack have already become foundational to modern cloud infrastructure. As businesses and organizations continue to migrate their workloads to the cloud, open-source tools will remain essential for ensuring interoperability, scalability, and security. The dominance of major cloud providers—such as Amazon Web Services (AWS), Google Cloud, and Microsoft Azure—however, raises concerns about the centralization of cloud computing resources. The open-source community may respond by developing decentralized cloud computing models, where users have greater control over their data and computing power. Federated computing and decentralized networks, such as those enabled by blockchain and P2P technologies, could offer an alternative to traditional cloud providers by leveraging distributed open-source platforms.

Security and governance will also be key considerations in the future of open-source software. As open-source projects become more widely adopted in enterprise environments, there is a growing need for better governance and security practices. High-profile vulnerabilities, such as the Log4j security flaw, have highlighted the risks associated with under-maintained open-source software dependencies. In response, there is likely to be a greater emphasis on securing the open-source supply chain, improving code auditing practices, and establishing industry-wide security standards. Initiatives such as Google's OpenSSF and efforts to create SBOMs demonstrate the increasing focus on ensuring the security and reliability of open-source software.

The globalization and diversification of the open-source community will also be a major trend in the coming years. While open-source software has traditionally been dominated by contributors from North America and Europe, efforts are being made to increase participation from underrepresented regions, such as Africa, Latin America, and Southeast Asia. Initiatives focused on open-source education, mentorship programs, and localized documentation are helping to bridge the gap and make open-source development more inclusive. The decentralization of the open-source ecosystem will likely result in a more diverse range of contributions, ensuring that open-source software meets the needs of users from different cultural and economic backgrounds.

Finally, the legal and regulatory landscape surrounding open-source software is expected to evolve. Governments and policymakers are increasingly recognizing the importance of open-source software in public infrastructure, cybersecurity, and digital sovereignty. Some governments have already adopted policies that encourage the use of open-source software in public institutions, citing benefits such as transparency, cost savings, and vendor independence. Legal challenges, such as software patents, licensing disputes, and regulatory compliance, however, remain important issues that could impact the future of open-source development. As governments and international organizations become more involved in shaping the open-source landscape, there will be ongoing discussions about how to protect the openness and freedom of software while addressing legal and ethical concerns.

The future of the open-source movement is full of possibilities, challenges, and opportunities. As technology continues to evolve, open-source software will remain at the forefront of innovation, shaping the development of AI, cloud computing, security, and decentralized networks. Sustainability, governance, and corporate influence will, however, require careful management to ensure that open-source software remains true to its core principles of transparency, collaboration, and accessibility. The expansion of open-source methodologies into new fields, from biotechnology to space exploration, suggests that the movement's impact will extend far beyond software, influencing the way knowledge and technology are created and shared across all aspects of society. In an increasingly digital world, the principles of open source will continue to play a vital role in defining the future of technology, ensuring that it remains open, inclusive, and driven by the needs of the global community.

DRAWBACKS AND CONTROVERSIES

The open-source movement has revolutionized software development, fostering collaboration, transparency, and innovation. Despite its many advantages, it is not without its drawbacks and controversies. As open-source software becomes increasingly integral to both private and public sectors, challenges related to security, sustainability, commercialization, governance, and ethical concerns have emerged. These issues have led to debates within the open-source community about how best to preserve its core values while addressing practical challenges that arise from widespread adoption.

One of the most significant drawbacks of open-source software is its sustainability and funding issues. Many open-source projects rely on volunteer developers who contribute their time and expertise without direct compensation. While some projects are backed by large corporations or nonprofit foundations, a vast number of smaller but essential open-source projects struggle to secure adequate funding. This can lead to a situation where critical software is maintained by a handful of unpaid developers who are unable to dedicate enough time to address security vulnerabilities, fix bugs, or implement new features. The Log4j vulnerability, which exposed millions of systems to security risks in 2021, highlights the dangers of underfunded open-source projects. Although many organizations depend on open-source software, they often fail to contribute financially or offer long-term support to ensure its sustainability.

Another major controversy surrounding open source is the security risks associated with publicly available code. While transparency allows for greater scrutiny and peer review, it also makes open-source software a target for malicious actors. Attackers can easily study publicly available source code to identify vulnerabilities and exploit them before they are patched. Additionally, the decentralized nature of open-source development means that security patches may not be applied consistently across all users. Supply chain attacks—where attackers inject malicious code into open-source dependencies—have become a growing concern. Incidents such as the SolarWinds attack and the hijacking of the npm package show how attackers can manipulate dependencies in widely used open-source libraries to spread malware. Without dedicated security teams to monitor vulnerabilities, open-source projects may struggle to maintain the same level of security as proprietary software backed by well-funded companies.

The commercialization and corporate influence over open-source projects have also sparked controversy within the community. Many large technology companies have embraced open-source software, integrating it into their products and even contributing to major projects. While this corporate involvement has helped drive development and adoption, it has also raised concerns about whether companies are genuinely supporting open-source principles or merely using them for profit. Some companies have adopted a "bait-and-switch" approach, initially offering software as open source before shifting to a more restrictive licensing model once they gain market dominance. This has led to debates about the ethics of open-core business models, where a basic version of the software is free, but advanced features or enterprise support require paid subscriptions.

Another drawback of open-source software is the fragmentation and lack of standardization. Because open-source projects are often driven by diverse and independent contributors, different projects may develop competing solutions to the same problem. This can result in fragmentation, where multiple versions of similar software exist without clear compatibility or interoperability. For example, the Linux ecosystem is notorious for its fragmented landscape, with numerous distributions that are not always compatible with one another. While diversity in software development can be beneficial, excessive fragmentation can make it difficult for users and businesses to choose a stable and reliable solution. Additionally, open-source software often lacks the cohesive user experience and polished interfaces found in proprietary software, which can be a barrier to adoption for non-technical users.

Governance and decision-making in open-source projects can also be a source of conflict and inefficiency. Unlike proprietary software, which is controlled by a single entity, open-source projects often rely on decentralized governance structures. While this can foster inclusivity, it can also lead to disputes over project direction, leadership struggles, and difficulties in reaching consensus. Some projects have experienced internal conflicts that resulted in "forks," where a group of developers breaks away to create a separate version of the software. In some cases, influential corporate sponsors or individual maintainers hold disproportionate power over project decisions, raising concerns about whether governance structures are truly democratic.

Another controversy in open-source software is the issue of licensing and IP rights. While open-source licenses are designed to promote freedom and collaboration, legal disputes have arisen over how these licenses are interpreted and enforced. Some companies and developers have been accused of violating open-source licenses by incorporating open-source code into proprietary products without proper attribution or compliance. The enforcement of open-source licenses, such as the GNU GPL, has led to lawsuits and legal battles over whether companies are properly adhering to the terms of the license. Additionally, some developers argue that traditional open-source licenses do not adequately protect against corporate exploitation, leading to the creation of more restrictive licenses that attempt to prevent large cloud providers from profiting off open-source software without contributing back to the community.

The ethical and ideological debates within the open-source community have also become increasingly prominent. While the movement was originally founded on the ideals of freedom and openness, there have been ongoing discussions about whether open-source software should impose ethical restrictions on its use. Some developers have proposed "ethical licenses" that prohibit the use of their software for military applications, surveillance, or other activities that they deem harmful. These ethical licenses have, however, faced pushback from those who argue that open-source software should remain neutral and unrestricted. The debate over whether developers should have control over how their software is used continues to be a divisive issue within the community.

Lastly, accessibility and usability concerns continue to be challenges for many open-source projects. While open-source software provides unparalleled freedom and flexibility, it often lacks the ease of use and comprehensive support that proprietary software offers. Many open-source applications have steep learning curves, require manual configuration, or lack detailed documentation, making them less accessible to non-technical users. Additionally, because open-source software is developed by a decentralized community, users may struggle to find reliable customer support when they encounter issues. While forums, wikis, and community-driven support channels exist, they may not always provide the same level of assistance as professional support services offered by proprietary software vendors.

REFERENCES

1. Copyleft. In: Wikipedia [Internet]. 2025 [cited 2025 Jan 22]. Available from: *https://en.wikipedia.org/w/index.php?title=Copyleft&oldid=1269361184*
2. Eric S. Raymond. In: Wikipedia [Internet]. 2024 [cited 2025 Jan 22]. Available from: *https://en.wikipedia.org/w/index.php?title=Eric_S._Raymond&oldid=1265549323*
3. GNU General Public License. In: Wikipedia [Internet]. 2025 [cited 2025 Jan 22]. Available from: *https://en.wikipedia.org/w/index.php?title=GNU_General_Public_License&oldid=1269775663*
4. GNU Manifesto. In: Wikipedia [Internet]. 2024 [cited 2025 Jan 22]. Available from: *https://en.wikipedia.org/w/index.php?title=GNU_Manifesto&oldid=1194660510*
5. Open Source Initiative [Internet]. [cited 2025 Jan 22]. Home Page. Available from: *https://opensource.org*
6. Linus Torvalds. In: Wikipedia [Internet]. 2025 [cited 2025 Jan 22]. Available from: *https://en.wikipedia.org/w/index.php?title=Linus_Torvalds&oldid=1268202809*
7. Linux. In: Wikipedia [Internet]. 2025 [cited 2025 Jan 22]. Available from: *https://en.wikipedia.org/w/index.php?title=Linux&oldid=1270710088*
8. Mozilla Public License. In: Wikipedia [Internet]. 2025 [cited 2025 Jan 22]. Available from: *https://en.wikipedia.org/w/index.php?title=Mozilla_Public_License&oldid=1269760251*
9. Open collaboration. In: Wikipedia [Internet]. 2025 [cited 2025 Jan 22]. Available from: *https://en.wikipedia.org/w/index.php?title=Open_collaboration&oldid=1270286640*
10. Open source. In: Wikipedia [Internet]. 2024 [cited 2025 Jan 22]. Available from: *https://en.wikipedia.org/w/index.php?title=Open_source&oldid=1265168128*
11. Open-source license. In: Wikipedia [Internet]. 2024 [cited 2025 Jan 22]. Available from: *https://en.wikipedia.org/w/index.php?title=Open-source_license&oldid=1266120677*

12. Open-source software. In: Wikipedia [Internet]. 2025 [cited 2025 Jan 22]. Available from: *https://en.wikipedia.org/w/index.php?title=Open-source_software&oldid=1270023835*

13. Open-source software development. In: Wikipedia [Internet]. 2024 [cited 2025 Jan 22]. Available from: *https://en.wikipedia.org/w/index.php?title=Open-source_software_development&oldid=1263458189*

14. Open-source software movement. In: Wikipedia [Internet]. 2024 [cited 2025 Jan 22]. Available from: *https://en.wikipedia.org/w/index.php?title=Open-source_software_movement&oldid=1262044047*

15. Richard Stallman. In: Wikipedia [Internet]. 2025 [cited 2025 Jan 22]. Available from: *https://en.wikipedia.org/w/index.php?title=Richard_Stallman&oldid=1267094247*

16. The Apache Software Foundation. In: Wikipedia [Internet]. 2025 [cited 2025 Jan 22]. Available from: *https://en.wikipedia.org/w/index.php?title=The_Apache_Software_Foundation&oldid=1270363160*

17. The GNU Operating System and the Free Software Movement [Internet]. [cited 2025 Jan 22]. Available from: *https://www.gnu.org/home.en.html*

18. The Open Source Definition. In: Wikipedia [Internet]. 2024 [cited 2025 Jan 22]. Available from: *https://en.wikipedia.org/w/index.php?title=The_Open_Source_Definition&oldid=1266422623*

CHAPTER 5

DEFENSIVE TOOLS

In today's hyper-connected world, personal data has become one of the most valuable commodities. Every click, search, and online transaction generates data that is collected, analyzed, and often monetized by corporations, governments, and cybercriminals. From targeted advertising and algorithmic profiling to mass surveillance and data breaches, the threats to digital privacy are ever-growing. While the Internet is designed to facilitate data collection, users are not powerless against it. A wide range of privacy-focused tools and technologies has emerged to help individuals regain control over their digital footprint and protect their sensitive information. Given this landscape, relying solely on built-in security features of mainstream services is no longer sufficient. Instead, proactive steps must be taken to minimize exposure and enhance digital privacy.

VPNS

VPNs have emerged as a crucial tool for safeguarding online privacy. A VPN is a technology that creates an encrypted connection between a user's device and a remote server, effectively masking their Internet activity from prying eyes. By rerouting Internet traffic through a secure tunnel, VPNs offer protection against hackers, government surveillance, and corporate tracking, making them an essential tool for anyone concerned about digital privacy.

The fundamental principle behind a VPN is encryption. When a user connects to a VPN, their data is encrypted before leaving their device, making it unreadable to third parties, including ISPs and malicious actors. This encryption ensures that even if the data is intercepted, it remains indecipherable.

The VPN server then forwards the encrypted traffic to its final destination—whether it's a Web site, an online service, or a remote network—before relaying the response back to the user. Since the data passes through the VPN server rather than being sent directly from the user's device, the destination sees the VPN server's IP address instead of the user's real one, effectively masking their location and identity.

The need for VPNs has grown exponentially due to the increasing threats to online privacy. Governments around the world have expanded their surveillance capabilities, monitoring citizens' online activities under the pretext of national security. In countries with strict censorship laws, authorities routinely block access to foreign Web sites and social media platforms. VPNs allow users in these regions to bypass restrictions and access uncensored information by tunneling their connection through servers located in countries with unrestricted Internet access. Similarly, journalists and activists rely on VPNs to communicate securely and evade state-sponsored monitoring, reducing the risk of persecution or harassment.

Beyond governmental surveillance, VPNs also protect against corporate data collection. Major technology companies track user activity to serve targeted advertisements and build detailed consumer profiles. ISPs, which serve as the gateway to the Internet, can log users' browsing history, sell their data to advertisers, or throttle connection speeds based on content type. In the absence of robust privacy laws in many countries, VPNs serve as an independent solution for users who wish to maintain control over their personal information.

Security is another major reason why VPNs have become indispensable. Public Wi-Fi networks, such as those found in cafes, airports, and hotels, are notoriously insecure. Hackers can exploit vulnerabilities in these networks to intercept data transmissions, steal login credentials, or distribute malware. By encrypting Internet traffic, a VPN ensures that sensitive information, such as passwords and financial transactions, remains secure even on unsecured networks. This makes VPNs particularly valuable for remote workers, business travelers, and anyone accessing sensitive data outside of a trusted network.

Not all VPNs are created equal, however. The effectiveness of a VPN depends on factors such as encryption protocols, logging policies, server distribution, and jurisdiction. This is why choosing a reputable, no-logs VPN provider is critical for ensuring true privacy. Despite their advantages, VPNs are not a silver bullet for online privacy. They do not protect users from tracking technologies such as browser fingerprinting, cookies, or malicious software. Moreover, some Web sites and streaming services actively block VPN traffic, making access more difficult. In response, VPN providers continuously innovate, developing obfuscation techniques to bypass detection. Governments in authoritarian countries have also attempted to curb VPN usage by blocking known VPN servers or requiring providers to register with state authorities, further intensifying the cat-and-mouse game between censors and privacy advocates.

FIREWALLS

The concept of firewalls emerged in the late 1980s, a time when the Internet was still in its infancy but already showing signs of becoming a new frontier for both innovation and risk. Early computer networks lacked proper security mechanisms, leaving systems vulnerable to intrusions. The first firewalls were relatively simple, relying on packet filtering to inspect data passing through a network. These early versions worked by analyzing packets—small units of data containing information about their source, destination, and protocol—to determine whether they should be allowed or blocked. As cyberattacks grew more sophisticated, however, so too did firewall technology. What started as basic rule-based filtering evolved into complex systems capable of deep packet inspection, stateful monitoring, and even behavioral analysis of network traffic.

A firewall functions as a mediator between trusted and untrusted networks. When a user accesses the Internet, data flows in both directions: outgoing traffic from the user's device to the destination server and incoming traffic from the server back to the user. Without proper security measures, malicious actors can exploit vulnerabilities, intercept sensitive information, or inject harmful code into these data exchanges. Firewalls mitigate these risks by analyzing traffic based on predefined security policies. They enforce rules that determine which connections are legitimate and which pose potential threats. When unauthorized access attempts or suspicious activities are detected, the firewall can block the traffic, log the event, or trigger alerts for further investigation.

The rise of Web applications, cloud computing, and encrypted communication posed new challenges, leading to the creation of next-generation firewalls (NGFWs). Unlike their predecessors, NGFWs possess deep packet inspection capabilities, allowing them to analyze the contents of data packets rather than just their headers. This enables them to detect malware, phishing attempts, and other sophisticated threats that traditional firewalls might miss. Furthermore, they incorporate intrusion prevention systems (IPSs) that proactively identify and block known attack patterns, preventing cybercriminals from exploiting vulnerabilities.

Another crucial development in firewall technology is application-layer filtering, which allows firewalls to recognize and control specific applications rather than just network traffic. This is particularly useful in corporate environments where organizations may want to restrict access to certain services or ensure that sensitive data is not transmitted through unsecured channels. With the increasing reliance on cloud computing and remote work, cloud-based firewalls have also gained prominence, offering scalable security solutions that protect distributed networks without requiring on-premises hardware.

Despite their effectiveness, firewalls are not infallible. They must be properly configured to strike a balance between security and usability. Overly restrictive firewalls can block legitimate traffic, disrupting business operations or user activities, while lenient configurations can leave networks vulnerable to attacks. Furthermore, firewalls alone cannot provide complete security; they must be used in conjunction with other cybersecurity measures, such as encryption, antivirus software, IDSs, and user awareness training.

The significance of firewalls extends beyond individual users and businesses. Governments and critical infrastructure rely on them to protect national security interests, financial institutions use them to safeguard sensitive transactions, and healthcare organizations depend on them to ensure patient data privacy. As cyber threats continue to evolve, so too must firewall technology, adapting to new attack vectors and integrating with emerging security frameworks. The future of firewalls lies in automation, AI, and ML, which will enhance their ability to detect anomalies, predict threats, and respond in real time.

How to Set Up a Firewall on Windows

Setting up a firewall on Windows is a crucial step in ensuring the security of your system, as it serves as a barrier between your computer and potential threats from the Internet or other networks. Windows includes a built-in firewall known as Windows Defender Firewall, which offers a robust level of protection while allowing users to configure rules and permissions based on their security needs.

The process of setting up a firewall on Windows begins with accessing the firewall settings. To do this, open the Control Panel and navigate to the "System and Security" section, where the "Windows Defender Firewall" option can be found. Upon selecting this, a new window presents an overview of the firewall status, indicating whether it is active for different network profiles, such as private, public, and domain networks. If the firewall is disabled, it is highly recommended to enable it immediately to prevent unauthorized access.

Once the firewall is active, it is important to understand its configuration options. The default settings are designed to allow most essential network activities while blocking potentially harmful connections. Advanced users may, however, wish to customize these settings to enhance security or allow specific applications to function correctly. To modify firewall rules, access the "Advanced Settings" section, which opens the "Windows Defender Firewall with Advanced Security" interface. This tool provides control over inbound and outbound rules, as well as connection security rules.

Inbound rules determine which incoming connections are permitted, whereas outbound rules regulate which connections the system can initiate. By default, Windows allows most outbound connections but restricts inbound traffic unless explicitly allowed. If an application requires network access, a new rule can be created by selecting "New Rule…" within the "Inbound Rules" or "Outbound Rules" section. The wizard that appears offers different rule types, including program-based rules that allow or block a specific executable file, port-based rules that regulate traffic on specific network ports, and predefined rules for commonly used applications.

For users who require stricter security measures, blocking all inbound and outbound traffic by default and allowing only necessary exceptions is an effective strategy. This can be done by changing the default behavior in the firewall properties, accessible from the "Advanced Security" window. Once set to block all traffic, users can manually create exceptions for trusted applications, ensuring that only explicitly permitted communications occur.

Another essential aspect of firewall configuration is monitoring. The Windows firewall provides logging capabilities that can be enabled in the "Monitoring" section. By activating logging, users can keep track of allowed and blocked connections, helping them identify potential security threats or troubleshoot connectivity issues.

For those who require additional protection, third-party firewalls offer enhanced features such as IDSs, application behavior monitoring, and more detailed traffic analysis. For most users, however, the built-in Windows Defender Firewall provides a sufficient level of security when properly configured.

Setting up a firewall on Windows involves enabling it, configuring inbound and outbound rules, adjusting default behaviors for stricter security, and enabling monitoring to track network activity. By taking these steps, users can ensure that their systems are protected from unauthorized access and potential cyber threats.

How to Set Up a Firewall on Linux Ubuntu

Setting up a firewall on Linux Ubuntu is an essential task for securing the system against unauthorized access and potential threats from the Internet. Unlike Windows, where the firewall is enabled and configured through a GUI by default, Ubuntu relies on a more flexible yet command-line-driven approach, primarily through the Uncomplicated Firewall (UFW), which acts as a front-end for the more complex iptables framework.

To begin, it is crucial to check whether UFW is installed and active on the system. By default, Ubuntu includes UFW, but it may not be enabled. To verify this, opening a terminal and executing the command `sudo ufw status` provides the necessary information. If the firewall is inactive, it must be enabled by running `sudo ufw enable`. This simple command ensures that Ubuntu starts filtering network traffic according to the default rules, which generally block incoming connections while allowing outgoing traffic.

Once the firewall is active, the next step involves configuring rules that control which connections are permitted and which are denied. UFW allows users to define rules using straightforward commands, making it accessible even for those without extensive networking knowledge. For example, to allow SSH access, which is essential for remote management, the command `sudo ufw allow ssh` or `sudo ufw allow 22/tcp` can be used. This creates a rule that permits incoming traffic on port 22, ensuring that remote users can connect securely. Similarly, if the system hosts a Web server, allowing HTTP and HTTPS traffic with `sudo ufw allow 80/tcp` and `sudo ufw allow 443/tcp` ensures that visitors can access the hosted content.

For those who wish to implement stricter security measures, it is possible to configure the firewall to deny all incoming and outgoing connections by default, only allowing explicitly specified traffic. This can be done with the commands `sudo ufw default deny incoming` and `sudo ufw default deny outgoing`. Once these restrictions are in place, individual applications must be granted permission explicitly. For example, allowing outgoing Web browsing requires enabling access to ports 80 and 443 with `sudo ufw allow out 80/tcp` and `sudo ufw allow out 443/tcp`.

Advanced users may want to configure specific rules based on IP addresses. If an administrator wants to allow SSH access only from a particular IP, such as 192.168.1.100, the command `sudo ufw allow from 192.168.1.100 to any port 22` ensures that only that machine can establish an SSH connection. Conversely, blocking a malicious IP address is as simple as executing `sudo ufw deny from [IP address]`.

After configuring the necessary rules, it is essential to review them to ensure the firewall is functioning as intended. This can be done using `sudo ufw status verbose`, which provides a detailed output of all active rules. If any rule needs to be removed or modified, `sudo ufw delete [rule]` allows for easy adjustments.

For those who prefer a graphical interface, Ubuntu offers GUFW, a graphical front-end for UFW that can be installed with `sudo apt install gufw`. Once installed, launching GUFW provides an intuitive interface where users can enable or disable the firewall, add or remove rules, and monitor traffic without using the terminal.

Finally, it is good practice to ensure that UFW starts automatically at boot, which is typically the case once enabled. Verifying this with `sudo systemctl enable ufw` ensures that the firewall remains active even after a system restart.

Setting up a firewall on Ubuntu involves enabling UFW, defining rules to allow or deny specific types of traffic, configuring advanced options such as IP-based filtering, and optionally using a graphical interface for ease of use. When properly configured, UFW provides a robust level of protection against unauthorized access while allowing necessary services to function seamlessly.

ANTIVIRUS

The origins of antivirus software date back to the early days of personal computing, when viruses were initially developed as experimental programs but quickly evolved into real threats capable of spreading and causing damage. The first known computer virus, known as Creeper, appeared in the 1970s, displaying a simple message without causing harm. As technology progressed, however, so did the complexity and destructiveness of malicious software. By the late 1980s and early 1990s, viruses such as Brain, Michelangelo, and CIH (Chernobyl) had demonstrated the need for dedicated security solutions. In response, the first commercial antivirus programs emerged, relying primarily on signature-based detection to identify known threats.

At its core, antivirus software functions by scanning files, programs, and system activities for signs of malicious behavior. Early antivirus programs relied on signature-based detection, which involved maintaining a database of known malware signatures—unique digital fingerprints of malicious files. When a user downloaded or executed a file, the antivirus software would compare it against its database to determine whether it matched any known threats. While effective against previously identified malware, this approach had a significant limitation: it could not detect new, unknown viruses that had not yet been added to the database.

As cyber threats became more sophisticated, antivirus technology evolved to incorporate heuristic analysis. Unlike signature-based detection, heuristic methods analyze the behavior of programs rather than their exact code, allowing antivirus software to identify potentially harmful files even if they have never been encountered before. By examining how a file behaves—whether it tries to modify system settings, replicate itself, or access sensitive data—heuristic analysis can detect suspicious activity and block potential threats before they cause harm. This approach proved particularly useful in combating polymorphic malware, which constantly modifies its code to evade traditional signature-based detection.

With the rise of zero-day attacks, in which cybercriminals exploit vulnerabilities before they are patched, modern antivirus programs have further enhanced their capabilities. Behavioral analysis and ML now play a crucial role in identifying threats in real time. Instead of relying solely on predefined rules, antivirus software can learn from vast datasets of malware behaviors, recognizing new attack patterns and proactively defending against them. Additionally, cloud-based antivirus solutions leverage collective intelligence by analyzing threats on a global scale, allowing users to benefit from real-time updates and shared threat intelligence without relying solely on local databases.

The increasing prevalence of ransomware and fileless malware has also driven advancements in antivirus technology. Traditional antivirus programs focused primarily on detecting and removing infected files, but modern threats often operate without leaving a tangible footprint on disk. Ransomware encrypts a user's files and demands payment for their release, while fileless malware operates entirely in memory, making it harder to detect. To combat these threats, contemporary antivirus solutions incorporate real-time monitoring, sandboxing, and anti-exploit technologies, which allow them to detect suspicious activity at the behavioral level, stopping malware before it can execute its payload.

Despite these advancements, antivirus software is not an infallible solution. Cybercriminals continuously develop new techniques to bypass security measures, using encryption, obfuscation, and social engineering tactics to deceive users and evade detection. Many modern attacks rely on phishing schemes, in which victims are tricked into downloading malicious files or providing sensitive information voluntarily. In such cases, antivirus software alone is insufficient; user awareness and safe browsing practices play a crucial role in maintaining security.

Another challenge is the increasing complexity of modern computing environments. Traditional antivirus solutions were designed for standalone systems, but today's digital landscape includes a vast array of interconnected devices, from smartphones and tablets to IoT devices and cloud-based services. Cybercriminals exploit vulnerabilities in these systems to launch attacks, making it necessary for antivirus software to evolve beyond simple file scanning. Many modern security suites now include features such as firewalls, anti-phishing protection, VPNs, and password managers, providing a more comprehensive approach to cybersecurity.

The future of antivirus technology lies in greater automation and AI. As cyber threats become more sophisticated, antivirus solutions will need to rely increasingly on AI-driven threat detection, predictive analytics, and automated response mechanisms. Rather than simply reacting to known threats, next-generation antivirus software will anticipate and neutralize attacks before they occur. Additionally, the integration of endpoint detection and response (EDR) solutions will enable continuous monitoring of devices, ensuring that even APTs can be identified and mitigated in real time.

Ultimately, antivirus software remains an essential component of any cybersecurity strategy. While no solution can offer absolute protection, combining a robust antivirus program with other security measures—such as firewalls, secure browsing habits, and regular system updates—provides the best defense against the ever-growing landscape of cyber threats.

Windows Defender

The origins of Windows Defender can be traced back to Microsoft AntiSpyware, a security tool released in 2005 as a response to the increasing threat of spyware, which was rapidly spreading through malicious Web sites, infected downloads, and deceptive software bundling. At that time, Windows systems were often criticized for their vulnerability to malware, and users frequently relied on third-party security programs to protect their devices. Recognizing the importance of built-in security, Microsoft rebranded and expanded its toolset, eventually integrating it directly into Windows operating systems as Windows Defender with the release of Windows Vista in 2006. Initially, its capabilities were limited to detecting and removing spyware, but as cyber threats evolved, Microsoft continuously enhanced its functionality, transforming it into a full-fledged antivirus solution.

With the release of Windows 10, Windows Defender underwent a significant transformation, rebranded as Windows Defender Antivirus, and later as Microsoft Defender Antivirus. This marked a major shift in Microsoft's security approach, as the software was no longer just an optional tool but an essential, always-on security component built directly into the operating system. Unlike traditional antivirus programs that require separate installation and manual updates, Windows Defender operates seamlessly in the background, providing real-time protection without requiring user intervention. Its automatic updates ensure that users always have the latest security definitions, protecting them from newly emerging threats without the need for additional subscriptions or software installations.

One of Windows Defender's key strengths is its real-time protection, which continuously scans files, applications, and downloads for potential threats. Unlike traditional antivirus programs that rely solely on signature-based detection, Windows Defender incorporates behavioral analysis and ML to identify suspicious activities and prevent malware from executing. This proactive approach is particularly effective against zero-day threats, which exploit unknown vulnerabilities before security patches are released. By leveraging Microsoft's vast cloud infrastructure, Windows Defender can quickly analyze and respond to emerging threats, distributing security intelligence across millions of devices in real time.

Another crucial feature of Windows Defender is its Windows Defender Firewall, which monitors network traffic and prevents unauthorized access to a system. Unlike conventional third-party firewalls, which often require manual configuration, Windows Defender Firewall is integrated directly into the Windows Security Center, offering automatic protection while allowing users to customize security settings as needed. It helps prevent hackers, malware, and unauthorized applications from establishing remote connections, reducing the risk of data breaches and unauthorized system control.

Windows Defender also includes exploit protection, a security feature designed to mitigate vulnerabilities in applications and the operating system. This component works by enforcing security policies that prevent common attack techniques, such as buffer overflow exploits and code injection attempts. Combined with controlled folder access, which protects important directories from unauthorized modifications, these features provide an added layer of defense against ransomware attacks, ensuring that sensitive files cannot be encrypted or altered without explicit permission.

One of the most significant advancements in Windows Defender's evolution is the introduction of Microsoft Defender SmartScreen, a feature that protects users from phishing attacks and malicious Web sites. SmartScreen analyzes URLs and downloads in real time, warning users if they attempt to visit potentially dangerous sites or download suspicious files. This functionality is particularly valuable in an era where cybercriminals frequently exploit human error through deceptive emails, fraudulent Web sites, and social engineering tactics. By integrating Web protection directly into Microsoft Edge and other Windows components, SmartScreen helps reduce the likelihood of users falling victim to phishing schemes and drive-by malware attacks.

Despite its numerous strengths, Windows Defender also has its limitations. While it provides solid protection for most users, advanced cybersecurity professionals may find its customization options somewhat limited compared to specialized third-party security suites. Some independent antivirus testing organizations have found that while Windows Defender offers excellent detection rates, it may have a slightly higher rate of false positives compared to other premium antivirus solutions. Additionally, because it is a built-in Microsoft product, it may not be as feature-rich as some paid security suites that offer additional tools such as VPNs, password managers, or identity theft protection.

Nevertheless, Windows Defender has proven to be a reliable and effective security solution, particularly for everyday users who require hassle-free, automatic protection. By continuously evolving and integrating the latest threat intelligence, Microsoft has transformed Windows Defender from a simple anti-spyware tool into a comprehensive security platform that competes with—and in some cases surpasses—many third-party alternatives. For most Windows users, especially those who practice safe browsing habits and keep their systems updated, Windows Defender provides more than sufficient protection, eliminating the need for additional antivirus software.

As cyber threats continue to evolve, Windows Defender is expected to further integrate with Microsoft's AI and cloud security initiatives, enhancing its ability to detect and respond to emerging dangers. The future of cybersecurity lies in automation, predictive analysis, and real-time threat mitigation—areas where Windows Defender is already making significant strides.

ANTI-MALWARE

Anti-malware software is designed to detect, prevent, and remove malware from a system. Its purpose is to protect devices from infection by malicious programs that can corrupt files, steal personal information, hijack computer resources, and even disrupt business operations. The rise of malware as a global cybersecurity concern has made anti-malware software a critical component of any security strategy. Without it, users and organizations expose themselves to a wide range of risks, from data breaches and financial loss to system crashes and reputation damage.

The evolution of anti-malware tools can be traced back to the early days of computing when viruses first emerged as a threat. Early antivirus programs were basic, primarily focused on detecting and removing known viruses by scanning files and identifying virus signatures, which are unique patterns or characteristics of malicious code. As the malware landscape expanded and more sophisticated threats emerged, however, the limitations of traditional antivirus software became evident. New malware types, such as rootkits, spyware, and ransomware, often use advanced techniques to evade detection, rendering signature-based detection alone inadequate.

To counter these advanced threats, modern anti-malware software has evolved to include a wide range of detection methods, such as heuristic analysis, behavioral monitoring, and ML. Heuristic analysis involves analyzing the behavior of programs rather than relying solely on known signatures. This approach allows anti-malware software to identify potentially malicious activities in files, even if the file itself has not been previously recognized as malware. By observing how a file interacts with the system—whether it attempts to replicate itself, make unauthorized changes to system files, or access sensitive data—heuristics can flag suspicious behavior for further inspection.

Behavioral monitoring takes the heuristic approach a step further, actively tracking system activities in real time to detect malicious behavior as it happens. This is particularly useful for identifying threats such as ransomware, which typically initiates harmful actions only when it is executed on the system. Behavioral monitoring allows anti-malware software to stop such programs before they can cause significant damage by recognizing harmful patterns as soon as they occur.

With the rise of sophisticated, polymorphic malware that can change its appearance to avoid detection, anti-malware programs now also incorporate ML algorithms. ML leverages vast amounts of data to train the software to recognize patterns and behaviors associated with malware. Over time, as the software encounters more threats, its ability to identify new and unknown types of malware improves, making it more effective at spotting emerging attacks. This technology enables anti-malware programs to predict and detect previously unseen threats, improving their ability to respond to new attack vectors.

One of the defining features of modern anti-malware software is its real-time protection. This feature ensures that the system is continuously monitored for potential threats, even when the user is not actively scanning for malware. Real-time protection works by intercepting malicious files before they can execute, preventing infections before they cause any harm. This proactive approach to cybersecurity is essential for maintaining system integrity and protecting against a wide range of cyber threats.

Another important aspect of anti-malware software is its ability to detect and remove adware and spyware, which are types of malware designed to monitor a user's activities, track their online behavior, and serve unsolicited advertisements. These programs often operate in the background without the user's knowledge, stealing personal information or invading privacy. Anti-malware software can scan for and remove these types of software, ensuring that users' online activities remain private and secure.

Anti-malware programs also provide protection against trojans, a type of malware that disguises itself as legitimate software to trick users into installing it. Once inside the system, trojans can perform a variety of malicious actions, such as stealing login credentials, installing additional malware, or granting remote access to cybercriminals. By identifying the characteristic behavior of trojans—such as attempts to establish unauthorized connections—anti-malware tools can neutralize them before they can cause any significant harm.

One particularly dangerous form of malware is ransomware, which encrypts the victim's files and demands payment in exchange for the decryption key. Ransomware attacks have become increasingly common and devastating, often targeting businesses, healthcare organizations, and government agencies. Anti-malware software has incorporated specialized tools to identify and block ransomware before it can encrypt files, preventing these types of attacks from reaching the point of data loss. Additionally, many anti-malware programs offer backup and recovery options, allowing users to restore their files from a secure backup in the event of a successful attack.

While anti-malware software is a vital tool for defending against digital threats, it is important to note that no program can provide 100% protection. Malware creators are constantly evolving their tactics, developing new techniques to bypass security measures, and exploiting vulnerabilities in software. As a result, it is essential to adopt a multi-layered approach to cybersecurity that includes not only anti-malware software but also firewalls, regular system updates, and safe browsing practices. Anti-malware software should be used in conjunction with other security measures to provide comprehensive protection against both known and unknown threats.

Additionally, it is crucial for users to exercise caution and follow best practices to reduce their risk of infection. This includes being wary of emails that could be phishing attempts, avoiding downloading files or software from untrusted sources, regularly updating passwords, and keeping operating systems and software up to date with the latest security patches.

Anti-malware software plays an essential role in protecting devices and data from the ever-growing landscape of cyber threats. As the nature of malware continues to evolve, so too does the technology used to combat it. By combining advanced detection methods, real-time monitoring, and ML, modern anti-malware programs provide users with a powerful defense against the wide array of malicious software that poses a threat to their systems. To ensure comprehensive protection, however, users must remain vigilant, implement multiple layers of security, and stay informed about emerging threats in the digital world.

DEFENDING AGAINST PHISHING AND SOCIAL ENGINEERING

In the age of information, where digital communication has become the cornerstone of modern life, the dangers of cybercrime have evolved to exploit human psychology rather than relying solely on technological vulnerabilities. Among the most pervasive and dangerous tactics employed by cybercriminals are phishing and social engineering—methods that manipulate individuals into revealing sensitive information, granting unauthorized access, or performing actions that compromise security. These attacks rely not on sophisticated malware or exploits but on the vulnerabilities of human nature, making them particularly difficult to defend against. Understanding how phishing and social engineering work, and knowing how to protect oneself, is essential for navigating the increasingly dangerous landscape of digital threats.

Phishing, a form of social engineering, involves the use of deceptive emails, messages, or Web sites to trick individuals into divulging sensitive information such as passwords, credit card numbers, or personal identification details. The term "phishing" comes from the idea of using a baited hook to lure in victims, much like how cybercriminals create seemingly legitimate scenarios to lure their targets. Phishing attacks are typically carried out through email, but they can also take place via phone calls (known as vishing, or voice phishing), text messages (known as smishing, or SMS phishing), or social media platforms. The key to these attacks is the deception: the attacker impersonates a trusted entity, such as a financial institution, government agency, or well-known company, in order to establish a sense of urgency or trust.

The tactics used in phishing attacks are diverse and constantly evolving. One common method is the use of spoofed email addresses or fake Web sites that look remarkably similar to legitimate sources, often with only subtle differences that might go unnoticed by an unsuspecting victim. For example, a phishing email might come from an address that appears to be from a bank, asking the recipient to click a link to "verify" their account details. The link directs the user to a Web site that looks identical to their bank's official site but is actually a fake page designed to capture login credentials. Once the victim enters their username and password, the attacker can gain access to their real account, causing financial or data loss.

In addition to phishing, social engineering is another pervasive threat in the digital age. While phishing specifically targets information through deceptive electronic means, social engineering is a broader term that encompasses a range of tactics designed to manipulate people into divulging confidential information or performing actions that they otherwise would not. Social engineering techniques are often more personalized and may involve phone calls, physical interaction, or other forms of direct communication. Attackers may pose as trusted individuals, such as colleagues, IT support personnel, or even family members, to exploit the target's trust.

Both phishing and social engineering take advantage of common human weaknesses, such as trust, curiosity, fear, and the desire to help. Cybercriminals understand that people are often the weakest link in security, and they craft their attacks to exploit these emotions. A sense of urgency, for example, is frequently used in phishing emails to prompt victims to act quickly without thinking critically about the legitimacy of the request. The goal is to lower the victim's defenses, making them more likely to make hasty decisions that compromise security.

Defending against phishing and social engineering attacks requires a combination of awareness, skepticism, and proactive security measures. The first line of defense is education. Users must be taught to recognize common signs of phishing and social engineering. For phishing, this means being suspicious of unsolicited emails that ask for personal information or urge immediate action. Users should be trained to look for subtle signs of deception, such as misspelled words, suspicious email addresses, and unusual URLs. When receiving emails that appear to be from trusted organizations, it is important to avoid clicking links or downloading attachments without first verifying the authenticity of the sender through a separate communication channel, such as by calling the company directly or logging in via the official Web site.

Similarly, users should be wary of unsolicited phone calls or messages requesting sensitive information. Even if the caller claims to be from a trusted organization, individuals should avoid providing information over the phone unless they are absolutely certain of the caller's identity. When in doubt, hanging up and calling the company's verified customer service number is always a safer option. Additionally, many organizations implement MFA, which requires more than just a password to access accounts, providing an extra layer of security even if login credentials are compromised through phishing.

Another effective defense against phishing and social engineering is the use of email filters and anti-phishing tools. Many email providers now offer built-in filters that detect phishing attempts and block or flag suspicious messages. These filters can identify and quarantine known phishing emails, preventing them from reaching the inbox in the first place. Many Web browsers also include anti-phishing protections that alert users if they attempt to visit a known malicious Web site. Keeping software up to date is another essential defense, as it ensures that security patches are applied to vulnerabilities that could be exploited by attackers.

On a larger scale, businesses and organizations should invest in security protocols and employee training programs to reduce the risk of social engineering attacks. Employees should be trained to recognize the signs of social engineering and follow established procedures for verifying the identity of external contacts. Companies should also implement access controls and physical security measures to prevent attackers from gaining physical access to sensitive areas or systems. Regular security audits and penetration testing can help identify vulnerabilities in an organization's defenses and address them before they can be exploited.

Ultimately, defending against phishing and social engineering attacks requires a combination of vigilance, technological tools, and a commitment to staying informed about evolving threats. While these attacks may never be fully eradicated, individuals and organizations that prioritize cybersecurity awareness and practice caution in their online interactions will be far less likely to fall victim to these deceptive tactics. In the digital age, knowledge is the best defense against phishing and social engineering, and it is essential that we all remain aware of the risks and proactive in our efforts to stay secure.

APP MANAGEMENT ON SMARTPHONES

As mobile devices and desktop applications become integral to everyday life, users are increasingly relying on a variety of apps to perform tasks, access information, and stay connected. While these applications offer tremendous convenience, they also introduce significant security and privacy concerns, particularly when it comes to the management of app permissions and authorizations. App management and authorizations refer to the processes and systems that govern how apps are installed, configured, and granted access to sensitive data or system resources. Effective app management and control over authorizations are essential for ensuring the security of a device and protecting user privacy from malicious or unauthorized access.

App management involves several key tasks, including the installation, monitoring, updating, and removal of apps. It also encompasses the management of app permissions, which define what resources or data an app is allowed to access. In modern operating systems such as Android and iOS, users have some level of control over which permissions an app can access, giving them the ability to deny or revoke specific permissions after installation. This approach empowers users to manage their privacy actively, ensuring that apps only access what is necessary for their intended functionality. For example, a photo-editing app may need access to the device's camera and storage to function properly, but it should not require access to the user's contacts or location. By allowing users to selectively grant or deny permissions, app management tools reduce the risk of unnecessary data exposure or malicious exploitation.

Many users, however, fail to exercise caution when granting permissions, often blindly accepting the default settings without considering the risks involved. This is where effective app management becomes essential. The first step in app management is to be selective about the apps that are installed on a device. Apps from untrusted sources, or those that are downloaded from unofficial app stores, carry an increased risk of being malicious. In addition to installing apps from trusted platforms, users should regularly review and update the apps they have installed, ensuring that they are using the most secure and up-to-date versions. Software updates often include critical security patches that address vulnerabilities, so keeping apps up to date is a key aspect of preventing exploitation.

The role of app permission management extends beyond the initial installation and grant of permissions. Users should regularly audit their apps and the permissions they have granted. Over time, apps may accumulate permissions for features or resources that are no longer relevant. For example, a social media app may no longer need access to a user's contacts or location if those features are no longer being used. By periodically reviewing permissions and revoking access to data that is no longer necessary, users can minimize their exposure to potential security and privacy risks.

Furthermore, many apps request access to background services, such as push notifications or location tracking. While these features can be useful, they also have the potential to track a user's movements, collect unnecessary data, or drain device resources. As part of effective app management, users should ensure that background services are only enabled for apps that genuinely require them. For example, a fitness tracking app may need continuous access to the user's location to monitor running routes, but a news app does not need to track location in the background. By reviewing background services and disabling them when not needed, users can improve device performance and reduce the risk of unauthorized data collection.

The security of app updates is another key aspect of app management. Just as users need to update their apps to maintain security, they must also be vigilant when it comes to app updates. Malicious actors may attempt to disguise malware within an app update, a technique known as trojanizing an update. To mitigate the risk of this type of attack, users should only update apps through official app stores, where updates are vetted and verified for safety. Additionally, users should enable automatic updates where possible to ensure they receive security patches promptly, reducing the likelihood of vulnerability exploitation.

Despite these proactive measures, third-party app permissions and authorizations can still present significant risks if the underlying app is compromised or poorly designed. Therefore, users should always download apps from reputable sources, avoid suspicious or unsolicited app requests, and be cautious about granting apps access to sensitive data, particularly when it is not essential for the app's core functionality. Additionally, the use of security software such as mobile security apps can provide an added layer of protection, scanning apps for potential threats before they are installed or run.

Effective app management and authorizations are critical for protecting both personal data and system security in the digital age. By exercising caution when installing apps, carefully managing permissions, and regularly reviewing authorizations, users can significantly reduce the risks posed by malicious or overreaching applications. Ultimately, the responsibility for safeguarding data and privacy lies with the user, who must remain informed about the potential dangers of app permissions and take proactive steps to manage their app ecosystem effectively. With the increasing reliance on apps in all aspects of life, the need for vigilant app management and responsible authorization practices has never been more important.

TWO-FACTOR AUTHENTICATION

2FA has emerged as a crucial security measure in the modern digital landscape, offering an additional layer of protection against unauthorized access. Traditional authentication methods, primarily based on a single password, have become increasingly vulnerable due to phishing attacks, data breaches, and brute-force techniques. As cyber threats evolve, relying solely on something the user knows—a password—has proven insufficient. 2FA mitigates these risks by requiring a second form of verification, typically something the user possesses or an inherent characteristic.

The fundamental concept behind 2FA is the combination of two distinct factors, which can be knowledge, possession, or inherence. Knowledge-based factors include passwords or security questions, while possession-based factors encompass physical devices such as smartphones, hardware tokens, or smart cards. Inherence-based factors include biometrics, such as fingerprints, facial recognition, or iris scans. By demanding two of these elements, 2FA significantly reduces the likelihood of an attacker gaining unauthorized entry, even if one factor, such as a password, is compromised.

The most common implementation of 2FA involves OTPs sent via SMS or generated through authentication apps such as Google Authenticator or Authy. While SMS-based 2FA remains popular due to its ease of use, it has notable vulnerabilities. Attackers can exploit SIM swapping techniques, intercept messages through SS7 protocol flaws, or use phishing tactics to trick users into revealing OTPs. Consequently, security experts recommend authentication apps or hardware security keys as more robust alternatives. Apps generate time-based OTPs that are device-specific, reducing the risk of interception, whereas hardware keys, such as YubiKey or Titan Security Key, provide even stronger protection by requiring physical interaction.

Despite its advantages, 2FA is not a perfect solution. Usability challenges can deter widespread adoption, as users may find the additional authentication step cumbersome. Losing access to the second factor, such as a misplaced phone or a damaged security key, can lock users out of their accounts, necessitating backup codes or alternative recovery mechanisms. Additionally, sophisticated phishing attacks, such as adversary-in-the-middle (AITM) attacks, can still bypass 2FA by intercepting credentials and session tokens in real time. These limitations have led to the development of more advanced security models, including MFA and passwordless authentication, which integrate biometric verification and cryptographic credentials.

In sectors with stringent security requirements, such as banking, healthcare, and government agencies, 2FA has become an industry standard. Financial institutions mandate it to protect online transactions, while corporate environments employ it to safeguard sensitive data and systems. Regulatory frameworks, including GDPR and the Payment Services Directive 2 (PSD2), emphasize strong authentication measures, further driving 2FA adoption.

As cyber threats continue to evolve, the role of 2FA remains indispensable. While not infallible, it represents a significant improvement over single-factor authentication by adding an extra barrier against unauthorized access. The future of authentication may shift toward passwordless solutions, leveraging biometrics and cryptographic keys, yet 2FA will likely persist as a foundational security measure for the foreseeable future. Balancing security with usability remains the primary challenge, requiring continuous innovation and user education to ensure effective protection in an increasingly digital world.

ALTERNATIVE SEARCH ENGINES

Alternative search engines have gained significant traction in recent years as concerns over privacy, data collection, and monopolization of information grow. While Google continues to dominate the search engine market with its vast index, advanced algorithms, and personalized results, its business model, heavily reliant on user data collection, has led many individuals and organizations to seek out privacy-focused or niche alternatives. These alternative search engines cater to users who prioritize anonymity, unbiased results, or specific functionalities that mainstream search engines do not provide.

One of the most well-known alternatives is DuckDuckGo, which has built its reputation on privacy. Unlike Google, DuckDuckGo does not track users, store personal search histories, or create detailed profiles for targeted advertising. Instead, it delivers search results by aggregating data from multiple sources, including Bing, Yahoo, and its own Web crawler, DuckDuckBot. The absence of tracking makes it an attractive choice for privacy-conscious users, but it also means that it lacks the level of personalization that Google provides. Additionally, because it relies on external sources, its search results may sometimes be less comprehensive or refined compared to Google's.

Another significant contender in the realm of privacy-centric search engines is Startpage. Unlike DuckDuckGo, which sources data from multiple platforms, Startpage offers a unique advantage by delivering Google search results without the tracking. Essentially, it acts as an intermediary between the user and Google, stripping away identifying information before submitting a query. This allows users to benefit from Google's powerful search capabilities while maintaining a higher degree of anonymity. Because Startpage relies entirely on Google, however, it is still subject to Google's indexing decisions, meaning censored or deprioritized content on Google may also be affected in Startpage's results.

For users seeking a search engine that aligns with open-source principles and community-driven indexing, Searx offers a compelling alternative. Searx is an open-source metasearch engine that allows users to host their own instances, effectively decentralizing the search process. Because it can aggregate results from various sources, including Google, Bing, and even academic databases, it provides a highly customizable experience. Its reliance on multiple third-party sources, however, means that availability and reliability can vary depending on the instance being used. Some major search engines actively block Searx requests, making it less consistent than proprietary options.

Beyond privacy-focused search engines, some alternatives prioritize ethical considerations and sustainability. Ecosia, for instance, is a search engine that uses its ad revenue to fund tree-planting initiatives. It operates using Bing's search index while ensuring that user data is not sold to advertisers. For those who want to support environmental causes simply by browsing the Web, Ecosia presents a unique and ethical alternative.

Another growing segment in the search engine market is Brave Search, developed by the team behind the Brave browser. Unlike DuckDuckGo, which relies on external data, Brave Search is working to build its own independent index. This effort aims to reduce reliance on major players such as Google and Microsoft while providing transparent and private search results. Brave Search also offers a paid version that eliminates ads, giving users even greater control over their experience.

From a functionality standpoint, there are also search engines that specialize in academic research, open-source knowledge, and censorship-resistant content. WolframAlpha, for example, is not a traditional search engine but rather a computational knowledge engine that provides direct answers based on structured data and algorithms. It is particularly valuable for students, researchers, and professionals needing precise calculations or factual information. Meanwhile, Qwant, a European search engine, emphasizes compliance with strict European Union privacy regulations while providing a visually distinct interface and category-based search results.

Despite the appeal of these alternatives, challenges remain. One of the main drawbacks of non-Google search engines is their relatively smaller Web indexes, which can sometimes lead to less comprehensive or relevant results. Additionally, many alternative search engines depend on Bing's infrastructure, making them indirectly reliant on Microsoft. Without a truly independent index that can rival Google's scale, these alternatives often struggle to provide the same breadth and depth of information.

Nonetheless, as privacy awareness increases and regulatory scrutiny on big tech companies intensifies, the demand for alternative search engines is expected to grow. Whether users prioritize privacy, ethical considerations, or specialized search functionalities, there is an increasing array of choices beyond Google. While none of these alternatives can completely replace Google's dominance in terms of scale and accuracy, they serve as important tools in diversifying the search ecosystem and offering users greater control over their online experience.

END-TO-END ENCRYPTION

E2EE has become a cornerstone of digital privacy and security, ensuring that data remains accessible only to its intended recipients. E2EE plays a crucial role in safeguarding user information by preventing third parties—including service providers, hackers, and even governments—from accessing the content of messages or stored files.

At its core, E2EE ensures that data is encrypted on the sender's device and remains in an unreadable state until it reaches the recipient, who is the only one with the necessary decryption key. This means that even if data is intercepted in transit or accessed on a company's servers, it remains unintelligible to anyone without the proper decryption credentials. Unlike traditional encryption methods, where service providers may hold encryption keys and thus have access to user data, E2EE removes this vulnerability by ensuring that keys remain exclusively with the communicating parties.

One of the most well-known applications of E2EE is in messaging platforms. Apps such as Signal, WhatsApp, and Apple's iMessage have implemented E2EE to protect user conversations from unauthorized access. Signal, in particular, has set a high standard in the field by using the Signal Protocol, an open-source encryption protocol that ensures messages are not only encrypted but also incorporate forward secrecy. Forward secrecy ensures that even if an encryption key is compromised in the future, past messages remain protected because each communication session generates new encryption keys. WhatsApp, which also utilizes the Signal Protocol, brought E2EE to the mainstream by implementing it for over two billion users worldwide. Concerns remain, however, about metadata collection, as even encrypted services may still gather information about who communicates with whom, at what time, and for how long.

Email encryption is another critical area where E2EE is making strides, though it faces more challenges than messaging encryption. Standard email protocols such as SMTP, IMAP, and POP3 do not inherently support E2EE, meaning that most email providers can access the content of emails stored on their servers. Services such as Proton Mail and Tuta have introduced built-in E2EE for email communication, ensuring that only the sender and recipient can read the content. Compatibility issues arise, however, when users attempt to send encrypted emails to recipients using traditional email providers, as not all systems support automatic decryption. Open-source encryption standards such as Pretty Good Privacy (PGP) and its successor, GnuPG, have provided a way to encrypt emails manually, but their complexity has hindered widespread adoption among non-technical users.

Cloud storage services have also integrated E2EE to protect user files from unauthorized access. Traditional cloud storage providers, such as Google Drive and Dropbox, encrypt data while it is stored on their servers, but they retain control over the encryption keys, meaning they can access user files if required. Privacy-focused alternatives, such as Tresorit, Sync.com, and MEGA, offer true E2EE, ensuring that only users have control over their decryption keys. A notable example is Cryptomator, an open-source tool that enables users to add client-side encryption to any cloud storage service, ensuring that files remain private even when stored on platforms that do not natively support E2EE.

While E2EE provides strong security benefits, it has also faced criticism and regulatory pressure. Governments and law enforcement agencies argue that E2EE can hinder criminal investigations by making it difficult to monitor communications between individuals engaging in illicit activities. Some governments have proposed measures requiring companies to implement backdoors—hidden access points that allow authorities to bypass encryption when needed. Cybersecurity experts warn, however, that any backdoor, regardless of its intended purpose, inherently weakens encryption and creates vulnerabilities that could be exploited by malicious actors.

Another challenge with E2EE is key management. Since only users have access to their encryption keys, losing them means permanently losing access to encrypted data. Unlike centralized encryption systems, where a company can reset passwords or restore access, E2EE does not allow for such recovery unless users have securely backed up their keys. This can be particularly problematic for encrypted email and cloud storage services, where a lost key means losing access to potentially critical data.

Despite these challenges, the importance of E2EE continues to grow as digital privacy concerns intensify. More services are adopting E2EE as a default security measure, and open-source initiatives are pushing for broader accessibility and ease of use. As encryption technology evolves, innovations such as ZKPs and homomorphic encryption may further enhance privacy by allowing computations on encrypted data without decrypting it. While E2EE is not a universal solution to all cybersecurity threats, it remains one of the most effective tools available for protecting user privacy in an increasingly interconnected world. Its widespread adoption is essential in the ongoing battle against mass surveillance, cybercrime, and unauthorized data collection, ensuring that individuals maintain control over their digital communications and personal information.

PASSWORD MANAGEMENT

Managing passwords effectively is one of the most critical aspects of online security, yet it remains one of the most overlooked. Poor password management habits, such as using weak passwords, reusing the same credentials across multiple sites, or storing them in insecure locations, expose users to significant security risks. A strong password strategy involves generating secure passwords, storing them safely, and updating them when necessary, all while balancing convenience and security.

One of the most important principles in password security is creating strong, unique passwords for every account. A strong password should be long, complex, and unpredictable, typically consisting of at least 12–16 characters that include a mix of uppercase and lowercase letters, numbers, and special symbols. The reason for this complexity is to prevent brute-force attacks, where hackers systematically try every possible combination until they gain access. A short or common password can be cracked in seconds using modern computing power, while a well-constructed password is significantly harder to break.

Despite knowing the importance of strong passwords, many users still fall into the habit of using simple, memorable phrases or reusing the same password across multiple accounts. This practice creates a dangerous vulnerability:

if one account is compromised, attackers can use the stolen credentials to access other services through credential stuffing attacks. This is particularly concerning given the frequent occurrence of data breaches, where large-scale leaks expose millions of usernames and passwords to cybercriminals. To mitigate this risk, it is essential to use unique passwords for each account, ensuring that a single breach does not jeopardize multiple services.

Given the difficulty of remembering multiple complex passwords, a password manager becomes an indispensable tool. Password managers securely store and generate passwords, eliminating the need for users to memorize multiple credentials. These tools encrypt stored passwords, requiring only a single master password to access them, significantly reducing the likelihood of human error. Well-established password managers, such as Bitwarden, 1Password, and KeePassXC, offer cross-platform compatibility, allowing users to securely retrieve their credentials across multiple devices while maintaining strong encryption. Some password managers also include features such as breach monitoring, alerting users if their credentials have appeared in a data breach, and enabling easy updates for compromised passwords.

Another crucial aspect of password management is enabling 2FA whenever possible. 2FA adds an additional layer of security by requiring a secondary verification method, such as a TOTP generated by an authentication app such as Authy or Google Authenticator, or a physical security key such as YubiKey. Even if an attacker manages to obtain a password, they will still need access to the second factor to successfully log in. While SMS-based 2FA is still widely used, it is generally less secure than authentication apps or hardware keys, as SMS messages can be intercepted or compromised through SIM-swapping attacks.

Updating passwords periodically is also a recommended practice, particularly for accounts containing sensitive personal or financial information. While frequent changes are not necessary if a password is strong and unique, it is advisable to update passwords if there is any suspicion of a breach or if the service provider has been compromised. Additionally, using passphrases—long combinations of random words that are easier to remember but still highly secure—can be an alternative for users who struggle with complex passwords. Passphrases such as "SunsetMangoLibrary$37" offer both strength and memorability without the weaknesses of predictable or short passwords.

For those looking to further enhance their security, adopting passwordless authentication methods may be an emerging alternative. Technologies such as biometric authentication, FIDO2 security keys, and passwordless login methods offered by companies aim to reduce reliance on traditional passwords. While these solutions are still gaining widespread adoption, they represent a promising future where users can authenticate securely without the risk of password-based attacks.

Ultimately, password management is a critical but often neglected aspect of digital security. By generating strong, unique passwords, using a password manager, enabling 2FA, and staying informed about security best practices, users can significantly reduce their risk of compromise. The key to effective password management is striking a balance between security and usability, ensuring that strong security measures do not become so cumbersome that users revert to unsafe habits. As cybersecurity threats continue to evolve, individuals and organizations must remain proactive in safeguarding their digital identities, making password hygiene a fundamental part of their online security strategy.

FINGERPRINT RECOGNITION

Fingerprint recognition has become one of the most widely used biometric authentication methods, offering a balance between security and convenience. Whether unlocking a smartphone, accessing secure facilities, or authorizing financial transactions, fingerprint authentication provides a quick and relatively secure alternative to traditional passwords and PINs. While fingerprints offer significant advantages in terms of usability and fraud prevention, they also raise critical concerns regarding privacy, data security, and potential vulnerabilities.

The primary advantage of fingerprint authentication is its convenience. Unlike passwords, which require memorization and can be forgotten, or security keys, which can be lost, fingerprints are always available to the user. Scanning a fingerprint is faster than entering a complex password, making authentication both seamless and efficient. This ease of use has contributed to its widespread adoption in consumer technology, with nearly all modern smartphones, laptops, and even payment systems integrating fingerprint scanners as an authentication option.

Security is another major benefit of fingerprint recognition. Because each individual's fingerprints are unique, they provide a more reliable form of identification than easily guessable passwords. Additionally, fingerprint-based authentication is resistant to many common cyber threats, such as phishing and brute-force attacks, which often exploit weak or reused passwords. Unlike passwords, which can be shared, stolen, or leaked in a data breach, fingerprints are inherently tied to the user, reducing the risk of credential compromise.

Despite its advantages, fingerprint authentication is not without its flaws. One of the most significant concerns is the immutability of biometric data. While passwords can be changed if compromised, fingerprints cannot. If a fingerprint template is leaked or stolen, there is no way for the individual to reset it like a traditional password. This makes biometric data an attractive target for cybercriminals.

Another security risk comes from spoofing and biometric forgery. While modern fingerprint scanners incorporate liveness detection to differentiate real fingers from artificial replicas, sophisticated attackers have demonstrated methods for creating high-quality fingerprint forgeries using materials such as latex, silicone, or even 3D printing. Certain types of fingerprint scanners, especially older or lower-quality models, remain vulnerable to these attacks. Advanced techniques, such as ultra-sonic fingerprint scanning, have improved security by mapping the fingerprint's depth and ridges more accurately, but no system is entirely foolproof.

The way fingerprint data is stored and processed also has significant privacy implications. Most modern devices use secure enclave technology, meaning fingerprint data never leaves the device and is not transmitted to external servers. Instead, the fingerprint is converted into a cryptographic hash, which is compared against the stored template for authentication. This approach minimizes the risk of data interception and unauthorized access. Some centralized systems, particularly in government and corporate environments, may, however, store fingerprints in databases, increasing the risk of mass-scale biometric theft in the event of a breach.

Another major concern is government surveillance and misuse. While fingerprint recognition is commonly used for secure authentication, it is also widely deployed in law enforcement and border control for identification purposes. Many countries maintain national fingerprint databases, and the expansion of biometric surveillance raises questions about civil liberties and data protection. Once collected, biometric data can be difficult to control, and there is the potential for misuse, whether by governments engaging in mass surveillance or private companies using fingerprints for tracking and profiling users.

Moreover, fingerprint recognition is not always reliable, as environmental factors can affect its accuracy. Dirt, moisture, cuts, or aging can alter fingerprint patterns, leading to failed authentication attempts. In extreme cases, individuals with worn or damaged fingerprints, such as construction workers or elderly individuals, may struggle to use fingerprint-based systems effectively. This highlights the need for backup authentication methods, ensuring that users are not locked out of their accounts or devices due to fingerprint recognition failures.

Despite these concerns, fingerprint authentication remains a valuable security tool when used appropriately and in combination with other security measures. MFA, which combines fingerprint recognition with a PIN, password, or hardware security key, significantly enhances security by ensuring that biometric authentication alone is not the sole factor protecting sensitive accounts. This layered approach mitigates the risk of fingerprint spoofing and ensures access control even if the biometric data is compromised.

Looking toward the future, fingerprint authentication will likely continue to evolve, with advancements in sensor technology, AI-driven liveness detection, and integration with other biometric modalities, such as facial recognition or iris scanning. As biometric security becomes more prevalent, however, regulatory frameworks must keep pace to address data protection concerns, ensuring that users have control over their biometric information and that companies handling such data implement robust security measures.

Fingerprint recognition is a powerful authentication method that balances security and usability, making it a popular choice for personal devices, financial transactions, and secure access control. Its immutability, potential for spoofing, privacy risks, and dependence on proper implementation, however, highlight the need for caution. Users and organizations must adopt fingerprint authentication as part of a broader security strategy rather than a standalone solution, combining it with encryption, MFA, and privacy safeguards to mitigate risks while benefiting from its convenience.

FACIAL RECOGNITION

Facial recognition has emerged as one of the most prominent and controversial biometric authentication methods in recent years. From unlocking smartphones to enabling seamless airport security checks, this technology offers a level of convenience and speed that traditional authentication methods struggle to match. While facial recognition provides a frictionless user experience, it also raises significant concerns regarding security, privacy, and ethical implications. The widespread deployment of facial recognition by both private companies and governments has sparked debates about its potential for misuse, making it a topic that requires careful consideration.

One of the key advantages of facial recognition is its efficiency and ease of use. Unlike passwords and fingerprint authentication, which require physical input from the user, facial recognition allows for seamless authentication without requiring direct interaction with a device. A simple glance at a smartphone or computer screen is enough to verify identity, reducing the friction of logging in to accounts, making payments, or accessing secure areas. This hands-free approach is particularly beneficial in scenarios where users may have limited mobility or need to authenticate quickly, such as when wearing gloves in cold weather or handling tasks that require rapid authorization.

In addition to convenience, security is a major selling point of facial recognition. Unlike passwords, which can be guessed, stolen, or reused across multiple accounts, a face is unique to each individual. Advanced facial recognition systems use complex algorithms to analyze thousands of facial features, including the distance between the eyes, the shape of the jawline, and the contours of the nose. Modern implementations, such as Apple's Face ID, incorporate depth mapping and infrared sensors to detect three-dimensional facial structures, making it difficult for attackers to bypass authentication with a simple photo or video.

While it has advantages, facial recognition technology also has its flaws. Spoofing and adversarial attacks pose significant challenges, particularly for systems that rely on standard image recognition. Early implementations of facial recognition were easily tricked by printed photos or high-resolution videos displayed on a screen. While modern systems have introduced countermeasures such as liveness detection, which distinguishes real faces from static images by detecting micro-movements, sophisticated attackers have demonstrated methods to deceive even advanced systems using deepfake technology, 3D-printed masks, or high-fidelity facial replicas.

Beyond direct security concerns, privacy risks associated with facial recognition are among the most pressing issues. Unlike passwords and fingerprints, which require intentional user input, facial data can be captured without consent. Public surveillance cameras, social media platforms, and corporate databases increasingly use facial recognition to track individuals, raising serious concerns about mass surveillance and the erosion of anonymity. Governments and law enforcement agencies in several countries have deployed large-scale facial recognition networks, enabling real-time monitoring of citizens without their knowledge. In places with weak data protection regulations, this can lead to significant abuses, including profiling, discrimination, or political repression.

Another concern is data storage and the risk of biometric leaks. Unlike passwords, which can be changed if compromised, facial data is permanent. If a database storing facial templates is breached, individuals have no way to "reset" their facial features to regain security. If such data falls into the wrong hands, it can be used for identity fraud or unauthorized tracking, or even manipulated to generate deepfake content.

The accuracy and bias of facial recognition systems also pose significant ethical and technical challenges. Studies have shown that many facial recognition algorithms exhibit racial and gender bias, performing significantly worse on women and individuals with darker skin tones compared to lighter-skinned males. This bias is largely due to imbalanced training data, where ML models are trained predominantly on faces from certain demographic groups. The implications of this bias are particularly alarming when facial recognition is used in law enforcement, where misidentification can lead to wrongful arrests or discrimination.

To mitigate these risks, some technology companies and governments have imposed restrictions on facial recognition technology. Major firms have halted or limited the sale of facial recognition software to law enforcement agencies due to concerns about misuse. Meanwhile, several cities around the world, including San Francisco and Boston, have enacted bans or moratoriums on the use of facial recognition in public surveillance. These policy measures highlight the growing awareness of the need to regulate biometric technologies to prevent potential abuses.

Despite these concerns, facial recognition continues to evolve, with privacy-preserving advancements aimed at reducing risks. Techniques such as on-device processing help enhance security by ensuring that facial data never leaves the user's device, reducing the likelihood of unauthorized access. Apple's Face ID, for example, stores facial templates within the Secure Enclave, an isolated chip designed to protect biometric data from external threats. Additionally, federated learning is being explored as a way to train facial recognition models without directly storing individual biometric data in central servers, helping balance security with privacy.

Looking ahead, the role of facial recognition in authentication and security will depend largely on how it is regulated and implemented. While it offers a highly convenient and secure alternative to traditional authentication methods, its risks cannot be ignored. The challenge lies in ensuring that facial recognition is deployed ethically, with strong protections against surveillance abuse, bias, and data exploitation. Organizations that adopt facial recognition should follow privacy-centric design principles, such as explicit user consent, local data storage, and MFA, to minimize vulnerabilities.

Facial recognition is a powerful but double-edged technology. While it provides speed, convenience, and enhanced security, it also introduces privacy risks, biases, and ethical concerns that must be carefully managed. As biometric authentication continues to integrate into daily life, striking a balance between innovation and user protection will be essential to ensuring that facial recognition remains a tool for convenience rather than a mechanism for surveillance and control.

LINUX TOOLS

Linux, an open-source operating system known for its flexibility, security, and privacy features, has become an increasingly popular choice for users concerned with protecting their personal data and maintaining their privacy. Unlike proprietary operating systems, Linux provides users with a high degree of control over the system, offering the ability to fine-tune security settings, modify source code, and select privacy-focused tools. For those who prioritize data protection and privacy, Linux offers a wide range of specialized tools designed to safeguard sensitive information and ensure a secure computing environment.

One of the key advantages of Linux is its customizability, which allows users to choose and configure privacy-focused tools that best suit their needs. Whether it's encrypting data, anonymizing Internet traffic, or securing communications, there are numerous Linux-specific tools that help users maintain a high level of privacy and security. Given the open-source nature of the Linux ecosystem, many of these tools are free to use and can be audited by anyone to ensure they are not introducing vulnerabilities or privacy risks.

One of the most essential categories of privacy tools on Linux is encryption software. Data encryption ensures that sensitive information is protected from unauthorized access, even if the device is compromised or lost. On Linux, one of the most widely used encryption tools is Linux Unified Key Setup (LUKS), a disk encryption standard that allows users to encrypt entire disk partitions. By encrypting data at the disk level, LUKS protects information such as personal files, passwords, and sensitive documents from being accessed by malicious actors or unauthorized users. When a Linux system is powered on, the user must enter a passphrase to unlock the encrypted disk, ensuring that data remains protected while the system is in use. LUKS can also be combined with other encryption tools, such as GnuPG, to encrypt individual files or email communications. GnuPG provides E2EE for files and messages, allowing users to secure sensitive data in transit, ensuring that only the intended recipient can decrypt and read the message.

For users concerned about anonymity while browsing the Internet, Linux offers several tools specifically designed to protect privacy and conceal users' identities. One of the most popular tools for anonymity is Tor. Tor is a free, open-source software that routes Internet traffic through a network of volunteer-operated servers, making it difficult for anyone to track a user's activity or identify their location. By encrypting traffic and bouncing it through multiple relays, Tor ensures that users can browse the Web anonymously, without leaving traces of their activities that could be used for surveillance or tracking. Tor is particularly useful for those living in regions with restrictive Internet policies, as it allows access to blocked Web sites and services while preserving privacy. While Tor provides a high degree of anonymity, it is important to combine it with other privacy practices, such as avoiding logging in to accounts with identifiable information, to ensure full privacy protection.

Another tool commonly used on Linux for Internet anonymity is the Invisible Internet Project (I2P), which operates in a similar way to Tor but focuses on providing anonymity for both users and services. While Tor is primarily designed for browsing the surface Web, I2P is intended for anonymous communication on hidden services within the I2P network. It is especially useful for users who wish to host their own anonymous Web sites or services while also maintaining their privacy. I2P also encrypts Internet traffic, routing it through multiple nodes to obscure the user's location and activity. Although it does not have the same widespread adoption as Tor, I2P is a valuable tool for users seeking a higher level of privacy and anonymity, particularly in areas with heavy surveillance.

For users concerned about online tracking and data mining, Linux offers a range of tools designed to block unwanted third-party trackers and advertisements. One of the most effective tools for this purpose is Pi-hole, a network-wide ad-blocker that functions as a DNS sinkhole. Pi-hole intercepts DNS queries for known ad-serving domains, blocking ads and trackers before they can even reach the user's device. By installing Pi-hole on a local network, users can block intrusive ads, tracking cookies, and other privacy-invasive elements across all devices connected to the network, including smartphones, tablets, and smart TVs. Pi-hole can be easily configured and customized to block specific types of content, enhancing users' online privacy and security.

Another tool for secure communication is Jitsi Meet, an open-source video conferencing tool that provides encrypted video calls. Jitsi is often favored by privacy-conscious users because it does not require creating an account to use the service, and it allows users to host their own secure video calls with E2EE.

Lastly, Linux users who prioritize secure file storage and sharing can benefit from tools such as Nextcloud and Syncthing. Nextcloud is an open-source cloud storage solution that allows users to store and share files securely. It offers E2EE and the ability to host the cloud service on personal servers, reducing reliance on third-party cloud providers. Similarly, Syncthing is a decentralized file synchronization tool that enables users to sync files securely between devices without relying on centralized servers. Both tools emphasize user control over their data and privacy, ensuring that sensitive files are kept safe from unauthorized access.

Linux offers a robust selection of tools and utilities specifically designed to enhance privacy and protect personal data. From encryption and anonymization to secure communication and ad-blocking, Linux provides users with a diverse range of options to safeguard their information in an increasingly surveillance-driven world.

REFERENCES

1. Antivirus software. In: Wikipedia [Internet]. 2025 [cited 2025 Jan 27]. Available from: *https://en.wikipedia.org/w/index.php?title=Antivirus_software&oldid=1269215168*
2. Ecosia - the search engine that plants trees [Internet]. [cited 2025 Jan 27]. Available from: *https://www.ecosia.org/*

3. End-to-end encryption. In: Wikipedia [Internet]. 2025 [cited 2025 Jan 27]. Available from: *https://en.wikipedia.org/w/index.php?title=End-to-end_encryption&oldid=1269104253*

4. Facial recognition system. In: Wikipedia [Internet]. 2025 [cited 2025 Jan 27]. Available from: *https://en.wikipedia.org/w/index.php?title=Facial_recognition_system&oldid=1268579072*

5. Fingerprint. In: Wikipedia [Internet]. 2025 [cited 2025 Jan 27]. Available from: *https://en.wikipedia.org/w/index.php?title=Fingerprint&oldid=1267364524*

6. Firewall (computing). In: Wikipedia [Internet]. 2025 [cited 2025 Jan 27]. Available from: *https://en.wikipedia.org/w/index.php?title=Firewall_(computing)&oldid=1272158100*

7. Microsoft Defender Antivirus. In: Wikipedia [Internet]. 2025 [cited 2025 Jan 27]. Available from: *https://en.wikipedia.org/w/index.php?title=Microsoft_Defender_Antivirus&oldid=1269639388*

8. Multi-factor authentication. In: Wikipedia [Internet]. 2025 [cited 2025 Jan 27]. Available from: *https://en.wikipedia.org/w/index.php?title=Multi-factor_authentication&oldid=1272268966*

9. Password strength. In: Wikipedia [Internet]. 2025 [cited 2025 Jan 27]. Available from: *https://en.wikipedia.org/w/index.php?title=Password_strength&oldid=1272011673*

10. Qwant [Internet]. [cited 2025 Jan 27]. Qwant. Available from: *https://www.qwant.com*

11. Searx. In: Wikipedia [Internet]. 2025 [cited 2025 Jan 27]. Available from: *https://en.wikipedia.org/w/index.php?title=Searx&oldid=1268123671*

12. Social engineering (security). In: Wikipedia [Internet]. 2025 [cited 2025 Jan 27]. Available from: *https://en.wikipedia.org/w/index.php?title=Social_engineering_(security)&oldid=1270444766*

13. www.startpage.com [Internet]. [cited 2025 Jan 27]. Startpage - Private Search Engine. No Tracking. No Search History. Available from: *https://www.startpage.com/*

14. Launchpad [Internet]. 2007 [cited 2025 Jan 27]. ufw in Launchpad. Available from: *https://launchpad.net/ufw/+index*

15. Uncomplicated Firewall. In: Wikipedia [Internet]. 2025 [cited 2025 Jan 27]. Available from: *https://en.wikipedia.org/w/index.php?title=Uncomplicated_Firewall&oldid=1267850824*

16. Virtual private network. In: Wikipedia [Internet]. 2025 [cited 2025 Jan 27]. Available from: *https://en.wikipedia.org/w/index.php?title=Virtual_private_network&oldid=1269644700*

17. Windows Firewall. In: Wikipedia [Internet]. 2023 [cited 2025 Jan 27]. Available from: *https://en.wikipedia.org/w/index.php?title=Windows_Firewall&oldid=1187079517*

18. Wolfram|Alpha: Making the world's knowledge computable [Internet]. [cited 2025 Jan 27]. Available from: *https://www.wolframalpha.com*

CHAPTER 6

Hackers and Hacking Tools

The terms "white hat" and "black hat" hackers are used to describe individuals who engage in hacking activities but with fundamentally different motivations, ethics, and goals. These terms originate from old Western movies, where the color of a character's hat symbolized their moral alignment—white for heroes and black for villains. In the context of cybersecurity, this dichotomy helps distinguish between those who use their skills for constructive, ethical purposes and those who exploit their knowledge for malicious intent.

WHITE HAT HACKERS: THE ETHICAL GUARDIANS

White hat hackers, also known as ethical hackers, are cybersecurity professionals who use their skills to protect systems, networks, and data from malicious attacks. They operate within the boundaries of the law and often work with organizations to identify vulnerabilities, strengthen defenses, and prevent cyber threats. Their primary goal is to improve security and safeguard sensitive information from unauthorized access or exploitation.

One of the key roles of white hat hackers is penetration testing, where they simulate cyberattacks on a system to identify weaknesses before malicious actors can exploit them. This proactive approach allows organizations to address vulnerabilities and implement robust security measures. White hat hackers also play a crucial role in developing secure software, conducting security audits, and educating employees about best practices for cybersecurity.

Many white hat hackers hold certifications such as Certified Ethical Hacker (CEH), Offensive Security Certified Professional (OSCP), or CompTIA Security+, which validate their expertise and commitment to ethical standards. They often work for government agencies, corporations, or cybersecurity firms, and some operate as independent consultants. Their work is guided by a strong sense of responsibility and a desire to contribute positively to the digital world.

White hat hackers are also instrumental in responding to cyber incidents. When a data breach or attack occurs, they analyze the situation, identify the root cause, and help mitigate the damage. Their efforts not only protect individual organizations but also contribute to the overall resilience of the global digital infrastructure.

BLACK HAT HACKERS: THE MALICIOUS EXPLOITERS

In contrast, black hat hackers are individuals who use their technical skills for illegal or unethical purposes. Their activities include stealing sensitive data, deploying malware, conducting ransomware attacks, and disrupting systems for personal gain or malicious intent. Black hat hackers operate outside the law and often target individuals, businesses, and governments to achieve their objectives.

The motivations behind black hat hacking can vary widely. Some hackers are driven by financial gain, seeking to profit from stolen data, fraudulent activities, or extortion. Others may be motivated by political agendas, aiming to disrupt operations or spread propaganda. Additionally, some black hat hackers engage in cybercrime for the thrill or notoriety, seeking to prove their skills or gain recognition within underground communities.

Black hat hackers employ a wide range of techniques to achieve their goals, including phishing, social engineering, brute-force attacks, and exploiting zero-day vulnerabilities. They often operate in organized groups or networks, sharing tools, knowledge, and resources to carry out large-scale attacks. The anonymity provided by the Internet makes it challenging to track and apprehend these individuals, although law enforcement agencies and cybersecurity experts continually work to combat their activities.

The impact of black hat hacking can be devastating. Data breaches can result in significant financial losses, reputational damage, and legal consequences for affected organizations. Individuals may suffer identity theft, financial fraud, or privacy violations. On a larger scale, black hat hacking can threaten national security, disrupt critical infrastructure, and undermine public trust in digital systems.

THE GRAY AREA: GRAY HAT HACKERS

Between the clear-cut categories of white hat and black hat hackers lies a gray area occupied by gray hat hackers. These individuals do not fit neatly into either category, as their actions may combine elements of both ethical and unethical behavior. Gray hat hackers often identify vulnerabilities in systems without authorization but may disclose their findings to the affected organization or the public rather than exploiting them for personal gain.

For example, a gray hat hacker might discover a security flaw in a widely used software application and publicly disclose it to pressure the developer into fixing the issue. While their intentions may be well-meaning, their methods can still cause harm, such as exposing systems to potential attacks before a patch is available. This ambiguity makes gray hat hacking a controversial topic within the cybersecurity community.

THE ROLE OF EDUCATION AND AWARENESS

The distinction between white hat and black hat hackers underscores the importance of education and awareness in the field of cybersecurity. By promoting ethical hacking practices and providing opportunities for individuals to develop their skills in a constructive manner, society can channel technical expertise toward positive outcomes. Initiatives such as bug bounty programs, which reward ethical hackers for discovering and reporting vulnerabilities, encourage responsible behavior and foster collaboration between security professionals and organizations.

At the same time, raising awareness about the risks and consequences of black hat hacking is essential to deter malicious activities. Educating individuals about cybersecurity best practices, such as using strong passwords, enabling 2FA, and recognizing phishing attempts, can help reduce the success rate of cyberattacks. Governments and organizations must also invest in robust cybersecurity measures and enforce laws to hold black hat hackers accountable for their actions.

THE EVOLVING LANDSCAPE OF HACKING

As technology continues to advance, the line between white hat and black hat hacking may become increasingly blurred. The rise of AI, IoT, and quantum computing presents new challenges and opportunities for both ethical and malicious hackers. White hat hackers must stay ahead of emerging threats and develop innovative solutions to protect digital systems, while black hat hackers may exploit new technologies to launch more sophisticated attacks.

In this evolving landscape, collaboration and information sharing are crucial. White hat hackers, cybersecurity researchers, and law enforcement agencies must work together to stay one step ahead of black hat hackers. By fostering a culture of ethical behavior and continuous learning, the cybersecurity community can ensure that technology is used as a force for good.

Ultimately, the battle between white hat and black hat hackers is a reflection of the broader struggle between security and exploitation in the digital age. By promoting ethical hacking practices, investing in cybersecurity education, and fostering collaboration, society can harness the power of technology to create a safer and more secure future.

TOOLS

Cybercriminals rely on a variety of specialized software to exploit vulnerabilities, steal sensitive data, and disrupt digital systems. These tools, often developed for legitimate security testing purposes, can be weaponized by malicious actors to conduct cyberattacks ranging from data breaches to ransomware infections.

Understanding these hacking tools is not just an academic exercise; it is a crucial aspect of cybersecurity defense. Ethical hackers, security researchers, and IT professionals study these programs to anticipate threats, identify weaknesses, and develop countermeasures. By recognizing how attackers operate, organizations and individuals can enhance their security posture and mitigate risks before they are exploited.

This section explores some of the most widely used hacking tools, explaining their capabilities, potential threats, and how cybersecurity experts leverage them to build stronger defenses. From penetration testing frameworks such as Metasploit to password-cracking utilities such as John the Ripper, each of these tools serves as a reminder that knowledge is the key to both offense and defense in the ever-evolving landscape of cybersecurity.

Metasploit

Metasploit is one of the most powerful and widely used penetration testing frameworks in cybersecurity. Initially developed by H.D. Moore in 2003 as an open-source project, it has since been acquired by Rapid7 and evolved into a robust platform for security professionals, ethical hackers, and malicious actors alike. Its versatility, extensive exploit database, and modular architecture make it an indispensable tool for assessing and improving system security.

Metasploit provides an automated way to discover, exploit, and validate vulnerabilities in a target system. Security researchers and penetration testers use it to simulate real-world attacks, allowing organizations to identify weaknesses before cybercriminals can exploit them. The framework includes a vast repository of exploits, payloads, and auxiliary modules that facilitate various types of attacks, such as remote code execution (RCE), privilege escalation, and credential harvesting.

One of Metasploit's key strengths is its modular design, which allows users to mix and match exploits and payloads to suit their needs. Exploits are prewritten scripts designed to take advantage of security flaws, while payloads determine the outcome of the attack, such as opening a backdoor or exfiltrating data. The Meterpreter payload, for example, is a powerful in-memory shell that enables attackers to execute commands, escalate privileges, and maintain control over a compromised system without leaving traces on disk.

Metasploit is also an essential tool for reconnaissance and vulnerability scanning. It integrates seamlessly with other security tools, such as Network Mapper (Nmap), making it easy to map networks, discover hosts, and identify open ports before launching attacks. Additionally, it includes auxiliary modules that can be used for brute-force attacks, social engineering simulations, and phishing campaigns.

The framework supports both command line and graphical interfaces, with Metasploit Framework (MSF) being the most commonly used version. Advanced users can interact with msfconsole, a powerful CLI that provides fine-grained control over exploits and payloads. For those who prefer a more user-friendly experience, Armitage, a graphical front-end, offers a streamlined way to manage attacks through an intuitive interface.

Beyond offensive capabilities, Metasploit is also a valuable tool for defensive security teams. Teams use it to test an organization's defenses and develop stronger security measures against real-world threats. The ability to simulate attacks in a controlled environment helps organizations improve their incident response and harden their infrastructure against potential breaches.

Despite its legitimacy as a penetration testing tool, Metasploit is often misused by cybercriminals. Hackers exploit its capabilities to automate attacks, compromise networks, and deploy malicious payloads. This dual-use nature underscores the importance of ethical hacking and the responsible use of security tools. Proper authorization and adherence to legal guidelines are essential when conducting penetration tests to avoid legal consequences.

Metasploit remains one of the most comprehensive and effective penetration testing frameworks available. Its extensive exploit database, flexible architecture, and integration with other security tools make it a must-have for ethical hackers and security professionals. Note, however, that with great power comes great responsibility. Understanding how Metasploit works not only empowers security teams to strengthen their defenses but also highlights the ever-present risks posed by adversaries who exploit the same tools for malicious purposes.

Cobalt Strike

Cobalt Strike is one of the most advanced and widely used tools for adversary simulation and post-exploitation activities. Initially developed by Raphael Mudge, it was designed to assist security professionals in conducting realistic attack simulations against networks and organizations. Over time, it has become a staple for penetration testers, ethical hackers, and, unfortunately, cybercriminals, who have weaponized its capabilities for malicious campaigns.

Unlike traditional penetration testing tools that focus on vulnerability discovery and exploitation, Cobalt Strike excels in post-exploitation, command and control (C2), and persistence. It is often used to assess an organization's ability to detect and respond to sophisticated threats. By mimicking the tactics, techniques, and procedures (TTPs) of advanced threat actors, security professionals can evaluate their defenses against real-world cyberattacks.

One of Cobalt Strike's defining features is its Beacon payload, which provides full control over compromised machines. Beacon is a modular, stealthy backdoor that allows attackers to execute commands, escalate privileges, move laterally across networks, and exfiltrate data while evading detection. It supports multiple communication channels, including HTTP, HTTPS, DNS, and SMB, enabling attackers to blend their activity with legitimate network traffic and bypass security defenses.

Cobalt Strike's GUI makes it accessible to both experienced and novice users. It provides an intuitive dashboard that facilitates team collaboration, allowing multiple operators to control and coordinate attacks in real time. The tool integrates with other penetration testing frameworks, such as Metasploit, enhancing its capabilities for initial exploitation and privilege escalation.

A key advantage of Cobalt Strike is its ability to simulate APTs. It includes built-in tools for covert operations, such as process injection, keystroke logging, and token impersonation, which are commonly used by nation-state actors and cybercriminal groups. The platform also supports obfuscation techniques that help evade EDR and antivirus solutions. These stealth capabilities make Cobalt Strike particularly effective in testing an organization's security posture against sophisticated threats.

Despite its legitimate use in security assessments, Cobalt Strike has become a favorite tool among cybercriminals, ransomware gangs, and nation-state hackers. Cracked versions of the software have been widely distributed on underground forums, leading to its misuse in real-world attacks. Hackers have leveraged Cobalt Strike Beacon to establish footholds in corporate networks before deploying ransomware or conducting data breaches. This widespread abuse has led cybersecurity vendors to develop specialized detection and mitigation strategies against Cobalt Strike-based attacks.

Defending against Cobalt Strike requires a combination of network monitoring, behavioral analysis, and proactive threat hunting. Since Beacon often communicates using encrypted or obfuscated traffic, security teams must analyze network anomalies and suspicious command executions. Endpoint protection solutions, memory forensics, and deception technologies can help detect and disrupt Cobalt Strike activity before it leads to significant damage.

Cobalt Strike is an indispensable tool for adversary emulation, providing deep insights into an organization's security resilience. Its capabilities have, however, also made it a double-edged sword, widely exploited by cybercriminals and state-sponsored hackers. As a result, defenders must stay ahead of emerging threats by understanding Cobalt Strike's techniques and implementing robust detection and response mechanisms.

ExploitDB

Exploit Database (ExploitDB) is a comprehensive archive of publicly disclosed exploits, security vulnerabilities, and proof-of-concept code. Maintained by Offensive Security, the same organization behind Kali Linux and the OSCP certification, ExploitDB serves as an invaluable resource for security professionals, ethical hackers, and penetration testers seeking to understand and mitigate threats.

Unlike penetration testing frameworks such as Metasploit or Cobalt Strike, ExploitDB does not provide an automated exploitation platform.

Instead, it functions as a vast, openly accessible library where users can search for known vulnerabilities affecting a wide range of software, operating systems, and network devices. Security researchers and ethical hackers rely on ExploitDB to find weaknesses in systems, while malicious actors may use it to identify potential attack vectors.

One of ExploitDB's key strengths is its well-structured and constantly updated database. Exploits are categorized by software name, Common Vulnerabilities and Exposures (CVE) ID, platform, and type, making it easy to locate relevant vulnerabilities. The repository contains thousands of exploits, ranging from simple DoS scripts to complex RCE payloads. Additionally, it includes privilege escalation techniques, SQL injection scripts, and local exploits that attackers can use to gain deeper access to a system.

The SearchSploit command-line tool, included in Kali Linux, provides an efficient way to query ExploitDB directly from the terminal. This feature is particularly useful for penetration testers working in an offline environment or on engagements where Internet access is restricted. By running a simple search command, security professionals can quickly retrieve exploits relevant to their target system and determine whether vulnerabilities exist that require patching.

ExploitDB is also a valuable educational tool for those studying cybersecurity. It offers insights into how vulnerabilities are discovered, how they can be exploited, and how defenses can be implemented. By analyzing exploit code, security teams can understand attack methodologies and proactively harden their systems against similar threats. For software developers, it serves as a reminder of common security pitfalls and the importance of secure coding practices.

Despite its benefits, ExploitDB presents some risks. Since it is an open database, anyone—including cybercriminals—can access it freely. Threat actors often use ExploitDB to find publicly available exploits for unpatched vulnerabilities, making it crucial for organizations to stay informed about newly disclosed security flaws. Regularly monitoring the database and applying patches promptly can help mitigate the risks associated with zero-day and publicly disclosed exploits.

ExploitDB is an essential resource for security professionals, researchers, and ethical hackers. It provides a transparent and organized repository of publicly disclosed exploits that can be used for both offensive security testing and defensive hardening. While it is a powerful tool for understanding vulnerabilities, its open-access nature highlights the ongoing challenge of cybersecurity—ensuring that knowledge is used for protection rather than exploitation.

Nmap

Nmap is one of the most powerful and widely used tools for network discovery, port scanning, and security auditing. Developed by Gordon Lyon (Fyodor) in 1997, it has since become an essential asset for penetration testers, system administrators, and security professionals looking to map networks, identify open ports, and assess vulnerabilities. Due to its versatility and efficiency, Nmap is often the first tool used in a cybersecurity assessment, forming the foundation for further exploitation or defense strategies.

Nmap functions as a network scanner, capable of detecting live hosts, discovering services, and determining operating systems running on target machines. It accomplishes this by sending packets to specified IP addresses and analyzing their responses. The tool is particularly useful for enumerating open ports and identifying services that may be vulnerable to exploitation. Whether scanning a single device or an entire corporate network, Nmap provides detailed insights into network configurations and potential security weaknesses.

One of Nmap's defining features is its extensive range of scanning techniques. It supports various scanning methods, including TCP connect scans, SYN (stealth) scans, UDP scans, and more advanced techniques such as fragmentation scanning and idle scanning. These options allow penetration testers to bypass firewalls, evade IDSs, and conduct stealthier reconnaissance. Additionally, Nmap can perform version detection, enabling users to determine the exact versions of services running on detected ports, which is critical for identifying outdated or vulnerable software.

Beyond basic scanning, Nmap is also equipped with the Nmap Scripting Engine (NSE), which enhances its functionality by allowing users to automate tasks and perform advanced security assessments. NSE scripts can be used for vulnerability detection, brute-force attacks, malware scanning, and even exploitation. The growing collection of scripts, contributed by the cybersecurity community, makes Nmap a highly adaptable tool for a wide range of security tasks.

While primarily a command-line tool, Nmap also offers a GUI known as Zenmap, which provides a more user-friendly experience for those unfamiliar with command-line operations. Zenmap allows users to visualize network topologies, manage scan results, and generate detailed reports, making it particularly useful for beginners or security teams that require organized documentation of their scans.

Not only is Nmap a tool for offensive security, but it also plays a crucial role in network defense. System administrators use it to audit their own networks, ensuring that unauthorized services are not exposed to the Internet. By regularly scanning their infrastructure, organizations can proactively close unnecessary ports, update vulnerable software, and strengthen firewall configurations to mitigate potential threats.

Despite its legitimate use, Nmap is often exploited by cybercriminals for reconnaissance before launching attacks. Hackers use it to identify weak points in a network, locate unpatched services, and gather intelligence for targeted intrusions. This dual-use nature means that organizations must understand not only how to use Nmap but also how to detect and respond to scans conducted against their own systems.

Nmap remains one of the most indispensable tools in cybersecurity. Its ability to perform fast, efficient, and comprehensive network scanning makes it a fundamental component of penetration testing and security auditing. Whether used for offensive or defensive purposes, mastering Nmap is essential for anyone involved in cybersecurity, as it provides critical insights into network security posture and potential vulnerabilities. As with any powerful tool, however, it must be used responsibly, ensuring that it serves as a means of protection rather than exploitation.

Angry IP Scanner

Angry IP Scanner is a popular open-source network-scanning tool known for its speed, simplicity, and ease of use. Designed for quickly scanning IP addresses and detecting active devices on a network, it is widely used by system administrators, penetration testers, and even cybercriminals for reconnaissance. Unlike more advanced tools, such as Nmap, which offer deep security analysis, Angry IP Scanner is focused on speed and efficiency, making it ideal for users who need quick network insights without complex configurations.

The primary function of Angry IP Scanner is to scan a range of IP addresses and identify which ones are online. It achieves this by sending ping requests to each IP and checking for a response. If a device replies, the tool can gather additional information, such as open ports, hostnames, MAC addresses, and even basic operating system detection. Users can customize the scan results by integrating fetchers, which allow additional data collection based on network responses.

One of the reasons for its popularity is its cross-platform compatibility. Angry IP Scanner is available for Windows, macOS, and Linux, and because it is written in Java, it can run on virtually any system that has the Java Runtime Environment (JRE). Additionally, it does not require installation, making it a portable tool that can be executed directly from a USB drive or external storage, which is useful for security professionals who need to perform on-the-go network scans.

Compared to more feature-rich scanners such as Nmap, Angry IP Scanner is designed to be lightweight and user-friendly. Its intuitive graphical interface allows even non-technical users to perform network scans with minimal effort. For advanced users, however, it also offers a command-line mode, enabling automated scans and integration into scripts for larger-scale network monitoring.

Although it is primarily used for legitimate network administration purposes, Angry IP Scanner is also frequently misused by hackers for reconnaissance. Cybercriminals use it to identify potential targets, scanning entire IP ranges to find active devices that may have open ports or weak security configurations. This makes it essential for network defenders to be aware of such tools and implement proper security measures, such as firewalls and IDSs, to detect and block unauthorized scans.

Despite its simplicity, Angry IP Scanner is an excellent tool for quick network discovery, especially when time is a factor. System administrators use it to troubleshoot network issues, identify unauthorized devices, and monitor network activity. Ethical hackers can integrate it into their penetration testing workflows to quickly map out targets before using more advanced tools for in-depth analysis.

Angry IP Scanner is a fast, portable, and easy-to-use network scanner that excels in speed and simplicity. While it lacks the deep security assessment features of tools such as Nmap, its efficiency makes it a valuable asset for both security professionals and IT administrators. As with all network-scanning tools, however, it must be used responsibly and within legal and ethical boundaries, as unauthorized scanning can be considered an attack in many environments. Organizations should remain vigilant by monitoring their networks for suspicious scanning activity and implementing strong security practices to mitigate potential threats.

Shodan

Shodan is a unique and powerful cybersecurity tool, often referred to as the "Google for hackers." Unlike traditional search engines that index Web pages, Shodan is designed to scan and index Internet-connected devices, including servers, webcams, industrial control systems (ICSs), databases, routers, IoT devices, and even unsecured security cameras. It provides detailed insights into exposed services and vulnerabilities, and so it is widely used by security researchers, penetration testers, system administrators, and, unfortunately, cybercriminals who seek to exploit misconfigured or unprotected systems.

Shodan works by continuously scanning the Internet for open ports and publicly accessible devices. It collects and categorizes information from these devices, such as IP addresses, banners, metadata, SSL certificates, and service versions. This allows users to search for specific technologies, manufacturers, or geographical locations to find exposed devices and assess their security posture. Unlike traditional vulnerability scanners such as Nmap and Metasploit, Shodan does not require users to perform active scans themselves; instead, they can simply search its database to find existing results, making reconnaissance much faster and more efficient.

One of Shodan's most critical applications is cybersecurity monitoring. Organizations can use it to audit their own infrastructure, identifying exposed services and ensuring that sensitive systems are not publicly accessible. IT administrators can track assets, detect unintended data leaks, and mitigate risks before attackers exploit them. Shodan's filtering capabilities allow users to narrow down results based on factors such as country, ISP, operating system, and device type, making it an essential tool for security assessments.

Shodan is particularly valuable in assessing the security of IoT devices, which are often poorly secured and left exposed to the Internet. Many IoT devices, such as smart cameras, industrial controllers, and even medical equipment, are deployed with default credentials or weak security settings, making them easy targets for cyberattacks. By searching for specific device types, security researchers can uncover large-scale vulnerabilities and push for better security practices among manufacturers and users.

Shodan is, however, also widely used by cybercriminals. Hackers leverage it to find unprotected servers, open databases, and remote access points (such as exposed RDP and SSH services) that they can exploit for attacks such as ransomware, botnet infections, and data breaches. Because it provides real-time intelligence on exposed infrastructure, it significantly reduces the effort required for attackers to identify weak targets. This dual-use nature highlights the ethical concerns surrounding tools such as Shodan—while it is an invaluable resource for security professionals, it also poses risks when used for malicious purposes.

To defend against threats posed by Shodan and similar tools, organizations should implement strong security measures, such as restricting access to critical services, enforcing authentication, disabling unnecessary ports, and using an IDS to monitor for suspicious activity. Security teams can also set up alerts on Shodan to notify them if their IP addresses or domains appear in search results, allowing them to address potential exposures before they are exploited.

Shodan is an incredibly powerful and versatile tool that provides unparalleled visibility into Internet-connected devices and their security status. While it is a vital resource for ethical hackers and security professionals, it is also a double-edged sword, often leveraged by cybercriminals to locate vulnerable systems. As the number of IoT and connected devices continues to grow, the importance of tools such as Shodan will only increase, making it essential for organizations to proactively monitor their Internet exposure and strengthen their cybersecurity defenses.

John the Ripper

John the Ripper is a highly versatile and powerful password-cracking tool that has earned its reputation as one of the most widely used and respected utilities in the field of cybersecurity. Developed by Openwall, John the Ripper is open-source software designed to detect weak passwords by performing brute-force attacks, dictionary attacks, and other password-cracking techniques. Its flexibility, efficiency, and extensive feature set make it an indispensable tool for security professionals, penetration testers, and system administrators.

One of the standout features of John the Ripper is its ability to work across multiple platforms. It is compatible with a wide range of operating systems, including Unix, Linux, macOS, and Windows, making it accessible to a broad user base. This cross-platform capability ensures that users can deploy the tool in diverse environments, whether they are auditing the security of a single system or conducting large-scale password audits across an entire network.

John the Ripper supports a vast array of password hash types, which is one of its most significant strengths. It can crack passwords encrypted with popular algorithms such as MD5, SHA-1, and bcrypt. Additionally, it can handle hashes from various applications and systems, including Unix/Linux shadow files, Windows LM and NTLM hashes, and even database passwords. This extensive support for different hash types makes John the Ripper a versatile tool that can be adapted to a wide range of scenarios.

The tool's performance is another area where it excels. John the Ripper is optimized for speed, leveraging advanced techniques such as single instruction, multiple data (SIMD) instructions and multi-threading to accelerate the cracking process. It also supports distributed computing, allowing users to harness the power of multiple machines to crack passwords more efficiently. This makes it particularly effective for tackling large and complex password lists.

John the Ripper's flexibility is further enhanced by its modular design. Users can extend its functionality by writing custom cracking modes or integrating external modules. This modularity allows security professionals to tailor the tool to their specific needs, whether they are conducting a simple dictionary attack or implementing a highly customized password-cracking strategy. The tool also includes a built-in scripting language, which enables users to automate tasks and create complex cracking routines.

One of the key advantages of John the Ripper is its active and supportive community. As an open-source project, it benefits from contributions by developers and security experts worldwide. This collaborative approach ensures that the tool is continuously updated with new features, improvements, and support for emerging hash types. The community also provides extensive documentation, tutorials, and forums where users can seek help and share knowledge.

Despite its many strengths, John the Ripper is not without its challenges. The tool requires a certain level of technical expertise to use effectively, particularly when dealing with advanced features or custom configurations. Beginners may find the learning curve steep, especially if they are unfamiliar with password-cracking techniques or CLIs. The availability of comprehensive documentation and community resources, however, helps mitigate this issue.

Another consideration is the ethical and legal implications of using John the Ripper. While it is a valuable tool for security professionals and system administrators, it can also be misused for malicious purposes. Users must ensure that they have proper authorization before conducting password audits or cracking attempts, as unauthorized use can lead to legal consequences.

John the Ripper is a robust and highly capable password-cracking tool that has stood the test of time. Its cross-platform compatibility, extensive hash support, and performance optimizations make it a go-to choice for security professionals. While it may require some technical expertise to master, its flexibility and active community support make it accessible to a wide range of users. When used responsibly and ethically, John the Ripper is an invaluable asset for enhancing the security of systems and networks.

Hashcat

Hashcat is a state-of-the-art password recovery tool that has established itself as one of the most powerful and efficient password-cracking utilities available today. Developed by Jens Steube, Hashcat is renowned for its speed, versatility, and advanced capabilities, making it a favorite among cybersecurity professionals, penetration testers, and ethical hackers. Unlike many other password-cracking tools, Hashcat is designed to leverage the full potential of modern hardware, including CPUs, graphics processing units (GPUs), and even specialized hardware such as field-programmable gate arrays (FPGAs) and application-specific integrated circuits (ASICs), to achieve unparalleled performance in cracking hashes.

One of Hashcat's most distinguishing features is its ability to harness the power of GPUs for password cracking. GPUs are inherently better suited for parallel processing tasks compared to CPUs, and Hashcat takes full advantage of this capability. By utilizing GPU acceleration, Hashcat can perform billions of hash calculations per second, significantly reducing the time required to crack complex passwords. This makes it particularly effective for brute-force attacks, dictionary attacks, and rule-based attacks, where speed is critical.

Hashcat supports an extensive range of hash types, making it one of the most versatile tools in its category. It can handle over 300 hashing algorithms, including common ones such as MD5, SHA-1, SHA-256, and bcrypt, as well as more obscure or proprietary hash types. Additionally, Hashcat is capable of cracking hashes from a wide variety of sources, such as operating systems (Windows, Linux, and macOS), databases, network protocols, and applications. This broad compatibility ensures that Hashcat can be used in a wide range of scenarios, from auditing password policies to recovering lost credentials.

The tool's flexibility is further enhanced by its support for multiple attack modes. Hashcat offers several attack strategies, including straight dictionary attacks, combinator attacks, mask attacks, hybrid attacks, and rule-based attacks. Each mode is designed to address specific cracking scenarios, allowing users to tailor their approach based on the complexity of the target hashes and the available resources. For example, rule-based attacks enable users to apply custom transformations to dictionary words, such as adding prefixes or suffixes or altering letter cases, which can significantly increase the chances of success.

Hashcat's performance is not limited to single-machine setups. It supports distributed cracking, allowing users to combine the computational power of multiple systems to accelerate the cracking process. This is particularly useful for large-scale password audits or when dealing with highly complex hashes. Additionally, Hashcat's integration with tools such as Hashtopolis enables users to manage distributed cracking networks efficiently, further enhancing its scalability.

Another notable feature of Hashcat is its user-friendly interface, despite being a command-line tool. While it may appear intimidating to beginners, Hashcat provides clear and detailed documentation, along with examples and tutorials, to help users get started. The tool also includes a built-in benchmarking feature, which allows users to test the performance of their hardware and optimize their cracking strategies accordingly. Over time, as users become more familiar with Hashcat's syntax and capabilities, they can unlock its full potential and leverage its advanced features.

Hashcat's active development and strong community support are also key factors contributing to its success. The tool is regularly updated with new features, performance improvements, and support for additional hash types. The Hashcat community is highly engaged, with forums, GitHub repositories, and social media channels where users can share knowledge, seek assistance, and collaborate on projects. This vibrant ecosystem ensures that Hashcat remains at the forefront of password-cracking technology.

Like any powerful tool, however, Hashcat comes with ethical and legal considerations. Its capabilities can be misused for malicious purposes, such as unauthorized access to systems or data breaches. Users must ensure they have proper authorization before conducting any password-cracking activities, as unauthorized use can lead to severe legal consequences. Responsible and ethical use of Hashcat is essential to maintain its reputation as a legitimate security tool.

Hashcat is a cutting-edge password recovery tool that combines speed, versatility, and advanced features to deliver exceptional performance. Its ability to leverage GPU acceleration, support for a wide range of hash types, and flexible attack modes make it an indispensable tool for security professionals. While it may require some initial effort to master, its comprehensive documentation and active community support make it accessible to users of all skill levels. When used responsibly, Hashcat is an invaluable asset for enhancing cybersecurity, auditing password policies, and recovering lost credentials.

Mimikatz

Mimikatz stands as one of the most influential and widely discussed tools in the realm of cybersecurity, renowned for its ability to extract sensitive credentials from Windows systems. Developed by Benjamin Delpy, this post-exploitation tool has become a cornerstone for both ethical hackers and malicious actors due to its unparalleled effectiveness in revealing plaintext passwords, hashes, and Kerberos tickets stored in memory. Its capabilities have made it a double-edged sword, celebrated by penetration testers for its utility in uncovering vulnerabilities and feared by defenders for its potential to facilitate devastating attacks. At its core, Mimikatz exploits the way Windows handles authentication, particularly through the Local Security Authority Subsystem Service (LSASS), which manages security policies and stores credentials in memory for single sign-on functionality. By targeting LSASS, Mimikatz can extract plaintext passwords, NTLM hashes, and Kerberos tickets, enabling attackers to perform pass-the-hash (PtH) or pass-the-ticket (PtT) attacks. These techniques allow adversaries to authenticate to other systems without needing the actual plaintext password, making lateral movement across networks significantly easier.

One of the most notorious features of Mimikatz is its ability to execute golden ticket and silver ticket attacks, which exploit weaknesses in the Kerberos authentication protocol. A golden ticket attack involves generating a valid Kerberos ticket-granting ticket (TGT) for any user, granting unrestricted access to the domain. A silver ticket, on the other hand, is a forged service ticket that provides access to specific services within the domain. These attacks are particularly devastating in Active Directory environments, as they can compromise the entire domain infrastructure, allowing attackers to escalate privileges and maintain persistence. Beyond credential extraction, Mimikatz includes modules for dumping certificates, manipulating Kerberos tickets, and bypassing security mechanisms such as Windows Defender Credential Guard. Its modular design allows users to load specific functionalities as needed, making it a highly versatile tool adaptable to various attack scenarios.

For ethical hackers and penetration testers, Mimikatz is an invaluable asset for assessing the security of Windows environments. By simulating real-world attacks, security professionals can identify vulnerabilities in credential management and authentication protocols. Mimikatz helps highlight weaknesses such as the storage of plaintext passwords in memory, the use of weak hashing algorithms, and insufficient protection against PtH attacks. Ethical hackers often use Mimikatz to demonstrate the potential impact of compromised credentials, showing how an attacker could move laterally across a network, escalate privileges, and gain access to critical systems. This information is crucial for organizations looking to improve their security posture and implement stronger defenses against credential-based attacks. The same capabilities that make Mimikatz a powerful tool for ethical hacking, however, also make it a favorite among malicious actors. Cybercriminals, APT groups, and ransomware operators have widely adopted Mimikatz due to its ability to extract credentials with minimal effort.

The accessibility of Mimikatz further contributes to its widespread use. As an open-source tool, it is readily available to anyone, including less technically skilled adversaries. Its effectiveness against default Windows configurations means that attackers can often exploit systems without needing to bypass advanced security measures. This ease of use, combined with its powerful capabilities, has cemented Mimikatz as a go-to tool for credential theft and lateral movement in cyberattacks. Defending against Mimikatz requires a multi-layered approach. Restricting access to the LSASS process is a critical first step, as it prevents tools such as Mimikatz from extracting credentials. Features such as Credential Guard, which isolates LSASS in a virtualized environment, can provide additional protection. Enabling Local Security Authority (LSA) protection is another effective mitigation, as it prevents unauthorized processes from accessing LSASS memory and requires administrative privileges to disable. Implementing the principle of least privilege is also essential, as it limits the impact of credential theft by ensuring users only have the permissions they need. Monitoring and detection play a crucial role in identifying suspicious activity, such as attempts to access LSASS or extract credentials. EDR solutions can help detect and respond to such activities, while regular monitoring and logging of authentication events can provide valuable insights into potential attacks. Patching and hardening systems are equally important, as they reduce the attack surface and mitigate the risk of credential-based attacks. Disabling outdated protocols such as NTLM and enforcing strong password policies can further enhance security.

The ethical use of Mimikatz cannot be overstated. Security professionals must ensure that they have proper authorization before using the tool in penetration tests or security assessments. Unauthorized use can lead to legal consequences and damage to systems or data. Organizations should also be transparent about their use of Mimikatz in security testing, clearly communicating the purpose and scope of assessments to build trust with stakeholders and ensure alignment with ethical and legal standards. Mimikatz is a tool that embodies both the challenges and opportunities in cybersecurity. Its ability to extract credentials and exploit authentication mechanisms makes it an essential tool for penetration testers and a significant threat in the hands of malicious actors. While its capabilities are impressive, they also highlight the importance of robust defenses and proactive security measures. By understanding how Mimikatz works and implementing appropriate mitigations, organizations can better protect themselves against credential theft and lateral movement. At the same time, ethical hackers and security professionals must use the tool responsibly, ensuring that their actions contribute to the overall goal of improving cybersecurity. In a world where credentials are often the keys to the kingdom, Mimikatz serves as both a reminder of the risks and a tool for strengthening defenses.

Aircrack-ng

Aircrack-ng is one of the most well-known and widely used tools for wireless network security auditing and penetration testing. It is an open-source suite of tools designed for assessing Wi-Fi network security by capturing packets, analyzing encryption weaknesses, and ultimately cracking WEP, WPA, and WPA2 security protocols. Its efficiency, versatility, and lightweight nature have made it an essential tool for cybersecurity professionals, ethical hackers, and network administrators.

One of the key strengths of Aircrack-ng is its ability to perform various attacks and tests on wireless networks. It includes utilities for monitoring network traffic, injecting packets, capturing handshakes, and launching deauthentication attacks. The suite is composed of multiple components, including

Airmon-ng, which is used to enable monitor mode on wireless interfaces; Airodump-ng, which is responsible for packet capture and network scanning; Aireplay-ng, which allows packet injection and replay attacks; and Aircrack-ng itself, which is responsible for cracking encryption keys.

A significant advantage of Aircrack-ng is its compatibility with various wireless adapters and its support for multiple operating systems, including Linux, Windows, and macOS. It is, however, most commonly used on Linux distributions such as Kali Linux, which comes with the tool pre-installed. The software's efficiency in key cracking depends heavily on the quality of the captured packets and the attack methodology. When dealing with WEP encryption, the tool can exploit vulnerabilities in the RC4 cipher to recover the key quickly. WPA/WPA2 encryption, however, requires a dictionary or brute-force attack on the captured handshake, making it a more time-intensive process unless the password is weak.

Another strong point of Aircrack-ng is its ability to perform real-time decryption and inject packets to accelerate the cracking process. This feature is particularly useful for ethical hackers and penetration testers conducting security assessments on wireless networks. The tool also supports GPU-based acceleration using CUDA and OpenCL, allowing for much faster password cracking when run on compatible hardware.

Despite its strengths, Aircrack-ng is not without its limitations. The effectiveness of password cracking depends on the complexity of the target network's security. Strong WPA2 passwords with long and complex passphrases are virtually impossible to crack without a precomputed wordlist or a significant amount of computational power. Moreover, the success of deauthentication and packet injection attacks depends on the capabilities of the wireless network card in use, as not all adapters support monitor mode and packet injection.

The tool requires a solid understanding of wireless networking and security concepts, making it less suitable for absolute beginners. Users must be familiar with command-line operations and have a working knowledge of network protocols to fully utilize the suite. The legality of using Aircrack-ng is another crucial consideration; while it is a powerful security auditing tool, unauthorized use to compromise networks is illegal in most jurisdictions.

Aircrack-ng remains a cornerstone of wireless network security testing. Its comprehensive suite of tools, flexibility, and high efficiency in exploiting Wi-Fi vulnerabilities make it a preferred choice among cybersecurity professionals.

While it does have some limitations related to hardware compatibility and the difficulty of cracking strong passwords, it is an indispensable tool for those seeking to evaluate and strengthen wireless network security.

Wireshark

Wireshark is one of the most powerful and widely used network protocol analyzers available today. It is an open-source tool that allows users to capture, inspect, and analyze network traffic in real time, making it an essential asset for network administrators, cybersecurity professionals, and forensic analysts. With its deep packet inspection capabilities and user-friendly graphical interface, Wireshark provides unparalleled visibility into network activity, enabling users to diagnose performance issues, detect security threats, and troubleshoot connectivity problems.

One of the standout features of Wireshark is its ability to capture network traffic from a wide range of network interfaces, including Ethernet, Wi-Fi, and Bluetooth. It supports hundreds of network protocols, from standard ones such as TCP, UDP, and HTTP to more complex protocols such as SIP, RTP, and TLS. The ability to dissect and analyze packets down to the smallest details makes Wireshark an indispensable tool for network troubleshooting. Users can examine packet headers, follow TCP streams, and identify anomalies that could indicate misconfigurations or security breaches.

Wireshark's powerful filtering capabilities are another major advantage. The software allows users to apply display filters to isolate specific types of traffic based on criteria such as IP addresses, ports, protocols, or payload contents. This makes it easier to focus on relevant data rather than sifting through massive volumes of captured packets. Additionally, Wireshark supports Berkeley Packet Filter (BPF) syntax for more precise capture filtering, allowing users to collect only the traffic they need.

Another key strength of Wireshark is its extensive customization and extensibility. Users can write their own dissectors for proprietary protocols, extend functionality with Lua scripting, and integrate it with other network analysis tools. This flexibility makes Wireshark adaptable to various use cases, from routine network diagnostics to in-depth forensic investigations. The ability to export capture files in multiple formats, including PCAP and JSON, ensures compatibility with other security and analysis tools.

Despite its many strengths, Wireshark does have some limitations. One of the biggest challenges is that it requires a strong understanding of networking concepts to be used effectively. While the interface is user-friendly, interpreting packet data correctly demands knowledge of protocols, network structures, and security principles. Beginners may find the sheer volume of captured data overwhelming, especially in high-traffic environments. Wireshark, however, offers extensive documentation and community support, helping users overcome the learning curve.

Another limitation is its reliance on promiscuous mode or monitor mode for capturing packets. On some systems, particularly Windows, certain network interfaces do not support these modes fully, restricting Wireshark's ability to capture all network traffic. Additionally, encrypted traffic, such as HTTPS or VPN traffic, cannot be easily analyzed without access to the encryption keys, limiting the tool's effectiveness for inspecting secure communications.

From a security standpoint, Wireshark should be used with caution. Since it captures all network traffic passing through an interface, it can expose sensitive data, such as passwords and authentication tokens, if proper precautions are not taken. This makes it a double-edged sword—while invaluable for security professionals, it can also be misused for malicious purposes. Organizations need to enforce strict access controls to ensure that only authorized personnel can use Wireshark for legitimate network analysis.

Wireshark remains the gold standard for network traffic analysis. Its depth of packet inspection, robust filtering capabilities, and extensive protocol support make it an essential tool for network troubleshooting, security analysis, and forensic investigations. While it does have a learning curve and requires proper hardware and permissions for full functionality, its benefits far outweigh its limitations. Whether used for optimizing network performance or investigating cyber threats, Wireshark continues to be an indispensable tool for IT professionals.

Reaver

Reaver is a specialized open-source tool designed to exploit a vulnerability in Wi-Fi Protected Setup (WPS), a feature found in many wireless routers. WPS was originally intended to simplify the process of connecting devices to a Wi-Fi network by allowing users to enter an eight-digit PIN instead of a full WPA/WPA2 passphrase. Reaver, however, takes advantage of a fundamental flaw in the WPS protocol, enabling attackers to recover the PIN and ultimately obtain the network's WPA/WPA2 password. Due to its effectiveness,

Reaver has been widely used by security researchers and penetration testers to assess the security of wireless networks.

One of the most significant advantages of Reaver is its ability to perform an offline brute-force attack against WPS-enabled routers without requiring an extensive wordlist or computational power. Instead of attacking WPA encryption directly, which can be time-consuming and resource-intensive, Reaver targets the WPS PIN, which has a much smaller keyspace and can often be cracked in a matter of hours. The attack works by systematically trying different PIN combinations, exploiting the fact that WPS authentication can be broken down into two separate four-digit segments, significantly reducing the total number of possible PINs.

Reaver is relatively easy to use, especially for those familiar with wireless security tools. It is typically run from a Linux-based system, such as Kali Linux, and requires a compatible wireless network adapter that supports monitor mode and packet injection. Once the tool is set up, it can scan for WPS-enabled networks and begin the brute-force attack automatically. Additionally, Reaver provides detailed output during the attack process, allowing users to track progress and identify whether the target router is vulnerable.

Despite its effectiveness, Reaver has several limitations. One of the primary challenges is that many modern routers have implemented security measures to mitigate WPS brute-force attacks. For example, some routers introduce lockout mechanisms that temporarily or permanently disable WPS after multiple incorrect PIN attempts. This significantly increases the time required to crack the PIN or renders the attack infeasible. Additionally, some manufacturers have completely removed WPS from their devices or implemented stronger protections, making Reaver ineffective against certain routers.

Another limitation is that Reaver requires a stable and strong Wi-Fi signal to function efficiently. Weak or unstable connections can result in increased packet loss, slowing down the attack or causing it to fail altogether. Furthermore, while Reaver can be an effective tool for security testing, it does not work against networks that have WPS disabled. Since many security-conscious users and organizations now disable WPS by default, the scope of Reaver's effectiveness is gradually shrinking.

From an ethical and legal standpoint, using Reaver without authorization is illegal in most jurisdictions, as it is explicitly designed to compromise network security. For ethical hackers, penetration testers, and security researchers, however, Reaver remains a valuable tool for identifying and addressing vulnerabilities in wireless networks. It serves as a critical reminder of the dangers of WPS and the importance of disabling it on routers to prevent unauthorized access.

Reaver is a powerful but increasingly limited tool for Wi-Fi security testing. Its ability to crack WPS PINs efficiently makes it a useful asset for penetration testers, but the growing adoption of security countermeasures has reduced its effectiveness. While it remains relevant for assessing older or misconfigured networks, its overall usefulness is diminishing as more routers implement WPS protections or disable the feature entirely. Nonetheless, it underscores the importance of keeping wireless networks secure and reinforces the necessity of disabling WPS to prevent potential attacks.

Empire

Empire is a post-exploitation framework designed for penetration testing, offering a powerful and modular approach to executing and managing attacks on compromised systems. Initially developed as PowerShell Empire, it provided a pure PowerShell agent-based post-exploitation environment, allowing attackers and security professionals to execute commands, escalate privileges, exfiltrate data, and maintain persistence on target machines. Over time, as security defenses improved and PowerShell became increasingly monitored in enterprise environments, the framework evolved to include Python-based agents and other evasion techniques, making it more versatile.

One of the biggest advantages of Empire is its modularity. The framework comes with a wide range of built-in modules for privilege escalation, credential dumping, keylogging, lateral movement, and persistence, among others. Users can easily deploy and manage multiple agents on compromised machines, execute scripts, and automate tasks through its C2 infrastructure. The framework's interactive console makes it easy to track active sessions, interact with infected hosts, and execute commands remotely. Additionally, it supports encrypted communications, ensuring that the command traffic between the attacker and compromised machines remains stealthy.

Empire's effectiveness is largely due to its ability to evade traditional security defenses. Since it heavily leverages in-memory execution, it avoids writing malicious files to disk, reducing the likelihood of being detected by traditional antivirus solutions. Moreover, its ability to use obfuscated PowerShell scripts and bypass application whitelisting makes it particularly effective in environments where PowerShell logging and monitoring are not properly configured.

As security tools have improved, newer versions of Empire have incorporated additional obfuscation and execution techniques to bypass EDR solutions.

Empire has several limitations, however. One of the biggest challenges is that modern security solutions have become increasingly adept at detecting and mitigating PowerShell-based attacks. Many enterprise environments now enforce strict PowerShell execution policies, enable logging and monitoring, and deploy endpoint protection tools that can flag or block Empire's activities. As a result, attackers must often combine Empire with additional techniques or frameworks to remain undetected.

Another limitation is that, because Empire is a post-exploitation framework, it requires an initial foothold on the target system. Unlike tools designed for initial compromise, such as phishing frameworks and exploit kits, Empire is primarily focused on what happens after access has been gained. This means it is typically used in conjunction with other tools, such as Metasploit or Cobalt Strike, to complete a full attack chain.

The legality and ethical implications of using Empire also cannot be ignored. While it is a powerful tool for security professionals and penetration testers, it has been widely adopted by malicious actors for cybercrime and espionage. As a result, security researchers using Empire in authorized engagements must ensure that they have explicit permission and adhere to ethical guidelines.

Empire is a highly effective and flexible post-exploitation framework for security professionals engaged in penetration testing. Its modular design, obfuscation capabilities, and C2 infrastructure make it a valuable tool for testing enterprise security defenses. The increasing awareness and detection of PowerShell-based threats, along with improved security measures, however, have made it more challenging to use successfully in modern environments. As cybersecurity evolves, Empire continues to be updated with new evasion techniques, but organizations must remain vigilant by implementing strong security monitoring, endpoint protection, and PowerShell restrictions to mitigate its effectiveness.

Social-Engineer Toolkit

The Social-Engineer Toolkit (SET) is a powerful open-source framework designed for penetration testers and security professionals to simulate social engineering attacks. Developed by Dave Kennedy, SET is widely used to test human vulnerabilities in cybersecurity, highlighting the fact that people—not just technology—are often the weakest link in security defenses. The tool is designed to automate various social engineering techniques, making it a valuable asset for ethical hackers conducting security assessments.

One of the standout features of SET is its extensive range of attack vectors. The toolkit includes modules for phishing attacks, credential harvesting, payload generation, and even SMS-based social engineering. One of the most commonly used functions is the spear-phishing module, which allows attackers to craft highly targeted emails with malicious attachments or links. By leveraging real-world phishing tactics, security professionals can assess how susceptible an organization is to email-based threats.

Another significant aspect of SET is its ability to clone Web sites to capture user credentials. Using the credential harvester module, attackers can create fake login pages that mimic legitimate Web sites. When unsuspecting users enter their credentials, SET captures the information in real time. This technique is particularly effective when combined with phishing campaigns, as it exploits user trust in familiar-looking Web sites.

SET also includes a Metasploit integration, allowing for the seamless deployment of exploits and payloads. Users can generate malicious payloads, such as backdoors and reverse shells, to test endpoint security and user awareness. Additionally, the toolkit supports the use of USB and SD card attacks, enabling attackers to create infected media devices that execute malicious code when inserted into a target system.

One of SET's more advanced features is its ability to conduct wireless access point attacks. This technique involves setting up rogue Wi-Fi networks that mimic legitimate networks in order to capture authentication details from unsuspecting users. This is particularly effective in environments where users frequently connect to public Wi-Fi without verifying its authenticity.

Despite its effectiveness, SET has several limitations. One of the biggest challenges is that modern security awareness training and phishing detection tools have made social engineering attacks more difficult to execute successfully. Many organizations now use email filtering, MFA, and user training programs to reduce the effectiveness of phishing campaigns. Additionally, browser security improvements, such as HTTPS enforcement and built-in phishing detection, make credential-harvesting attacks more challenging.

Another limitation is the ethical and legal considerations surrounding SET. While it is a legitimate tool for penetration testing, social engineering attacks involve direct interaction with human targets, making them riskier from a legal and ethical standpoint. Unauthorized use of SET can lead to serious legal consequences, and even authorized operations must be carefully planned to avoid unintended harm.

SET requires a good understanding of social engineering principles and attack methodologies to be used effectively. While the tool automates many attack techniques, success depends largely on how well crafted the attack is. Simply using SET without proper reconnaissance and social engineering expertise may result in ineffective campaigns.

SET remains one of the most powerful tools for testing human security vulnerabilities. Its wide range of attack modules, phishing capabilities, and Metasploit integration make it an essential tool for penetration testers. Its effectiveness is, however, increasingly challenged by improved security awareness and technical defenses. Ethical and legal considerations also play a crucial role in how SET is used, requiring responsible deployment in controlled environments. Despite these challenges, SET continues to be a critical tool for evaluating and improving an organization's security posture by addressing the human factor in cybersecurity.

Evilginx

Evilginx is a powerful and widely used phishing framework designed for AITM attacks, allowing attackers and security professionals to bypass MFA and capture user credentials and session cookies. Unlike traditional phishing tools that rely solely on credential harvesting, Evilginx takes a more advanced approach by acting as a reverse proxy between the target user and the legitimate Web site. This enables it to intercept login credentials, authentication tokens, and session cookies in real time, effectively bypassing security mechanisms such as MFA.

One of the most significant advantages of Evilginx is its ability to conduct MITM phishing attacks without requiring malware or keyloggers. Instead of presenting a static phishing page that simply captures credentials, Evilginx proxies real-time Web traffic between the victim and the legitimate Web site, creating a highly convincing attack scenario. When a victim enters their login information, Evilginx captures not only the username and password but also the authentication token, which can be used to hijack the session without needing the MFA code.

The framework is highly customizable and supports phishlets, which are configurations that define how Evilginx interacts with different target Web sites. Users can create or modify phishlets to target specific services such as Google, Microsoft, Facebook, and banking platforms. Since the tool proxies traffic directly from the real Web site, victims see the legitimate site's content, making detection much harder. The use of HTTPS encryption with valid SSL/TLS certificates further adds to the illusion of legitimacy, as victims are less likely to recognize that they are being attacked.

Another major advantage of Evilginx is its stealth and effectiveness against modern authentication methods. Because it captures session cookies instead of relying solely on stolen passwords, it can bypass MFA solutions such as SMS-based codes, authenticator apps, and push notifications. Once an attacker obtains a session cookie, they can impersonate the victim without triggering additional authentication challenges, as long as the session remains active.

Despite its strengths, Evilginx has some limitations. One of the biggest challenges is that modern security measures are increasingly detecting and mitigating AITM attacks. Many Web services now implement additional security mechanisms, such as detecting unusual session activity, requiring reauthentication for high-risk logins, and enforcing short-lived session cookies that become invalid after a short period. These countermeasures reduce the window of opportunity for attackers using Evilginx.

Another limitation is that deploying Evilginx requires significant technical expertise. Setting up a working Evilginx server involves configuring domain names, obtaining SSL certificates, and fine-tuning phishlets to ensure seamless proxying. Security teams and penetration testers must also be cautious when using the tool, as its effectiveness depends on properly replicating the target Web site's behavior without triggering security flags.

From an ethical and legal perspective, Evilginx is a double-edged sword. While it is a legitimate security testing tool for penetration testing, it has been widely adopted by cybercriminals for credential theft and account hijacking. Unauthorized use of Evilginx to conduct phishing attacks is illegal in most jurisdictions and can result in severe legal consequences. Ethical security professionals must obtain explicit authorization before using Evilginx in penetration tests, ensuring that their assessments comply with legal and ethical guidelines.

Evilginx is one of the most effective tools for modern phishing attacks, particularly when bypassing MFA. Its ability to intercept real-time authentication sessions makes it a valuable tool for security researchers testing enterprise defenses. Its increasing detection by security systems, the technical complexity of setting it up, and the ethical considerations surrounding its use, however, make it a tool that must be handled responsibly. As cybersecurity defenses continue to evolve, organizations must implement robust monitoring, session hijacking detection, and additional authentication mechanisms, such as FIDO2-based security keys, to mitigate the risks posed by AITM phishing attacks.

Low Orbit Ion Cannon

Low Orbit Ion Cannon (LOIC) is an open-source network stress testing and DoS tool that gained notoriety due to its use in large-scale cyberattacks. Originally developed for network administrators to test server robustness and bandwidth capacity, LOIC was later adopted by hacktivist groups such as Anonymous for conducting distributed denial-of-service (DDoS) attacks. The tool is designed to generate massive amounts of network traffic, overwhelming a target server or Web site, effectively rendering it unreachable.

One of LOIC's defining characteristics is its ease of use. Unlike more sophisticated DDoS tools that require advanced configuration, LOIC features a simple GUI that allows users to launch an attack with minimal effort. Users can enter the target's IP address or URL, select an attack method (TCP, UDP, or HTTP flood), set the attack intensity, and begin flooding the target with traffic. This simplicity makes LOIC accessible even to individuals with little to no technical expertise, contributing to its widespread use in hacktivist campaigns.

Another key feature of LOIC is its ability to generate high volumes of traffic. By sending a rapid series of connection requests or data packets to a target system, LOIC consumes the server's resources and bandwidth, ultimately degrading performance or causing complete downtime. The tool supports multiple attack modes, including TCP flood, which overloads a target with TCP connection requests; UDP flood, which sends massive amounts of UDP packets; and HTTP flood, which repeatedly requests Web pages from a target server, exhausting its processing capacity.

Despite its effectiveness in launching volumetric attacks, LOIC has several major limitations. One of the most critical drawbacks is that it does not provide anonymity. Unlike more advanced DDoS tools that route traffic through proxy networks or botnets, LOIC sends attack traffic directly from the user's IP address. This makes it easy for security teams, law enforcement, and ISPs to trace the attack back to its origin. Many individuals who participated in LOIC-driven attacks have been identified and arrested due to this lack of anonymity.

Another limitation is that modern security defenses have significantly reduced LOIC's impact. Many organizations now deploy DDoS mitigation solutions, such as rate limiting, traffic filtering, and Web application firewalls (WAFs), which can detect and block LOIC-generated traffic. Additionally, content delivery networks (CDNs) and cloud-based anti-DDoS services automatically absorb and distribute attack traffic, reducing the likelihood of successful service disruption.

A key factor limiting LOIC's effectiveness in large-scale attacks is that it does not operate as a botnet. Unlike botnet-driven DDoS tools, which use thousands or millions of infected devices to generate distributed attack traffic, LOIC relies on individual users manually launching attacks from their own systems. To amplify attacks, users often participate in voluntary botnets, such as the "HiveMind" mode, which allows LOIC instances to be controlled remotely by a single operator. This approach still, however, requires a large number of participants to be effective, making it less powerful than botnet-driven DDoS campaigns.

From an ethical and legal perspective, LOIC is highly controversial. While it was originally intended for legitimate network testing, its widespread use in cyberattacks has made it synonymous with hacktivism and illegal activities. In most jurisdictions, using LOIC to attack a Web site or server without authorization is illegal and can result in severe legal consequences, including fines and imprisonment. Even participating in a LOIC-driven DDoS attack as part of a hacktivist movement can lead to prosecution, as authorities can easily trace the source of attack traffic.

LOIC is one of the most well-known DDoS tools, but its effectiveness has diminished due to modern security countermeasures and its lack of anonymity. While it is still used for stress testing and educational purposes, its association with hacktivist attacks has made it a controversial tool. Organizations seeking to protect themselves from LOIC-style attacks should implement DDoS mitigation strategies, traffic filtering, and network monitoring to detect and neutralize threats. For security professionals and ethical hackers, LOIC serves as a reminder of the importance of responsible cybersecurity testing and the legal risks associated with unauthorized use.

Mirai Botnet

Mirai Botnet is one of the most infamous and destructive botnets in cybersecurity history, known for hijacking IoT devices to launch massive DDoS attacks. Originally developed in 2016 by three hackers, Mirai was designed to infect vulnerable IoT devices, including routers, IP cameras, and digital video recorders (DVRs), turning them into remotely controlled “zombies” that could be used to overwhelm targeted networks with traffic. The botnet’s code was later leaked online, leading to the emergence of multiple Mirai variants and widespread adoption by cybercriminals.

One of the key characteristics of Mirai is its ability to automate the process of discovering and infecting vulnerable IoT devices. It does this by scanning the Internet for devices that use default or weak credentials, such as factory-set usernames and passwords. Once a device is compromised, Mirai installs itself and blocks remote administrative access to prevent other malware from taking control. This self-propagating nature allows the botnet to grow rapidly, infecting thousands or even millions of devices within a short period.

Mirai is particularly dangerous because it exploits the inherent security weaknesses of IoT devices. Many IoT manufacturers prioritize ease of use over security, shipping products with hardcoded credentials and minimal authentication protections. Because IoT devices often lack robust security updates, Mirai can remain on infected devices indefinitely, unless they are manually reset or patched. Furthermore, since these devices are always connected to the Internet, Mirai botnets have a continuous source of attack power, making them highly effective for sustained DDoS campaigns.

Despite its power, Mirai has several limitations. The original version of the botnet was designed primarily for volumetric DDoS attacks, meaning it floods a target with a high volume of traffic rather than exploiting application-layer vulnerabilities. While this makes it highly effective against unprotected networks, modern DDoS mitigation services such as Cloudflare and Akamai can absorb and filter out much of Mirai’s attack traffic. Additionally, once the Mirai source code was made public, cybersecurity researchers developed countermeasures to detect and neutralize infections more effectively.

Another limitation is that Mirai only targets devices running Linux-based operating systems, particularly those using BusyBox. While this still encompasses a significant portion of IoT devices, it excludes many modern cloud-based services and enterprise-grade infrastructure. Additionally, many ISPs and device manufacturers have taken steps to mitigate Mirai infections by enforcing stronger default security measures, requiring password changes, and deploying firmware updates.

From a legal and ethical standpoint, Mirai's use is entirely illegal unless employed for authorized security research in a controlled environment. The botnet has been leveraged by various cybercriminal groups for ransom denial-of-service (RDoS) campaigns, extortion schemes, and cyber warfare. The original creators of Mirai were eventually caught and sentenced, but since the code was leaked, numerous modified variants continue to circulate, leading to ongoing threats against IoT infrastructure.

Mirai Botnet is one of the most significant cybersecurity threats linked to IoT security weaknesses. Its ability to infect a vast number of vulnerable devices and launch high-volume DDoS attacks has made it a favorite tool among cybercriminals. Modern DDoS mitigation techniques, increased IoT security awareness, and improved manufacturer security practices, however, have helped reduce its overall effectiveness. Nonetheless, as long as insecure IoT devices exist, Mirai and its successors will continue to pose a threat, emphasizing the urgent need for stronger IoT security policies, mandatory firmware updates, and better authentication mechanisms to prevent future botnet-driven attacks.

IDA Pro

Interactive Disassembler (IDA) Pro is one of the most powerful and widely used tools for reverse engineering, malware analysis, and binary disassembly. Developed by Hex-Rays, IDA Pro is an advanced disassembler and debugger that allows security researchers, analysts, and software developers to deconstruct compiled programs, understand their inner workings, and identify vulnerabilities or malicious behavior. It is particularly valuable for reverse engineering closed-source applications, analyzing malware, and performing security audits.

One of IDA Pro's key strengths is its ability to disassemble machine code into human-readable assembly language. When a program is compiled, its source code is transformed into low-level instructions that are difficult to interpret. IDA Pro takes this compiled binary and translates it into assembly language, allowing analysts to reconstruct the logic of the original program.

This is crucial for understanding how a program functions, especially when dealing with malware, obfuscated binaries, or proprietary software without access to source code.

IDA Pro stands out from other disassemblers because of its interactive and dynamic analysis features. Unlike basic static disassemblers, IDA Pro allows users to annotate code, rename functions and variables, add comments, and track execution flow. This makes the process of reverse engineering more structured and manageable. Additionally, IDA Pro features a built-in graphing system that visually represents function calls and code execution paths, making it easier to navigate complex binaries.

Another major advantage of IDA Pro is its support for multiple architectures and platforms. It can analyze binaries compiled for a variety of processor architectures, including x86, x64, ARM, MIPS, and PowerPC, making it extremely versatile. Whether analyzing Windows executables, Linux ELF files, macOS binaries, or embedded system firmware, IDA Pro provides a comprehensive platform for reverse engineering across different systems.

IDA Pro also includes an integrated debugger, which allows for dynamic analysis in addition to static disassembly. The debugger enables researchers to step through code, set breakpoints, inspect memory, and analyze how a program behaves at runtime. This is particularly useful for malware analysis, as it helps identify how malicious software executes, which system calls it makes, and how it interacts with the operating system. The debugger supports both local and remote debugging, meaning analysts can debug applications running on different machines or even on embedded devices.

One of the most powerful extensions of IDA Pro is the Hex-Rays decompiler, which converts assembly code into a higher-level pseudocode representation that resembles C. This feature makes reverse engineering much easier, as analysts can interpret the code more quickly than working directly with assembly instructions. The decompiler significantly reduces the complexity of reverse engineering by reconstructing functions, loops, and conditional statements in a more readable format.

Despite its many strengths, IDA Pro has several limitations. One of the biggest drawbacks is its high cost. IDA Pro is a commercial tool, and its full version with the Hex-Rays decompiler is expensive, making it inaccessible for many independent researchers and smaller organizations. While a free version (IDA Free) exists, it is limited in functionality, lacks advanced features, and does not support modern architectures such as x64.

Another limitation is that IDA Pro requires significant expertise to use effectively. Reverse engineering is a complex discipline, and while IDA Pro provides powerful features, it does not automate the process of understanding a binary. Analysts need deep knowledge of assembly language, operating systems, and program execution to make full use of the tool. The steep learning curve means that beginners may struggle to leverage IDA Pro's full capabilities.

Additionally, while IDA Pro is a static analysis tool, it is not always effective against obfuscated or heavily protected binaries. Many modern software applications and malware use anti-analysis techniques, such as encrypted code sections, self-modifying code, or virtual machine–based obfuscation, which can make disassembly difficult. While IDA Pro can still analyze these binaries, additional tools such as dynamic instrumentation frameworks (e.g., Frida or DynamoRIO) or specialized unpackers may be required.

From a legal and ethical standpoint, IDA Pro is a legitimate tool used by security professionals for vulnerability research, malware analysis, and forensic investigations. It is, however, also widely used by cybercriminals, software pirates, and exploit developers to analyze software protections, reverse-engineer copy protection mechanisms, and develop software exploits. Because of this, some companies implement anti-reverse engineering techniques to deter IDA Pro analysis, such as code encryption, obfuscation, and runtime checks to detect when a program is being analyzed.

IDA Pro is one of the most powerful tools for reverse engineering and binary analysis, offering advanced disassembly, debugging, and decompilation capabilities. Its support for multiple architectures, interactive features, and the Hex-Rays decompiler make it an essential tool for malware analysts, security researchers, and vulnerability hunters. Its high cost, steep learning curve, and challenges with obfuscated binaries, however, are notable drawbacks. Despite these limitations, IDA Pro remains an industry-standard tool, and for those who can afford and master it, it provides unmatched capabilities in reverse engineering and cybersecurity research.

Ghidra

Ghidra is a powerful open-source reverse-engineering tool developed by the U.S's NSA and publicly released in 2019. It is designed to assist security researchers, malware analysts, and software developers in decompiling and analyzing binaries, making it a direct competitor to IDA Pro. Since its release,

Ghidra has gained widespread adoption due to its feature-rich environment, extensibility, and cost-free availability.

One of Ghidra's key strengths is its advanced disassembly and decompilation capabilities. It allows users to analyze binaries compiled for various architectures, including x86, x64, ARM, MIPS, PowerPC, and even specialized embedded systems. The tool takes raw machine code and translates it into human-readable assembly language, helping analysts understand the behavior of compiled programs. Additionally, Ghidra includes a powerful decompiler that converts assembly into a C-like pseudocode representation, making reverse engineering significantly easier by allowing users to reconstruct program logic more quickly.

Unlike traditional command-line disassemblers, Ghidra features a modern GUI that streamlines the reverse-engineering process. It provides a modular workspace, where users can interactively rename variables, add comments, analyze function flow, and apply custom scripts to enhance analysis. Ghidra also offers a graph-based function call analysis, similar to IDA Pro, which visually maps relationships between functions, making it easier to track execution paths.

One of Ghidra's most unique and powerful features is its collaborative reverse-engineering support. Unlike IDA Pro, which primarily operates as a standalone tool, Ghidra includes built-in multi-user functionality that allows teams of analysts to work on the same binary simultaneously. This is particularly useful for large-scale malware analysis or vulnerability research projects where multiple people need to share findings in real time.

Another major advantage of Ghidra is its extensibility. Since it is open source, users can modify its code, add plugins, and develop custom scripts to extend its functionality. Ghidra supports scripting in Python and Java, enabling researchers to automate repetitive tasks, integrate additional analysis techniques, and improve workflow efficiency. This level of customization is a significant advantage over proprietary tools such as IDA Pro, which restrict modifications unless additional paid licenses are obtained.

Ghidra also includes a built-in debugger, though it is not as mature as those found in IDA Pro or dedicated debugging tools such as GDB or WinDbg. Initially, Ghidra did not include native debugging support, but recent updates have introduced debugging capabilities that allow users to step through code, set breakpoints, and inspect memory at runtime. While still evolving, this feature enhances Ghidra's usefulness for analyzing live processes and tracking malware execution behavior.

Despite its strengths, Ghidra does have some limitations. One notable drawback is that its decompiler, while powerful, is not as refined as IDA Pro's Hex-Rays decompiler. In some cases, Ghidra may produce less accurate or more fragmented pseudocode, requiring additional manual effort to interpret. This gap, however, is closing as Ghidra continues to be updated and improved by the open-source community.

Another limitation is that Ghidra requires significant system resources, particularly for large binaries. The software is written in Java, which can lead to higher memory usage and occasional performance issues compared to IDA Pro, which is optimized for performance. While modern hardware can mitigate these concerns, users working with massive firmware images or complex executables may experience slower analysis times.

Security concerns have also been raised regarding Ghidra's origins as an NSA-developed tool. Some users initially speculated that it might contain backdoors or hidden telemetry, though extensive community scrutiny has not found any such issues. Since the source code is publicly available, security researchers can audit it to verify its integrity, making it a trustworthy option for most reverse-engineering tasks.

From an ethical and legal perspective, Ghidra is a legitimate and widely accepted tool for security research, malware analysis, and vulnerability discovery. Its release has significantly democratized access to advanced reverse-engineering tools, making high-quality binary analysis accessible to individuals and organizations that previously could not afford expensive proprietary software such as IDA Pro. Like any reverse-engineering tool, however, it can be misused for software piracy, exploit development, or cybercrime, which raises concerns about its potential abuse.

Ghidra is a game-changer in the world of reverse engineering, offering a powerful and free alternative to proprietary tools. Its disassembly, decompilation, collaboration features, and extensibility make it an invaluable resource for security researchers, especially those working in malware analysis and vulnerability research. While it still has room for improvement, particularly in debugging and decompilation accuracy, its open-source nature ensures continuous development and improvement by the global cybersecurity community. For anyone involved in reverse engineering, Ghidra is an essential tool that rivals commercial alternatives while being completely free and highly customizable.

OllyDbg

OllyDbg stands as a remarkable and enduring tool in the realm of debugging and reverse engineering, particularly for Windows applications. Its creation by Oleh Yuschuk in 2001 marked the beginning of a new era for software analysis, offering a level of accessibility and power that was previously unmatched. Over the years, OllyDbg has cemented its place as a go-to resource for developers, security researchers, and reverse engineers, thanks to its intuitive design, comprehensive feature set, and adaptability. Despite the lack of updates since 2013, its continued relevance is a testament to its effectiveness and the strong community that supports it.

The user interface of OllyDbg is one of its most praised aspects, designed with both simplicity and functionality in mind. The layout is clean and organized, featuring multiple panes that display essential information such as disassembled code, registers, the stack, memory dumps, and breakpoints. This multi-pane approach allows users to monitor and interact with a program's execution in real time, providing a clear and detailed view of its inner workings. The interface is highly customizable, enabling users to adjust the layout and appearance to suit their preferences. Context menus and keyboard shortcuts further enhance usability, making common tasks quicker and more efficient. This thoughtful design ensures that OllyDbg is accessible to beginners while remaining powerful enough for advanced users.

OllyDbg is a feature-rich debugger that excels in providing deep insights into binary code. Its real-time disassembler is a standout feature, converting machine code into human-readable assembly language, which is invaluable for understanding how a program operates at a low level. The debugger supports step-by-step execution, breakpoints, and runtime analysis, allowing users to trace the flow of a program and identify critical functions. The memory dump viewer is another powerful tool, enabling users to inspect and modify a program's memory during execution. This capability is particularly useful for analyzing how data is stored and manipulated. Additionally, OllyDbg's support for plugins extends its functionality, allowing users to add custom features or integrate it with other tools, making it a highly versatile solution.

For reverse engineering, OllyDbg is an indispensable tool. Its ability to trace program execution, analyze control flow, and identify key functions makes it ideal for dissecting software. The debugger can handle packed and encrypted executables, which are often used to obfuscate code and deter reverse engineering. By setting breakpoints and stepping through the code, users can uncover the original instructions and gain a deeper understanding of the program's behavior. The built-in assembler is another notable feature, allowing users to modify disassembled code directly within the debugger. This capability is particularly useful for patching software, fixing bugs, or bypassing security checks. Combined with its memory editing tools, OllyDbg provides a comprehensive environment for both analyzing and modifying binary code.

The community surrounding OllyDbg is one of its greatest strengths. Over the years, users have developed a wealth of plugins, scripts, and tutorials that enhance the tool's functionality and make it easier to use. This active and supportive community has played a significant role in keeping OllyDbg relevant, even in the absence of official updates. The extensibility of OllyDbg is another major advantage, as users can write their own plugins using the provided API. This flexibility allows for the addition of custom features or integration with other tools, making OllyDbg adaptable to a wide range of tasks and workflows.

OllyDbg is, however, not without its limitations. The most significant of these is its lack of support for 64-bit executables. As modern software increasingly adopts 64-bit architectures, this limitation can be a hindrance for users working with newer applications. To fill this void, x64dbg has emerged as the modern, open-source spiritual successor that reverse engineers use today for 64-bit Windows environments.

Additionally, the tool has not been updated since 2013, which means it may not be fully compatible with the latest versions of Windows or modern software protections. These limitations can pose challenges for users, particularly those working on cutting-edge projects.

Another challenge is the learning curve associated with OllyDbg. While the interface is user-friendly, mastering its advanced features requires a solid understanding of assembly language, Windows internals, and debugging techniques. Beginners may find it overwhelming at first, but the wealth of tutorials, documentation, and community resources available can help ease the learning process. With time and practice, users can unlock the full potential of OllyDbg and leverage its capabilities to tackle complex debugging and reverse-engineering tasks.

OllyDbg is a powerful and widely used debugger, despite its age and limitations. Its intuitive interface, robust feature set, and extensibility make it an invaluable tool for software developers, security researchers, and reverse engineers. While the lack of 64-bit support and updates may pose challenges, its strengths far outweigh its weaknesses. For anyone involved in debugging or reverse engineering on the Windows platform, OllyDbg is a tool that deserves a place in their toolkit.

AndroRAT

AndroRAT, short for Android Remote Administration Tool, is a powerful and controversial piece of software designed to provide remote control and surveillance capabilities over Android devices. Initially released in 2012 by a developer known as "JustinCase," AndroRAT was created as an open-source project, ostensibly for educational and research purposes. Its capabilities have, however, also made it a tool of choice for malicious actors, leading to its widespread use in cyberattacks and unauthorized surveillance. The dual nature of AndroRAT—as both a legitimate tool for security testing and a potential weapon for cybercriminals—has made it a subject of significant interest and concern in the cybersecurity community.

The primary function of AndroRAT is to provide remote access to an Android device, allowing an attacker or administrator to perform a wide range of actions without the device owner's knowledge. Once installed on a target device, AndroRAT operates stealthily, often disguising itself as a legitimate application to avoid detection. It can collect a variety of sensitive data, including call logs, text messages, GPS location, and even audio recordings from the device's microphone. Additionally, it can take photos using the device's camera, retrieve browsing history, and monitor social media activity. This extensive data collection capability makes AndroRAT a potent tool for surveillance, whether used for legitimate purposes or malicious intent.

One of the key features of AndroRAT is its ability to establish a persistent connection between the target device and the attacker's server. This connection allows the attacker to send commands and receive data in real time, providing a high degree of control over the compromised device. The tool supports a variety of communication methods, including SMS, HTTP, and sockets, making it adaptable to different network environments. Its flexibility and ease of use have contributed to its popularity among both security researchers and cybercriminals. For security professionals, AndroRAT can be used to test the vulnerabilities of Android devices and develop countermeasures. In the wrong hands, however, it becomes a dangerous tool for espionage and data theft.

The open-source nature of AndroRAT has played a significant role in its evolution and widespread adoption. By making the source code publicly available, the original developer enabled others to modify and improve the tool, leading to the creation of numerous variants and custom versions. This has allowed AndroRAT to remain relevant despite advancements in Android security. The open-source model, however, also means that malicious actors can easily access and weaponize the tool, contributing to its misuse in cyberattacks. The availability of tutorials and guides on how to deploy AndroRAT has further lowered the barrier to entry, enabling even inexperienced individuals to carry out sophisticated attacks.

Despite its capabilities, AndroRAT is not without limitations. Its effectiveness depends heavily on the attacker's ability to deceive the target into installing the malicious application. This often involves social engineering tactics, such as disguising the app as a legitimate service or exploiting the target's trust. Additionally, modern versions of Android have introduced stronger security measures, such as app sandboxing, permission controls, and Google Play Protect, which can detect and block malicious applications such as AndroRAT. These security enhancements have made it more challenging for attackers to successfully deploy the tool on newer devices.

The ethical implications of AndroRAT are a significant point of discussion. While it can be used for legitimate purposes, such as penetration testing and security research, its potential for abuse cannot be ignored. Unauthorized use of AndroRAT constitutes a violation of privacy and is illegal in most jurisdictions. Security professionals who use the tool must do so responsibly, with proper authorization and within the bounds of the law. The misuse of AndroRAT has led to numerous cases of data breaches, identity theft, and unauthorized surveillance, highlighting the need for robust cybersecurity measures and public awareness.

AndroRAT is a powerful and versatile tool that exemplifies the dual-use nature of technology. Its capabilities for remote access and data collection make it a valuable resource for security researchers, but also a dangerous weapon in the hands of cybercriminals. The open-source nature of the tool has fueled its evolution and widespread use, while also raising ethical and legal concerns. As Android devices continue to dominate the mobile market, tools such as AndroRAT will remain relevant, underscoring the importance of cybersecurity vigilance and responsible use. Whether used for good or ill, AndroRAT serves as a reminder of the fine line between innovation and exploitation in the digital age.

zANTI

zANTI is a comprehensive and widely recognized mobile penetration testing toolkit developed by Zimperium, designed to simulate cyberattacks on network infrastructures and identify vulnerabilities. Originally released as a tool for security professionals, zANTI gained popularity for its user-friendly interface and powerful capabilities, making it accessible to both seasoned penetration testers and those new to cybersecurity. The toolkit is available for Android devices, allowing users to turn their smartphones or tablets into portable penetration testing devices. While zANTI is intended for ethical hacking and security assessments, its capabilities have also attracted attention from malicious actors, highlighting the dual-use nature of such tools.

zANTI is designed to assess the security of Wi-Fi networks and connected devices. It provides a suite of network scanning and exploitation tools that can identify vulnerabilities, intercept network traffic, and simulate various types of attacks. One of its standout features is its ability to perform MITM attacks, which allow users to intercept and analyze data transmitted over a network. This capability is particularly useful for identifying unencrypted communications, weak authentication mechanisms, and other security flaws. Additionally, zANTI includes tools for network mapping, port scanning, and service enumeration, providing a comprehensive overview of the target network's structure and potential weaknesses.

The user interface of zANTI is one of its most appealing aspects, designed to simplify complex penetration testing tasks. The app features a clean and intuitive layout, with clear menus and visualizations that guide users through the process of setting up and executing attacks. This accessibility has made zANTI a popular choice for educational purposes, as it allows students and aspiring security professionals to learn about network security in a hands-on manner. The toolkit also includes preconfigured attack modules, which automate many of the steps involved in penetration testing, further lowering the barrier to entry for beginners.

One of zANTI's key strengths is its ability to simulate real-world attack scenarios, helping organizations identify and address vulnerabilities before they can be exploited by malicious actors. For example, the toolkit can test the effectiveness of a network's defenses against common threats, such as password cracking, session hijacking, and rogue access points. By providing detailed reports on discovered vulnerabilities, zANTI enables security teams to prioritize and remediate issues, ultimately strengthening the overall security posture of the network. This proactive approach to cybersecurity is essential in an era where data breaches and network intrusions are increasingly common.

The power and accessibility of zANTI, however, also raise ethical and legal concerns. While the toolkit is intended for legitimate security testing, its capabilities can easily be misused for malicious purposes. Unauthorized use of zANTI to intercept communications, steal sensitive data, or disrupt network operations constitutes a violation of privacy and is illegal in most jurisdictions. The availability of such tools on mobile platforms further complicates the issue, as it lowers the technical barrier for potential attackers. This has led to calls for stricter regulations and oversight to prevent the misuse of penetration testing tools such as zANTI.

Another limitation of zANTI is its dependence on the capabilities of the Android device it runs on. While the toolkit is powerful, its performance is constrained by the hardware and software limitations of mobile devices. For example, complex attacks or large-scale network scans may be slower or less effective on a smartphone compared to a dedicated penetration testing machine. Additionally, modern network security measures, such as encrypted communications and IDSs, can mitigate many of the attacks simulated by zANTI. As a result, the toolkit is most effective when used as part of a broader security assessment strategy, rather than as a standalone solution.

The development and distribution of zANTI also highlight the importance of responsible disclosure and ethical use in the cybersecurity community. Zimperium, the company behind zANTI, has emphasized the tool's intended use for legitimate security testing and has implemented measures to discourage misuse. For example, the app requires root access on the Android device, which adds a layer of complexity and reduces the likelihood of casual misuse. Nonetheless, the availability of zANTI and similar tools underscores the need for ongoing education and awareness about the ethical implications of penetration testing.

zANTI is a powerful and versatile mobile penetration testing toolkit that has made significant contributions to the field of network security. Its user-friendly interface, comprehensive feature set, and ability to simulate real-world attacks make it a valuable resource for security professionals and educators. The dual-use nature of zANTI, however, also poses ethical and legal challenges, as its capabilities can be exploited for malicious purposes. As cybersecurity threats continue to evolve, tools such as zANTI will remain essential for identifying and addressing vulnerabilities, provided they are used responsibly and within the bounds of the law. The ongoing debate over the use and regulation of such tools reflects the broader challenges of balancing innovation, security, and ethics in the digital age.

REFERENCES

1. Aircrack-ng [Internet]. [cited 2025 Feb 5]. Available from: *https://www.aircrack-ng.org/*
2. Angry IP Scanner - the original IP scanner for Windows, Mac and Linux [Internet]. [cited 2025 Feb 5]. Available from: *https://angryip.org/*
3. Black hat (computer security). In: Wikipedia [Internet]. 2025 [cited 2025 Feb 5]. Available from: *https://en.wikipedia.org/w/index.php?title=Black_hat_(computer_security)&oldid=1272594155*
4. Cobalt Strike [Internet]. [cited 2025 Feb 5]. Cobalt Strike | Adversary Simulation and Red Team Operations. Available from: *https://www.cobaltstrike.com*
5. EmpireProject/Empire [Internet]. EmpireProject; 2025 [cited 2025 Feb 5]. Available from: *https://github.com/EmpireProject/Empire*
6. Ghidra [Internet]. [cited 2025 Feb 5]. Available from: *https://ghidra-sre.org/*
7. Grey hat. In: Wikipedia [Internet]. 2025 [cited 2025 Feb 5]. Available from: *https://en.wikipedia.org/w/index.php?title=Grey_hat&oldid=1273457596*
8. Hacker. In: Wikipedia [Internet]. 2024 [cited 2025 Feb 5]. Available from: *https://en.wikipedia.org/w/index.php?title=Hacker&oldid=1258648544*
9. Hacker culture. In: Wikipedia [Internet]. 2024 [cited 2025 Feb 5]. Available from: *https://en.wikipedia.org/w/index.php?title=Hacker_culture&oldid=1244550236*
10. Hacktivism. In: Wikipedia [Internet]. 2025 [cited 2025 Feb 5]. Available from: *https://en.wikipedia.org/w/index.php?title=Hacktivism&oldid=1271477959*
11. hashcat - advanced password recovery [Internet]. [cited 2025 Feb 5]. Available from: *https://hashcat.net/hashcat/*
12. IDA Pro [Internet]. [cited 2025 Feb 5]. Available from: *https://hex-rays.com/ida-pro*

13. John the Ripper password cracker [Internet]. [cited 2025 Feb 5]. Available from: *https://www.openwall.com/john/*

14. Singh N. karma9874/AndroRAT [Internet]. 2025 [cited 2025 Feb 5]. Available from: *https://github.com/karma9874/AndroRAT*

15. Gretzky K. kgretzky/evilginx2 [Internet]. 2025 [cited 2025 Feb 5]. Available from: *https://github.com/kgretzky/evilginx2*

16. Low Orbit Ion Cannon. In: Wikipedia [Internet]. 2025 [cited 2025 Feb 5]. Available from: *https://en.wikipedia.org/w/index.php?title=Low_Orbit_Ion_Cannon&oldid=1272692790*

17. Metasploit [Internet]. [cited 2025 Feb 5]. Metasploit | Penetration Testing Software, Pen Testing Security. Available from: *https://www.metasploit.com/*

18. Mimikatz. In: Wikipedia [Internet]. 2025 [cited 2025 Feb 5]. Available from: *https://en.wikipedia.org/w/index.php?title=Mimikatz&oldid=1271057141*

19. Mirai (malware). In: Wikipedia [Internet]. 2024 [cited 2025 Feb 5]. Available from: *https://en.wikipedia.org/wiki/Mirai_(malware)*

20. Nmap: the Network Mapper - Free Security Scanner [Internet]. [cited 2025 Feb 5]. Available from: *https://nmap.org/*

21. OffSec's Exploit Database Archive [Internet]. [cited 2025 Feb 5]. Available from: *https://www.exploit-db.com/*

22. OllyDbg v1.10 [Internet]. [cited 2025 Feb 5]. Available from: *https://www.ollydbg.de/*

23. Shodan [Internet]. [cited 2025 Feb 5]. Shodan. Available from: *https://www.shodan.io*

24. t6x. t6x/reaver-wps-fork-t6x [Internet]. 2025 [cited 2025 Feb 5]. Available from: *https://github.com/t6x/reaver-wps-fork-t6x*

25. trustedsec/social-engineer-toolkit [Internet]. trustedsec; 2025 [cited 2025 Feb 5]. Available from: *https://github.com/trustedsec/social-engineer-toolkit*

26. White hat (computer security). In: Wikipedia [Internet]. 2025 [cited 2025 Feb 5]. Available from: *https://en.wikipedia.org/w/index.php?title=White_hat_(computer_security)&oldid=1271677737*

27. Wireshark [Internet]. [cited 2025 Feb 5]. Wireshark · Go Deep. Available from: *https://www.wireshark.org/*

CHAPTER 7

The Dark Web, Tor Network, and Invisible Internet Project

The dark Web is a hidden part of the Internet that is not indexed by traditional search engines and requires special software, such as Tor, to access. It exists as an encrypted network that provides anonymity to its users, making it a space for both privacy-conscious individuals and those engaging in illicit activities. Unlike the surface Web, which consists of publicly accessible Web sites, or the deep Web, which includes private databases and content behind paywalls, the dark Web operates on a decentralized network designed to obscure the identities and locations of its users.

Originally developed for secure government communications, the technology behind the dark Web has since been adopted by activists, journalists, and individuals seeking to bypass censorship. It serves as a refuge for whistleblowers and those in oppressive regimes who need a secure platform for communication. Its anonymity, however, also makes it a breeding ground for black markets, cybercriminal activity, and illicit trade, fostering a reputation that is often associated with danger and illegality.

Despite its notoriety, the dark Web is not inherently malicious. It is a tool—one that can be used for good or ill, depending on the intentions of those who navigate its hidden corridors. Understanding the dark Web requires separating myth from reality, recognizing both its potential for protecting privacy and its risks in enabling criminal activity.

THE GOOD SIDE

The dark Web is often portrayed as a shadowy underworld filled with illicit activities, from drug trafficking to cybercrime. While it is true that anonymity on the dark Web can facilitate illegal enterprises, this hidden part of the Internet also serves as a vital tool for those seeking privacy, security, and freedom in an increasingly surveilled digital world. For journalists, activists, whistleblowers, and individuals living under oppressive regimes, the dark Web offers a crucial platform for communication, protection, and access to uncensored information.

One of the most significant positive uses of the dark Web is providing a secure channel for journalists and whistleblowers to exchange information. In countries where press freedom is restricted and government surveillance is pervasive, reporting on corruption, human rights abuses, or political scandals can be dangerous. Journalists risk harassment, imprisonment, or worse. Platforms such as SecureDrop, which is accessible via the Tor network, allow whistleblowers to safely submit sensitive information to media organizations without fear of being traced. This has led to major investigative reports uncovering corruption and wrongdoing worldwide, demonstrating the power of the dark Web as a force for transparency and accountability. In authoritarian countries, governments frequently monitor Internet activity and block access to information that contradicts official narratives. The dark Web provides a way to bypass these restrictions, enabling activists to share their stories, coordinate efforts, and access uncensored news. The anonymity afforded by the Tor network and other privacy tools makes it possible for these individuals to speak out without risking immediate detection and persecution.

Beyond activism and journalism, the dark Web serves as a safe space for individuals in need of privacy, particularly those in vulnerable situations. Victims of domestic abuse, LGBTQ+ individuals in hostile environments, and those suffering from stigmatized medical conditions may find solace in anonymous forums and support groups hosted on the dark Web. Unlike mainstream social media, where online activity can be easily tracked and exploited, these platforms offer a refuge where people can seek help, share experiences, and receive guidance without fear of exposure.

Another ethical use of the dark Web is its role in counter-surveillance and cybersecurity. Researchers and security experts use dark Web forums to study emerging cyber threats, track stolen data, and develop strategies to protect organizations and individuals from cyberattacks. Law enforcement agencies also monitor illicit activities on the dark Web to dismantle criminal networks, seize illegal marketplaces, and apprehend perpetrators of cybercrime. In this sense, understanding and utilizing the dark Web is not just a matter of criminal activity but a means of enhancing security and digital resilience.

The ability to communicate securely and access uncensored information is now more crucial than ever. The dark Web, though often misunderstood, plays a key role in protecting these fundamental rights. Rather than dismissing it as a dangerous digital underworld, it is essential to recognize its positive contributions and the important role it plays for those who rely on it to stay safe, informed, and free.

THE DARK SIDE

The dark Web has long been associated with secrecy, anonymity, and hidden activity, making it a breeding ground for illicit enterprises and cybercrime. While it does offer privacy and security for those who need protection from surveillance, it is also exploited by criminals who take advantage of its obscurity to conduct illegal business with minimal risk of detection. The same encryption and anonymity that safeguard whistleblowers and activists also enable drug trafficking, human trafficking, illicit markets, and a host of cybercrimes that pose serious threats to individuals and societies worldwide.

One of the most notorious aspects of the dark Web is its role in facilitating black markets, where illegal goods and services are bought and sold with little oversight. Marketplaces such as the now-defunct Silk Road pioneered the sale of drugs, counterfeit documents, weapons, and even hitman services, using cryptocurrency transactions to maintain anonymity. Despite law enforcement crackdowns on major platforms, these marketplaces continue to reappear, making it difficult to permanently dismantle the underground economy. The decentralized nature of the dark Web ensures that when one site is taken down, others quickly emerge to take its place, sustaining an ever-evolving digital black market.

Human trafficking and exploitation are among the darkest and most disturbing aspects of the dark Web. Hidden forums and Web sites facilitate the sale of illegal pornography, creating an ecosystem where criminals operate beyond the reach of traditional law enforcement. The anonymity of the dark Web allows perpetrators to connect with buyers, exchange illegal content, and communicate without fear of immediate detection. While international agencies and cybersecurity experts have made significant efforts to track and dismantle these networks, the very nature of the dark Web makes it an ongoing challenge.

Cybercrime is another significant threat that thrives in the depths of the dark Web. Hackers and cybercriminals use hidden forums to sell stolen data, hacking tools, and malware that can be deployed to attack businesses, governments, and individuals. Massive data breaches have led to the sale of millions of stolen credit card numbers, personal information, and login credentials, fueling identity theft and financial fraud on a global scale. Ransomware-as-a-service, where cybercriminals rent out ransomware tools to less experienced attackers, has also become a lucrative industry, enabling even those with minimal technical skills to launch devastating cyberattacks against unsuspecting victims.

Terrorist organizations and extremist groups have also leveraged the dark Web to recruit members, spread propaganda, and communicate outside of traditional monitoring channels. Encrypted messaging services and hidden forums provide a safe haven for radical groups to discuss plans, share violent ideologies, and coordinate attacks without the risk of surveillance. While counterterrorism agencies actively monitor these spaces, the constantly shifting nature of the dark Web makes it difficult to track and shut down such operations entirely.

Despite ongoing efforts by law enforcement to combat illicit activities on the dark Web, its resilience and adaptability present a continuous challenge. While some criminal enterprises have been dismantled, new ones quickly emerge, taking advantage of the anonymity and encryption that make this hidden corner of the Internet so difficult to regulate. The dark Web remains a double-edged sword, providing both a refuge for those seeking privacy and a platform for those engaging in some of the most nefarious activities imaginable.

The existence of the dark Web forces society to grapple with complex ethical and legal questions about online privacy, law enforcement, and digital freedoms. While it is a tool that can be used for good, it is undeniable that its dark side harbors some of the most dangerous and harmful activities in the digital world. Understanding its risks is crucial in the ongoing effort to combat cybercrime, protect vulnerable populations, and ensure that anonymity does not come at the cost of public safety.

THE TOR NETWORK

The Tor network is a powerful tool designed to provide anonymity and privacy online by routing Internet traffic through a series of encrypted relays. Initially developed by the U.S. Naval Research Laboratory in the 1990s to protect government communications, Tor has since evolved into an open-source project used by millions worldwide. By masking users' IP addresses and encrypting their data multiple times through a decentralized network of volunteer-operated nodes, Tor allows individuals to browse the Internet anonymously and access content that might otherwise be restricted or censored. While it is often associated with the dark Web and illicit activity, the Tor network plays a crucial role in safeguarding digital privacy, enabling free speech, and protecting individuals from surveillance.

In countries where political regimes restrict free speech and block certain Web sites, Tor allows citizens to access uncensored news, communicate safely, and share information without fear of government reprisal. This has been particularly valuable for journalists, activists, and dissidents who rely on secure, anonymous communication to expose corruption, report human rights violations, and organize resistance against oppressive authorities.

Beyond its role in promoting free speech, Tor is a crucial tool for privacy-conscious individuals seeking to protect their online identity. In an era where mass surveillance has become the norm, many people use Tor to prevent tracking by corporations, governments, and cybercriminals. Unlike traditional browsers, which collect vast amounts of personal data, Tor minimizes digital footprints and prevents advertisers from monitoring browsing habits. This makes it an essential resource for whistleblowers, investigative journalists, and anyone who values online anonymity.

Another ethical application of the Tor network is its use in cybersecurity research and defense. Security experts and ethical hackers use Tor to study cyber threats, monitor cybercriminal activities, and develop strategies to enhance online safety. Law enforcement agencies also leverage the Tor network to conduct undercover investigations, track criminal enterprises, and infiltrate illegal online marketplaces. In this sense, Tor is not just a tool for privacy but also a means of strengthening cybersecurity efforts and countering digital threats.

Despite its many positive uses, the Tor network is also exploited for illicit purposes. Its ability to provide anonymity makes it an attractive platform for cybercriminals, drug traffickers, and other malicious actors seeking to evade law enforcement. The dark Web, which operates within the Tor network, hosts black markets, forums for cybercrime, and other illegal services that rely on encrypted communication to function. This has led to a common misconception that Tor is primarily a tool for criminals, overshadowing its legitimate and beneficial applications. While many Tor advocates argue that the network itself is neutral—neither inherently good nor bad—the lack of oversight allows harmful activities to persist, creating a moral and legal challenge for authorities attempting to regulate online anonymity.

The Tor network remains a double-edged sword, offering both unparalleled privacy and a safe haven for criminal activity. While it is a crucial tool for protecting free speech, circumventing censorship, and enhancing cybersecurity, it also poses significant challenges in the fight against cybercrime and illegal online activities. The debate over Tor's ethical implications continues, raising important questions about the balance between privacy, security, and the need for accountability in an increasingly digital world. Ultimately, Tor is not the problem itself but rather a reflection of the broader issues surrounding Internet freedom, regulation, and the struggle between anonymity and law enforcement.

Accessing the Tor Network

Accessing the Tor network requires downloading and using Tor Browser, a specialized Web browser designed to anonymize your Internet activity by routing your traffic through multiple encrypted relays. To begin, you must visit the official Tor Project Web site at *https://www.torproject.org* using a regular Web browser such as Chrome, Firefox, or Edge. It is crucial to download Tor only from the official Web site to avoid counterfeit versions that could contain malware or compromise anonymity.

Once on the Tor Project Web site, select the appropriate version of Tor Browser for your operating system—Windows, macOS, Linux, or Android. After downloading the installation file, follow the on-screen instructions to install the browser. On Windows and macOS, this typically involves running the downloaded file and following the installation prompts. On Linux, you may need to extract the compressed archive and run Tor Browser manually. Android users can install the browser through the Google Play Store or by downloading the APK directly from the Tor Project Web site.

After installation, launch Tor Browser. The first time you open it, you will be presented with two options: "Connect" and "Configure." Most users can simply click "Connect," allowing the browser to establish a secure connection to the Tor network automatically. If you are in a country where Tor is blocked, however, you may need to click "Configure" and follow additional steps to bypass restrictions using bridges or obfuscation techniques. The browser will then attempt to connect by routing your Internet traffic through a series of decentralized volunteer-operated nodes, encrypting it at multiple layers to ensure anonymity.

Once connected, you can browse the Internet as you would with any other browser. Tor Browser automatically blocks tracking scripts, prevents fingerprinting, and disables plugins that could compromise anonymity. By default, it directs users to DuckDuckGo as the search engine, since it does not track search history or personal data. To access `.onion` Web sites—services and platforms that exist exclusively within the Tor network—you must enter their specific `.onion` URLs into the address bar. These sites are not indexed by regular search engines, so finding them typically requires directories or community forums dedicated to listing `.onion` services.

To enhance privacy and security while using Tor, it is essential to follow best practices. Avoid logging in to personal accounts, such as email or social media, as doing so can link your identity to your Tor activity. Never download files from untrusted sources or enable browser plugins, as these could reveal your real IP address or expose you to malware. Additionally, using Tor does not make you completely anonymous if your Internet activity contains identifiable information, so it is crucial to remain cautious about what you share online.

Tor is a powerful tool for protecting online privacy and circumventing censorship, but it is not without risks. Because of its ability to anonymize users, the network is also used for illegal activities. As a result, some ISPs or governments may monitor or restrict Tor usage. If you need an extra layer of privacy, you can use Tor in combination with a VPN to mask the fact that you are accessing the network. VPNs should, however, be chosen carefully, as some may log user data or compromise security.

By understanding how to properly set up and use the Tor network, users can take advantage of its privacy features while minimizing risks. Whether for protecting sensitive communications, accessing censored content, or simply browsing anonymously, Tor provides a valuable tool for maintaining online freedom in an increasingly monitored digital landscape.

SILK ROAD

Silk Road was a revolutionary yet controversial online marketplace that emerged as the first major darknet market, operating on the Tor network and utilizing Bitcoin for transactions. It was launched in 2011 by a man under the pseudonym "Dread Pirate Roberts," and quickly became a focal point for discussions about online privacy, cryptocurrency, and the dark Web's potential for both freedom and criminal activity. Unlike conventional e-commerce platforms, Silk Road provided a decentralized and anonymous space for users to buy and sell goods, primarily illicit drugs, but also other contraband items, hacking tools, counterfeit documents, and, to a lesser extent, legal goods. Anonymity was maintained through the use of Tor, which concealed the identities of both buyers and sellers, and Bitcoin, which provided pseudonymous, though not entirely untraceable, transactions.

The marketplace's existence raised ethical and legal questions regarding online governance, the role of cryptography in facilitating crime, and the limits of law enforcement in cyberspace. Advocates of Silk Road argued that it was not merely a black-market drug bazaar but an experiment in libertarian ideals, where individuals could engage in voluntary transactions free from state intervention. Some even suggested that by allowing the direct trade of drugs without the risks of street violence, it was a safer alternative to the traditional narcotics trade. The creator himself, in his libertarian philosophy, envisioned it as a means to promote individual freedoms and limit government overreach. Law enforcement agencies, however, viewed it as a dangerous hub for illegal activity that enabled drug trafficking, money laundering, and other cybercrimes, undermining established laws and regulations designed to protect public health and safety.

The FBI ultimately shut down Silk Road in October 2013, arresting the creator, Ross Ulbricht, in a dramatic operation in a San Francisco library. The trial that followed was highly publicized, with him convicted on charges of money laundering, conspiracy to commit computer hacking, and conspiracy to traffic narcotics. He was sentenced to life in prison without the possibility of parole, a punishment that many critics viewed as excessively harsh, considering he had never directly sold drugs or committed violent crimes. The case also highlighted the growing capabilities of law enforcement in tracking cryptocurrency transactions and unmasking Tor users, dispelling the illusion that Bitcoin provides absolute anonymity.

Despite its closure, Silk Road left a lasting impact on the Internet and the world of digital black markets. Its takedown did not stop the proliferation of darknet marketplaces; instead, it inspired numerous successors, such as Silk Road 2.0, AlphaBay, and Dream Market, each implementing stronger security measures and attempting to refine the model previously introduced. The rise and fall of these markets demonstrate an ongoing cat-and-mouse game between cybercriminals and law enforcement, with each new marketplace being targeted and eventually dismantled by authorities. As quickly as one is taken down, however, another rises in its place, revealing the resilience of the darknet economy.

Beyond its criminal implications, Silk Road played a significant role in demonstrating the potential of Bitcoin as a real-world currency. Prior to its emergence, Bitcoin was largely an obscure concept discussed within cryptography and tech circles, but its use on Silk Road showed that it could function as a medium of exchange. This, in turn, attracted attention from regulators and financial institutions, accelerating discussions on cryptocurrency regulation, blockchain tracking technologies, and the need for digital financial oversight.

The legacy of Silk Road is a complex one. On one hand, it provided a proof of concept for decentralized, anonymous markets, shaping the future of digital commerce and cryptographic financial tools. On the other, it reinforced concerns about the dark Web's capacity to facilitate crime, leading to intensified efforts to monitor and regulate online anonymity. The debate over online privacy, government surveillance, and the ethics of digital marketplaces continues today, with Ulbricht's case still serving as a touchstone for discussions about Internet freedom and justice. Whether one views Silk Road as a pioneering libertarian experiment or a dangerous criminal enterprise, its impact on cybersecurity, law enforcement, and digital currencies is undeniable.

THE INVISIBLE INTERNET PROJECT

I2P is an anonymous, decentralized network designed to facilitate private and secure communication. It operates as an overlay network, meaning it runs on top of the existing Internet but remains separate from it. Unlike traditional browsing, which exposes users to surveillance and tracking, I2P encrypts data and routes it through multiple tunnels, making it extremely difficult to trace the origin or destination of any communication. I2P differs from other anonymity-focused networks such as Tor in its structure and purpose. While Tor is primarily used to access the surface Web anonymously, I2P is designed as a self-contained ecosystem with its own Web sites, known as eepsites, and services that operate exclusively within the network. I2P utilizes a fully decentralized P2P model where every user contributes to routing traffic, making it more resistant to attacks or censorship.

The core functionality of I2P relies on unidirectional tunnels, which separate inbound and outbound traffic to prevent any single relay from knowing both the sender and receiver. Messages sent through I2P are encrypted from end to end, passing through multiple randomly selected nodes before reaching their destination. This ensures that even if a node is compromised, it cannot access the entire communication path. The decentralized nature of I2P makes it more difficult to monitor compared to Tor, which uses a centralized directory of relays. This, however, also makes I2P more complex to set up and maintain, requiring users to manually configure applications to work within the network.

I2P serves as a critical tool for activists, journalists, and individuals in oppressive regimes who need to communicate securely without fear of surveillance. It provides a censorship-resistant platform for sharing information, hosting Web sites, and engaging in P2P file sharing. Many privacy-conscious users rely on I2P for secure messaging through applications such as I2P-Bote and Susimail, which allow for encrypted, anonymous communication. File-sharing platforms such as BitTorrent have also been adapted to function within the I2P network, enabling users to exchange data without exposing their identities.

Despite its legitimate uses, I2P has also attracted individuals seeking to engage in illicit activities. Like Tor's dark Web, I2P hosts underground marketplaces, cybercriminal forums, and other hidden services that take advantage of the network's anonymity. Law enforcement faces significant challenges in tracking illegal activities within I2P due to its decentralized architecture and strong encryption. While I2P itself is a neutral technology, its potential for misuse has sparked debate over the ethical implications of providing absolute online anonymity.

One of the major drawbacks of I2P is its limited user base and slower speeds compared to Tor and traditional Internet browsing. Because I2P traffic is routed through multiple encrypted tunnels and relies on user-contributed bandwidth, network performance can suffer, making tasks such as video streaming and large downloads impractical. The complexity of setting up I2P also discourages mainstream adoption, as users must manually configure browsers, email clients, and torrent applications to work within the network.

Compared to Tor, I2P offers distinct advantages in terms of anonymity and resistance to attacks. While Tor relies on a known set of relay nodes that could potentially be compromised, I2P's P2P model distributes network participation across all users, making it more resilient. Because I2P has received less scrutiny from security researchers compared to Tor, however, some experts argue that its security model has not been as rigorously tested. Tor is better suited for accessing the traditional Internet anonymously, while I2P is more effective for secure communication within a closed, hidden network.

The future of I2P depends on its ability to overcome technical barriers and attract a larger user base. Developers continue to work on improving usability, performance, and integration with existing applications to make I2P more accessible. As concerns over mass surveillance and censorship increase, interest in decentralized, anonymous networks is likely to grow. Regulatory and legal challenges, however, could arise as governments seek to monitor or restrict anonymous online activity. While I2P remains a niche tool compared to Tor, its decentralized design offers a promising alternative for those seeking maximum privacy and security online.

REFERENCES

1. I2P Anonymous Network [Internet]. [cited 2025 Feb 7]. Available from: *https://geti2p.net/en/*
2. Silk Road (marketplace). In: Wikipedia [Internet]. 2025 [cited 2025 Feb 7]. Available from: *https://en.wikipedia.org/w/index.php?title=Silk_Road_(marketplace)&oldid=1272862536*
3. The Tor Project | Privacy & Freedom Online [Internet]. [cited 2025 Feb 7]. Available from: *https://torproject.org*
4. Tor (network). In: Wikipedia [Internet]. 2025 [cited 2025 Feb 7]. Available from: *https://en.wikipedia.org/w/index.php?title=Tor_(network)&oldid=1274381023*

Index

B

C

D

Bei Fragen zur Produktsicherheit wenden Sie sich bitte an:
If you have any questions regarding product safety,
please contact:

Walter de Gruyter GmbH
Genthiner Straße 13
10785 Berlin
productsafety@degruyterbrill.com